British Film Editors

BRITISH FILM EDITORS

'The Heart of the Movie'

Roy Perkins
and
Martin Stollery

 Publishing

'Most of the directors I've worked with needed someone to talk to who is deep inside the heart of the movie.'

Mick Audsley, film editor

First published in 2004 by the
BRITISH FILM INSTITUTE
21 Stephen Street, London W1T 1LN

The British Film Institute is the UK national agency with responsibility for encouraging the arts of film and television and conserving them in the national interest.

Cover design by Mark Swan
Cover images (clockwise from top left): Noreen Ackland, Peter Tanner, Frank Clarke and Richard Best (images courtesy of Roy Perkins).

Set by Fakenham Photosetting Limited, Norfolk
Printed in the UK by St Edmundsbury Press, Bury St Edmunds, Suffolk

British Library Cataloguing-in-Publication Data
A catalogue record for this book is available from the British Library

ISBN 1 84457 008 8 (pbk)
ISBN 1 84457 007 X (hbk)

Contents

Acknowledgments

The authors' first and biggest debt is to the many editors who kindly agreed to be interviewed for this book, and we are particularly grateful to Alfred Cox of the Guild of British Film Editors. The second biggest debt is to the BECTU History Project for allowing us access to their invaluable transcripts and interviews with editors.

Roy Perkins would like to thank Dai Vaughan for his continuing interest in this project, Jack Tucker of ACE (American Cinema Editors) for help in the United States, and Vivien Pottersman for her professional input.

Martin Stollery would like to thank Helen Eyers for all her help as the book neared completion, and Peter Krämer for useful comments on part of Chapter 4.

This book is jointly authored. Roy Perkins conducted the interviews and wrote the Introduction, chapters 1, 2 and 6, and the Select Glossary. Martin Stollery wrote chapters 3, 4 and 5, and the Appendix.

Introduction

What actually is the editor's contribution to a film? Walter Murch, the American editor of *Apocalypse Now* (1979), has been described by Francis Coppola as 'the essential collaborator on what are probably the best films I worked on: *The Conversation* and *The Godfather Part II*' (quoted in Murch, 1995, p. ix). British film-maker and historian Kevin Brownlow has referred to the editor's 'hidden power' and the process of film editing as 'directing for the second time' (1968, p. 280), while the film industry itself acknowledges the contribution of editors in terms of status (front instead of end credits) and remuneration. Yet few academics have considered writing about editors, whereas the other key figures in production, particularly the director, have received extensive critical recognition. As film scholar Alan Lovell has pointed out, although there has been an abundance of work published on individual film-makers (that is, directors) and on the history, context and analysis of British cinema over the past twenty-five years, significant gaps remain (2001). One of the most creative figures in film production, the film editor, has been particularly poorly served. Tony Lawson, who edited *Barry Lyndon* (1975), *Cross of Iron* (1977) and *Bad Timing* (1980) for Stanley Kubrick, Sam Peckinpah and Nicolas Roeg respectively, has remarked that 'editing has been left out of the constant stream of words on film for too long' (1998).

With the advent of multi-skilling, and as a new generation of digitally literate film-makers has begun to question the delineation of roles in film production, it is time to take stock of how film editors, directors and producers have worked together in the past, and to consider how new technology will affect working relationships in the future. Director Mike Figgis, for example, has attempted to forge a new digital film aesthetic in *Time Code* (2000) and *Hotel* (2002) and, in so doing, liberate his films from what he considers to be the constraints imposed by editing:

> The editing process has become something that has a huge effect on the way we tell stories. The editor has become an incredibly important person in the process of story telling because of editing techniques, not because of the story. And we accept it. We accept editing as being the language of film-making. It's actually not; it doesn't have to be (quoted in Reed, 2000).

Most of the editors interviewed for this book consider editing to be inextricably linked with storytelling. They would probably agree with Figgis' assessment of the importance of their role in the production process but would reject his notion of editing as an end rather than a means. Their role is a self-effacing one, which aims to serve the best interests of the material, representing, in the words of editor Terry Rawlings, 'another creative, contributory force on the film'. The long lists of established editors' credits attest to the variable quality of the material they have to work with, but their skills and experience, which sometimes exceed the quality of the films they edit, are usually valued by the directors and producers who engage them. Clearly there is a compelling need for critics and academics to develop a more informed view of film-making which takes proper account of the crucially important phase of post-production, and to reassess established notions of film authorship which have ignored the work of the editor as a distinctive creative input.

There are directors, such as Coppola quoted above, who publicly recognise the crucial support they receive from editors, and a few – like Alexander Mackendrick – have questioned the almost obsessive (and usually exclusive) focus on the directing role.[1] Other directors are reluctant to acknowledge the creative importance of editing, and one editor felt unable to contribute to this book because of the sensitivity of the relationship. But the considerable cultural capital invested by the discipline of film studies over the past forty years in author-led critiques of cinema, and their propagation through the popular media, have effectively masked out other significant roles in the production process.

Film critic Philip French's observation that most British feature directors do not work enough to gain an international profile (2000, p. 6) stands in stark contrast to the busy working careers of outstanding British cinematographers such as Roger Pratt and Roger Deakins, and picture and sound editors such as Antony Gibbs, Anne Coates, Thom Noble, Peter Honess and Mike Le-Mare, all now based in California. The Hollywood majors also employ British film editing 'doctors' to re-cut productions that for various reasons have run into difficulties. For example, Stuart Baird was called in to re-work *Mission: Impossible II* (John Woo, 2000) and Lesley Walker was asked to re-cut *Born Yesterday* (Luis Mandoki, 1993) from scratch in a space of five weeks. Many of these British technicians have received international acclaim – since 1960 winning three times as many Academy Awards for editing and cinematography as for directing – as well as scores of nominations. Others have been granted membership of the American Cinema Editors' guild (ACE), and the Career Achievement Award presented to Antony Gibbs by ACE in 2002 stands in stark contrast to his critical anonymity in the UK. A later generation of technicians trained to the exacting standards of

British public service broadcasting – editors like Tariq Anwar, *American Beauty* (Sam Mendes, 1999); Masahiro Hirakubo, *Trainspotting* (Danny Boyle, 1996); Frances Parker, *Band of Brothers* (TV series, 2001); and Martin Walsh, *Chicago* (Rob Marshall, 2002) – are also increasingly in demand beyond the UK film and television industry.

This book is an attempt to redress an imbalance of critical interest, rather than diminish the significance of the director. Although there are references to documentary editors, extended discussion of the documentary field (which is now rarely independent of television broadcasting) lies beyond the scope of this book. The focus of interviews and analysis has been on feature film production and discussion has inevitably strayed beyond the UK, reflecting the shift from studio-based employment to international freelancing. There are more similarities than significant differences in production practice between Britain and Hollywood, and although attempts have been made to foreground examples drawn from British film-making, the American production context has been cited where relevant. Of the thirty or so editors who were consulted in the preparation of this book, few had previously been interviewed in their own right, except to supply commentaries on the careers of directors they had worked with; and the fact that one Oscar-winning editor was 'flattered to be included' indicates both the level of regard that he has for his peers and the sense that a wider understanding of this pivotal role is long overdue.

The approach taken by this book is to integrate the editors' voices thematically and historically, predominantly through the use of specially recorded interviews, as well as previously transcribed material from the BECTU History Project archives. Chapter 1 attempts to explain the exclusion of editors from most written accounts of film-making and Chapter 2 examines the role and process of editing as described by contemporary practitioners. Chapters 3 and 4 explore key moments and phases of film history, looking at British editors' work in a range of different production contexts, and Chapter 5 traces stylistic developments from the 1930s to the 90s. Chapter 6 looks at the impact on editing produced by the transition from film to digital technologies, and considers the future of editing. Our intention throughout has been to foregound the voices of editors themselves.

R.P.

NOTES

All unattributed quotations from editors are drawn from the interviews conducted for this book.

1. In an interview with Alexander Mackendrick, Theresa Fitzgerald (1990, p. 16) reported on the director's reaction to a showing of his films at the Quimper Film Festival: 'Mackendrick himself, though enjoying the Festival, takes an ironic attitude to such auteurist reverence. He deprecates the "utterly unjustified cult of the director".'

1

Editing, Authorship and Collaboration

PROBLEMS OF RECOGNITION 1

Our work is by and large unnoticed and consequently misunderstood.
Tariq Anwar, editor, *The Madness of King George* (Nicholas Hytner, 1994),
American Beauty

Film editing, considered by director and editor Stuart Baird to be the 'only thing that is particular and original to film-making', although technically allocated to the editor, is assumed to be the artistic responsibility of the director. In the numerous references to editing technique, editors themselves are rarely mentioned. Win Sharples Jr, in his 1977 article on international film editing, pointed out that in both the *The International Encyclopaedia of Film* and *The Oxford Companion to Film*, whose combined entries on the craft of editing amounted to 4,000 words, not one editor was mentioned by name (p. 7). Sharples' survey has not been updated, and nor significantly have the attitudes he complains of, at least in British writing about film. In the United States two separate volumes of interviews with leading Hollywood editors have now been compiled by Vincent LoBrutto (1991) and Gabriella Oldham (1992), and there is a developing awareness of editing culture reflected in numerous American websites devoted to film. Michael Ondaatje (2002a) offers a unique insight into the relationship between writing and film editing, the product of his discussions with the distinguished American film editor Walter Murch with whom he collaborated on *The English Patient* (Anthony Minghella, 1996). In the UK, however, there remains little evidence of historical, theoretical or technological discussion of film editing beyond those who practise it.[1] Don Fairservice's book (2001) is a much-needed addition to film literature by one of the UK's most distinguished television editors; and Declan McGrath's impressively illustrated collection of interviews (2001) provides a valuable international perspective. However, Dai Vaughan's incisive portrait of Stewart McAllister (1983) – now unfortunately out of print – is the only written study devoted to the career of a British film editor.

Vaughan is, like Fairservice, a highly regarded editor and his book is an acknowledgment of the creative contribution made by McAllister to the British documentary movement. Vaughan's contention was that the quality and character of the best wartime films directed by Humphrey Jennings owed significantly to McAllister's editing; and this was borne out by interviews conducted with members of the Crown Film Unit. Producer Ian Dalrymple concluded that 'without McAllister, there would have been no Humphrey Jennings' (quoted in Vaughan, 1983, p. 7). Yet despite in some way embodying the 'spirit of Jennings' – in the estimation of producer Edgar Anstey (quoted in Vaughan, 1983, p. 7) – McAllister was, and has remained, largely absent in the discussions of the films he edited. The conventional approach of aggregating all editing decisions to the director ('Jennings holds a shot, Jennings cuts away to', etc.) extends also to specialised discussions of sound. For example, Vaughan (1983, p. 4) points out that Karel Reisz and Gavin Millar (1968) failed to mention McAllister even in an analysis of the sound editing of *Listen to Britain* (Humphrey Jennings and Stewart McAllister, 1942).[2] According to Ken Cameron, who worked on many of the wartime documentaries, McAllister's overall contribution to *Listen to Britain* was significant: 'there's no doubt that Mac made a tremendous contribution to that film. He told Humphrey what he needed – "Humphrey, go out and shoot this" – and Humphrey did it' (quoted in Vaughan, 1983, p. 83). Vaughan's book, despite much original research, appears to have had little impact on film scholarship in the twenty years since its publication. The Summary of Information on Film and Television (SIFT) Reference List at the British Film Institute library contains forty-one book, article and film screening references to Jennings. Of the four SIFT references to McAllister one is a National Film Theatre screening in November 1983, coinciding with the launch of Vaughan's book, and the other three are biographical and obituary notices that appeared in the trade union journal *Film and Television Technician* (February 1963, p. 38; January 1964, p. 14; December 1983, p. 8).

Wherever the true creative 'power' lies in film production – whether documentary or fiction – public and critical perception place it with the director, a legacy of the auteur theory. The publicity in July 2000 (*Time Out*, 2000, p. 100) for a re-edited version of *Wild Side* (Donald Cammell, 1995), for example, was couched in the following terms:

FROM THE CREATOR OF 'PERFORMANCE'
'IT'S NOT ABOUT SEX, IT'S ABOUT POWER'
DONALD CAMMELL'S
WILD SIDE [18]
THE DIRECTOR'S CUT

'CULT CLASSIC'
FILM OF THE WEEK
THE GUARDIAN

Apart from the problem of assigning sole creative responsibility for *Performance* (Nicolas Roeg, Donald Cammell, 1968) to one of its co-directors, what is notable here is that it is Donald Cammell who is being advertised (although it was editor/producer Frank Mazzola who re-edited *Wild Side* after Cammell's death). The 'maverick' director, once constructed by auteurist critics as a figure opposed to the system of production, has now been co-opted into it as a function of film marketing. Andy Medhurst has proposed why academic and media fascination with the director continues, despite the existence of other approaches:

> The reasons for the persistence of auteurist approaches to the cinema are not hard
> to understand. The idea that the director is solely responsible for a film's meaning
> is a comforting fantasy, restricting a potentially threatening diversity of
> interpretation, and giving secondary status to other analytical frameworks, such as
> production context, genre, audience, or ideology, which might put spanners in the
> works (1991, p. 37).

The status of the director rather than the producer or writer as the vital element in the film-making process was systematically argued by François Truffaut and other young critics writing in the French film review *Cahiers du cinéma* from the mid-1950s to the early 60s. They set out to demonstrate that even in Hollywood certain directors – Ford, Hawks, Hitchcock, Ray, Minnelli – exhibited stylistic or thematic consistencies across a range of films. The ability to achieve this, despite working with different crews and in varying production contexts, was evidence of the directors' personal authorship of those films. Although Truffaut subsequently emphasised that the auteur theory was 'merely a polemical weapon for a given time and place' (quoted in Sarris, 1992, p. 585), this did nothing to impede Andrew Sarris' enthusiasm for elaborating auteurism so influentially in American film criticism from 1962. The critical focus on the author/director helped establish film studies as a university discipline in both the United States and the UK. By 1989 David Bordwell felt able to write that: 'On the whole, the institutional context of academic film studies has been the result of explicatory, chiefly "auteur"-centred criticism' (p. 53).

A key text in the development of British auteurism was Peter Wollen's *Signs and Meanings in the Cinema* (1969, now in its fourth edition), which remains required reading on many film and media courses. Wollen argued that cinema is closer to literature than to any other art form, a critical position which implies the creative redundancy of all contributors except the author/director. The non-directorial roles in film production, according to Wollen, impede auteurist analysis:

> A great many features of films analysed have to be dismissed as indecipherable because of 'noise' from the producer, the cameraman or even the actors . . . Sometimes these separate texts – those of the cameraman or the actors – may force themselves into prominence so that the film becomes an indecipherable palimpsest . . . inaccessible to criticism (1998, p. 71).

The use of the word 'noise' here marks a disjunction between film theory and professional film practice. The contribution to production value made by leading cinematographers – and of course editors – is precisely why they are hired. There is no requirement that in the interests of critical purity they shed their creative and interpretive skills at the production threshold. Dai Vaughan has pointed out that the auteur theory set out to restore to Hollywood directors an artistic status denied them by the conditions of production (1983, p. 12). Later modifications to auteurism claimed to reject its individualising (and reactionary) tendencies by distinguishing between the film 'text' and the film director, for example, the *Howard Hawks text* and *Hawks the man*. Vaughan considers this to be no more than a subterfuge:

> The auteurists have created a criticism in which no one but the director may be discussed . . . and film, the most collaborative of the arts, is stuck with a literature which cannot at any level handle the idea of collaboration (1983, p. 13).

Tom Priestley, editor of *Isadora* (Karel Reisz, 1968) and co-editor of *Tess* (Roman Polanski, 1979), and a past visiting tutor at the National Film School, has given considerable thought to what he sees as a contradiction between the academic representation of film production, and his own long experience of it:

> Film studies is something that emerged – not an integral part of film-making – but something that has been attached to it, based on a whole set of preconceptions and their sort of 'auteur' ideas of the lonely creative man. This is so unlike the experience of film-making, that you wonder where they got it from.

The challenge that the collaborative nature of film production poses for the critic lies in the portrayal of the 'author-director' as sole creator. There could hardly be two cultural activities more dissimilar than literature and film-making, in both

Tom Priestley at work on a
Steenbeck machine in the 1970s

their production and reception: one solitary, and the other dependent on the
intervention of skilled technicians, finance, technology and, increasingly, audience previews. Auteurism does not recognise the idea of collective authorship
or creative synergy: the possibility that two people (say, a director and editor)
can achieve more working together than in a fixed hierachy of artist/director and
technician. Within the film industry itself it is routinely acknowledged that production is a collaborative process. The historic legacy of the 'giants of editing'
is now increasingly appreciated by film-makers, as Mick Audsley, film editor of
Dangerous Liaisons (Stephen Frears, 1988) and *Twelve Monkeys* (Terry Gilliam,
1995) points out:

> Think of Dede Allen, who has witnessed the Hollywood studio film going to the
> independents – *Bonnie and Clyde* etc. – and then coming back again into the studio
> system. Through all that, her name, and others – Anne Coates and Thelma
> Schoonmaker – are widely known in film circles. Their contribution is inestimable
> and if you talked to the directors of those films, they would corroborate this.

Within film studies, however, this notion has only gradually begun to filter
through into theoretical debates about film authorship.

There are signs of the emergence of a more progressive approach in recent
film writing, notably in Duncan Petrie (1996a) and (1996b). Petrie's books mark
an advance in that they pay serious attention to roles other than that of director. Brian McFarlane (1997) also profiles figures in the industry apart from
directors and actors, as does Colin Belfrage (n.d.). But although some of the

earlier excesses of auteurism have been moderated, its reductive view of the production process is still in evidence in much contemporary British writing about film, particularly in regard to film editing. Brian Spittles on John Ford, for example, offers a more developed approach by prefacing his analysis of Ford the auteur with a chapter on his 'film family': 'A film, however, is a collaborative adventure. Writers, cameramen, producers, composers, designers can all contribute to the overall conception of the work in hand' (2002, p. 17). Spittles writes in some detail about the great cinematographers, but there is no reference in his book to Dorothy Spencer, Jack Murray, Otho Lovering or any of the accomplished editors who worked on the feature films discussed. Instead, he cites a quotation from Ford's daughter, Barbara, as evidence of the monopoly over editing exercised by director and producer: 'My father was the second greatest editor who ever lived. Zanuck was the greatest' (2002, p. 67). The suggestion that the editing role on Ford's films was relegated to the joining up of shots by anonymous technicians is undermined by Don Fairservice's rigorous analysis (2001, pp. 269–73) of Dorothy Spencer's impeccably timed dialogue editing on *Stagecoach* (John Ford, 1939), achieved by working within the classic structure of wide, two-shot and close-ups provided by the director. Spencer, who also edited for Lubitsch and Hitchcock, received an Academy Award nomination for her work on *Stagecoach*, the first of four accolades in a career that spanned fifty years.

The purpose of emphasising collaboration is not to downgrade the role of the director, but to identify and understand the significance of each role within a complex interactive process. An efficient system of film production is based on the differentiation of skills, and the principle that specialisation enhances competence. A producer and director hiring a cinematographer, for example, will also in practice have contracted a complete camera crew – a specialised unit of many years' combined experience. This is also true of other departments such as post-production, where an editor will choose the assistants and usually the sound editing crew. A production company need not buy the skills of a highly regarded film editor (rumoured to earn between $5,000 and $20,000 per week in Hollywood) or pay more than minimum union rates, if the job of simply cutting to a director's prescription could be done by a computer-operator or an assistant film editor. A crew list that included a well-established cinematographer, production designer, line producer and editor would substantially increase a project's chances of securing the essential completion guarantee[3] – especially for a first-time (or a notoriously 'profligate') director. Completion bond companies have power to approve the director as well as heads of other departments, and their judgments are based on long experience of the structure of film production.

PROBLEMS OF RECOGNITION 2

> I don't think Mike Bradsell ever got his due credit for the amount he contributed
> to those Ken Russell pictures.
> Stuart Baird, editor, *Tommy* (Ken Russell, 1975), director, *US Marshals* (1998)

This observation by Stuart Baird, who worked as an assistant to film editor
Bradsell on some of Russell's successful early films, underlines the anonymity
of the editing role. Even if Bradsell had received acknowledgment beyond the
confines of the cutting room, writers on cinema have always had difficulty in
finding a language which expresses the contribution of the editor, overshadowed as it is by the image of the director. Popular perception of the role
of director has been reinforced by studio publicity photos where a 'name'
director is shown in poses that signify control over every aspect of production;
for example, looking through a viewfinder, sitting with the editor, or, most familiar of all, standing on the set and pointing authoritatively while the
cinematographer listens attentively. Screenwriter William Goldman has noted
how film promotion reinforces the creative status of a director in the eyes of
the media:

> They don't send production designers out on hype tours. It's the star or the
> director. So when the star says, 'I made up my part', or the director explains that
> he had this vision and voilà, it's now up there on the screen for you all to see and
> admire, that's what gets reported (1984, p. 102).

Richard Best, who edited *The Dam Busters* (Michael Anderson, 1955) and *Ice
Cold in Alex* (J. Lee Thompson, 1958), has described how the iconic image of
Eisenstein holding film in one hand and scissors in the other drew him into the
industry in the 1930s but also blinded him to the existence of a separate film
editing role.[4]

The less tangible contribution of film editors continues to be largely unrecog-
nised. An occasional tokenistic reference to the director's 'gifted editor' (adopting
the possessive form) only serves to reinforce the director's total ownership of the
editing process. The separation of function between, say, a cinematographer and
director is more immediately comprehensible and when critics do attempt to
identify the contribution of various departments, they usually credit the more visible roles. Tariq Anwar has contrasted the levels of recognition given to editors
with the higher profile enjoyed by directors of photography (DPs):

> I recall a TV critic once praising a cameraman for the 'timing' of his shots. All that
> gets noticed in editing and commented on, is the pace. Photography is the most

lauded of all the departments and I think it's the only one that has a presence outside of a film as well as within it. The photographed frame is the result of many people's work, like the director, laboratory [grader], design, make-up, etc., and yet the quality of the image is invariably attributed to the DP.

The relative visibility of the cinematographer was also noted by Tony Lawson, who edited with Kubrick and Peckinpah before cutting *The Butcher Boy* (Neil Jordan, 1997). He wrote to the magazine *Sight and Sound* in response to a review of that film, perplexed by the critic's attribution of rhythm and pacing to the cinematography:

> (Leslie) Dick uses words like 'stunning momentum', 'breakneck pace' and 'beautiful sudden rhythm', but then attributes these effects to 'the function of the cinematography'. In fact, all the words she uses more properly describe the function of editing. It is all too rare that film editing is commented on in reviews, and to find cinematography mistakenly praised for its effects is galling (1998, p. 68).

When interviewed later, Lawson acknowledged the difficulty of explaining precisely what the editing process involves. He was also concerned that revealing editing techniques might detract from the illusion and magic of cinema. Mick Audsley, too, is conscious of the problem of describing the editor's role:

> What's difficult to get across to people is that it's not just a button you switch, and out comes a good scene, or a good film editorially ... To me it's a stumbling through your responses, your feelings of what you have been presented with and trying to re-articulate it for the audience, to create the sort of journey you want them to go through.

He identifies a distinct editorial role, far removed from the image of the silently acquiescent film technician. For Audsley the responsibility of the editor is to balance the needs of the film with the wishes of the director, while retaining a strong sense of how the film will play for the audience.

Even those involved in film production may not fully understand the editor's contribution. Bernard Gribble, who edited *The Man in the White Suit* (Alexander Mackendrick, 1951), and Jonathan Morris, long-time collaborator with Ken Loach, both maintain that it wasn't until directors started coming into the cutting room and became more actively involved in the editing process, that even they really understood the transformations that can take place during editing.[5] For reviewers and academics who write about film, the problem of assessing

Mick Audsley, Stephen Frears'
regular collaborator, in 2003

editorial input is acute. Historian and film-maker Kevin Brownlow has cau-
tioned against the danger of misinterpretation:

> Editors are passed over by film historians because their work, when successful, is
> virtually unnoticeable. No historian, without knowing the problems, without
> knowing the director's working methods, or without being an editor himself, could
> possibly evaluate the editor's contribution (1968, p. 286).

The seamless quality of the final film will actually obscure an understanding of
the editor's role, and unless one had access to all of the shot film, marked-up
scripts, the different stages of the cut and a record of conversations that took
place during editing, it would be impossible to quantify the relative contributions of the editor, director or producer to the final version. According to Stuart
Baird the audience is unlikely anyway to be interested in tracing the editor's and
director's journey through the various drafts of the cut, and so the projected
film is widely considered to represent the director's original intention:

> It all looks so inevitable, so the audience assumes – why would they not? – *that* was
> the way it was always intended to be. You try to explain that it didn't look anything
> like that when it was first put together. It all looks so smooth, it all looks like it was
> in continuity, the director intended to go from there, to there …

The illusion of the director's smooth transference of a project from page to screen is reinforced by reading published scripts which derive from the finally released film. These give little indication of changes that may have taken place during shooting or post-production, as Roger Crittenden has pointed out: 'The free scripts given by *Sight and Sound* over the past year or two are, as far as I can tell, all based on the finished film and definitely not the original screenplay' (2000, p. 58).

The general assumption that directors 'edit' their films arises not only from the necessity to simplify the complexity of post-production, but also from the critical imperative to emphasise the creative authority of the director. Auteurists have argued that directors such as Ford and Hitchcock produced great films regardless of who they worked with, and have taken the other roles for granted. But, like most directors, they cast their key collaborators with as much care as their actors. Hitchcock's long partnership with editor George Tomasini – whom the director apparently wished to place under exclusive contract – and composer Bernard Herrmann, resulted in many of the director's finest films.[6] Ford also worked with Hollywood's best technicians, and benefited from the input of the distinguished editors already mentioned. Frank Clarke, supervising editor at MGM-British, recalls that in cutting *Mogambo* (John Ford, 1953) he had to employ all of his skills, including the supervision of additional shooting, to complete the film:

> The close-ups we did in the boat, did it back on the river . . . He [Ford] hadn't covered it very well, you know, certain things, skimped it . . . We went back on our own and shot the extras [additional material]. He didn't even know we'd done them, I don't think . . . He left it to me really. He thought the way he'd shot it was good enough, you know, 'just put it together'. But we had to work on it . . . We wanted to do things with it, so you had to shoot some more.

Mogambo may illustrate Ford's well-documented economy of shooting coverage, and it is possible that he lacked interest in this project. But whatever the shooting ratio, and however minor an example of Ford's work, Clarke's commitment to *Mogambo* demonstrated the professionalism that characterised all of his work, which included editing for George Cukor, Anthony Asquith, Terence Young and John Guillermin. Clarke expected to be creatively involved, and as a supervising editor he carried weight with many distinguished directors. When he was uniquely 'closed down' by Michelangelo Antonioni while cutting *Blow-Up* (1966), he completed the film but refused the editing credit, arguing that it should be transferred to the director. Antonioni's view of the editor as 'a pair of hands' is not generally shared by directors, and is certainly not accepted by any of the editors interviewed for this book. However, auteurists continue to claim that the director, if present during cutting 'directs' the editing, and if absent has predetermined the cutting points during shooting by restricting coverage or 'editing in camera'.[7] Both propositions offer an over-simplified view of post-production which will be addressed in Chapter 2.

Many editors are disinclined to go on record and state the level of their contribution to particular films, because of a sensitivity to the feelings of directors they have worked with before, and may want to work with again. In the highly competitive climate of film-making, self-publicity on the part of screenwriters, editors or cinematographers can work against their interests. Freelance technicians seek continuing employment contracts, and rocking the boat is unlikely to be helpful. Stuart Baird has referred to the close, almost secretive ties that can exist between editor and director: 'An editor's relationship with his director is very protective because it's the next job that comes along.' In fact editors often work on more productions than directors are able to, and thus benefit creatively and financially from this continuity of employment.[8] But even a world-class editor of the standing of Anne Coates has noted the insecurity of freelancing: 'Everybody always feels that they are never going to work again.'

Nevertheless, editors like Tom Priestley and Tony Lawson feel that academics and professional critics should engage more with the complexities of film-making. The 'unhealthy divide that exists between film-makers and film critics', referred to in Murphy (2001, p. xi), expressed concern about the critical under-evaluation of British film. But this statement also reflects the frustration felt by many practitioners with the remoteness of film theory from film practice, the obscurity of much of its writing, and the low level of interest in anyone except directors and actors. The paucity of critical recognition given to editors reflects an essentially 'top down' view of production perpetuated by much British writing on film, which Tom Priestley has alluded to – a kind of 'snobbism' that places a divide between the craftsman-technician and the artist-director – the old dichotomy between hand and brain (see Appendix: Filmographies).

Editors, designers, cinematographers, sound recordists – all understand the collaborative nature of the production process, and they represent far more than the inert technical backdrop assumed by so much critical theory. The thousands of hours of experience that technicians bring to a production clearly informs their dialogue with the director, and the subtlest of those interactions is between director and editor. In the words of Terry Rawlings, co-editor of *Alien* (Ridley Scott, 1979) and editor of *Chariots of Fire* (Hugh Hudson, 1981): 'A director will take the credit, but he takes the brickbats as well. I think they deserve to take the credit if they have done a good film, but I wish they would acknowledge the help they receive from their editors.'

NOTES

All unattributed quotations from editors are drawn from the interviews conducted for this book, apart from Richard Best's reference to the image of Eisenstein which is taken from his interview for the BECTU History Project.

1. Two important British books on film editing are by Ernest Walter (1973), who wrote an excellent manual for those interested in the technique of editing on film, and by Roger Crittenden (1981), now Deputy Director of the National Film and Television School, where he has taught editing for many years.

2. *The Technique of Film Editing* (1953) was originally solely authored by Reisz. Although written before Reisz had any direct experience of professional film editing, this book is notable for its contributions from editors including Jack Harris, Geoffrey Foot and Reginald Beck.

3. This is the financial underpinning required before a film can go into production. A specialist company guarantees the financiers (for a percentage fee related to the direct costs of production) that the film will be completed and delivered in accordance with the distribution agreement.

4. A similar image of Jean-Luc Godard holding a strip of film up to the light underscores the director's engagement with film editing, but it has obscured the contribution of editor Cécile Decugis to the films of Godard, Rohmer and Truffaut. It is paradoxical that Truffaut, the most enthusiastic early exponent of auteurism, appeared to show little interest in post-production when he became a director. According to Decugis: 'Truffaut rarely came into the cutting room because he did not like it very much' (quoted in McGrath, 2001, p. 66).

5. Broader understanding of the editor's role may develop with releases of DVD versions of feature films. Certainly *The Hamster Factor and Other Tales of Twelve Monkeys* (Keith Fulton, Louis Pepe, 1995), a documentary co-released with the feature film, presents a comprehensive picture of Mick Audsley's editorial contribution to *Twelve Monkeys*.

6. George Tomasini's wife, Mary Brian, interviewed in the mid-1990s, talked about the close working relationship between her husband and the director over nine key films: 'Mr Hitchcock always gave George first cut. He wanted to see his interpretation.' Tomasini rejected Hitchcock's attempt to put him under exclusive contract: 'Sometimes the screenplays that he [Hitchcock] was doing didn't come together very quickly, and George liked to work. So Mr Hitchcock said that they would make an agreement that he could do pictures for other directors in between, but after a picture was finished Mr Hitchcock would have first dibs on him. He said, "I'll let the film pile up for you." So that's the way it worked' (quoted in Igel, 2002).

7. Rudi Fehr, who worked with Hitchcock, Huston, Walsh, Vidor, Curtiz – none of whom came into the cutting room – edited Hitchcock's *I Confess* (1953) and *Dial*

M for Murder (1954), and says that neither film was cut in the camera (LoBrutto, 1991; Oldham, 1992). However, he does point to *Rope* (1948), with its uniquely constructed series of long takes designed to work like a continuous shot, as a technical example of cutting in the camera (Oldham, 1992). This experiment in dispensing with editing is generally considered interesting if unsuccessful.

8. American editor Carol Littleton has pointed out the disparity in experience between directors and other grades: 'There are few directors who have a large body of work, Steven Spielberg, John Huston, but most don't. Editors, cinematographers, production designers, and so on essentially have more experience than directors do' (quoted in Oldham, 1992, p. 75).

2

The Film Editor's Role

SOME COMMON MISCONCEPTIONS

> I suppose it's the old back-room stuff, the cutting room floor, people who cut
> things up. In fact what we do is exactly the opposite – we build things up.
> Mick Audsley, editor, *Dirty Pretty Things* (Stephen Frears, 2002), *Twelve
> Monkeys*

The popular image of the film director combines the authorial and the author-
itative: both the inspiration behind the filmed project, and the controller of cast
and crew. It is therefore unsurprising that the supporting role of the editor is
generally understood to be that of a technical pair of hands, a functionary who
cuts to the director's prescriptions. The work is assumed to combine the mechanical process of joining together largely predetermined sequences with that of
cutting the film down to length. But as Mick Audsley points out above, editing
is initially more concerned with constructing than with reducing, a role that is
both creative and technical. In practice, most directors require much more than
a compliant cutter, and the process of selecting an editor normally takes into
account the kind of experience they can bring to a production. The long and
illustrious career of editor Anne Coates, for example, provides a depth of experience which would be highly valued by the producer/director teams that engage
her. She might not appear to be the obvious choice to work with younger British
and American directors but, as she has pointed out, 'They're only employing you
for what you can bring' – in her case experience that spans fifty years working
with directors ranging from David Lean in the UK to Steven Soderbergh in Hollywood.

The extent to which film narrative and shot structure are predetermined
depends partly on the effectiveness of any storyboarding drawn prior to shooting, and whether at the editing stage the script works as originally intended. As
Terry Rawlings has pointed out, storyboarding is a valuable *aide-mémoire* for the
director in terms of shot coverage, but will usually serve as no more than a guide
during the final cutting: 'If it's all drawn out, the directors can tick them off –

"we've covered this, covered this", but once you start editing, it takes on another life. But you do have all the ingredients to play with.' The activity that Rawlings refers to, of manipulating picture and sound to produce new meanings, is what makes film editing so compulsive:

> I'm endlessly amazed at what you can do with the same film. You get, say, twenty set-ups in a sequence and you can do anything with them within reason. Change the emphasis, the meaning. Change the music, and it all means something else.

Even on a low shooting ratio, the scope for editorial interpretation remains high. American editor David Saxon attempted to describe the complexity of film editing by using a mathematical example:

> With everything already created and on film, what is left for the editor to do? After all, anyone can put it together, no? Let's see what the editor does. Take an example. Say there are 10 shots and that they may be arranged in any possible way. Incredibly, there are 3,628,800 different ways to assemble just those 10 shots. We're not talking about cutting, just arranging. Add one more shot and you have almost 40 million possibilities (1984, p. 11).

Each shot comprises twenty-four frames per second of cinema running time, so even a ten-second trim contains 239 cutting points. In a feature film the choice of shot combinations is partly suggested by script. But in action sequences, car chases, battles, fantasies and montages, where there is little or no shot continuity, the range of editing possibilities becomes almost unlimited.

A director who wants to limit the range of editing options and restrict the possibility of re-cutting must plan for the shooting of uninterrupted sequences (see Chapter 1, note 7). *Russian Ark* (Alexander Sokurov, 2003) has successfully created a model of the feature film as one continuous ninety-minute take with the use of Steadicam and high-definition video. Earlier attempts by Miklós Jancsó, for example, to construct films with continuous camera movements were limited to the camera magazine's running time of ten minutes. These long takes would have required considerably fewer edits than the number of picture cuts ranging between one and three thousand that usually constitute a feature film. However, the relationship between length of shot, shooting ratio and the amount of editing required can be misleading. A director working on a higher shooting ratio consisting largely of re-takes, offers less scope for editorial interpretation than a director working to a lower ratio using a classic shot/reverse shot structure. The possibility of inter-cutting determines the degree of editorial complexity here, not the shooting ratio.

In a tightly scripted dialogue scene with restricted shooting coverage, the choice of cutting points can be enormously varied, and an apparently uncomplicated scene between two people eating can be transformed by inspired editing into something memorable. Assembled one Sunday morning and relying on a simple shot structure that alternates between Albert Finney and Joyce Redman, editor Antony Gibbs, whose credits include *The Loneliness of the Long Distance Runner* (Tony Richardson, 1962) and *Ronin* (John Frankenheimer, 1998), considers the eating scene in *Tom Jones* (Tony Richardson, 1963) to be one of his most successful:

> People talk about it today – they talk about the eating scene and I feel pretty smug about it. I mean of all the things I've ever done, that has given millions of people so much pleasure that I'm very happy with it.

On a first glance the editing of this scene looks as though it may have been designed during shooting, but closer analysis reveals the concealed art of meticulous editing. The placing of the narration, 'Heroes – whatever high ideals we may have of them . . .', briefly cues a roguish smile from the head-bandaged Albert Finney, and introduces a voluptuous sequence in which sex masquerades as dining. There is no dialogue to orchestrate the cuts – only the voracious sounds of eating and an editing rhythm which traces the eating gestures of Finney and Redman, who start and complete each other's actions in alternating cuts. Gibbs made no subsequent changes to this scene, 'except to remove three feet of tricksy one-frame inter-cuts at the very end' (quoted in Sharples Jr, 1977, p. 13).

The actual process of editing often determines how a scene will develop, irrespective of cutting points indicated in the script. For example, cutting earlier rather than later from an establishing shot to a succeeding closer shot may present an opportunity for including additional shots, and so forth. Each editing decision informs the next, influenced by rhythm, performance and continuity. Gibbs' editing of the eating scene underlines how a well-directed sequence is in the end still reliant on the improvisation and timing of the editor. *Tom Jones* reflects Gibbs' mature editing skills, and few directors who have not themselves been editors would have been able to maximise its full potential. Edward Dmytryk, a Paramount editor turned director, remarked on the editorial pretensions often expressed during meetings of the Directors Guild of America in the late 1960s:

> In our own guild the annual meetings invariably erupt with cries of, 'Let's fight for the right to control the cutting of our pictures.' It's been interesting to note that these cries almost always come from our youngest, least experienced members,

men who would probably strangle in their own trims if they were placed at the
bench and told, 'There, go ahead, cut' (quoted in Koszarski, 1977, p. 379).

Ultimate control of the final cut may well not reside with the film-makers
at all, but with the studios and distributors. Even so, the invisibility of film
editors, in both film theory and sometimes conveniently in film practice
where reputations are at stake, belies their often crucial and creative contribution.

INTENTION, ACCIDENT AND DISCOVERY

A film critic may perhaps, while sitting alone in the darkened auditorium, ascribe
all kinds of directorial intentions and aesthetic characteristics to the films being
viewed. But because film criticism rarely takes account of the practice of film-
making, little recognition is given to the way in which chance and interaction
can inflect the finished film. Editor Terry Rawlings remarked on the occurrence
of chance in post-production:

> This myth that gets built up by film critics: when you've worked closely with a
> director and you've struggled over a sequence, and it comes out and they say, 'the
> meaning behind that sequence is summed up as so and so', and you think – we got
> there by accident. You know, we'd struggled with that so hard, that in the end these
> things just happened. We didn't aim to do this. So much is written into what they
> see which never existed in the first place.

He underlines the value of experimentation and describes how this, facilitated
by computer-based editing, influenced the cutting of Catherine Zeta-Jones' and
Sean Connery's performances in *Entrapment* (Jon Amiel, 1999):

> When she [Zeta-Jones] goes under the strings, the dissolves I originally had as cuts.
> I played with it for ages and I suddenly got this idea, that I wanted it to be like he
> was being absolutely seduced by her, and it was all drifting into one thing, which he
> snaps her out of in the end. And the dissolves worked so well, because I was
> playing with them on the machine. I thought, 'God this is fantastic,' I wasn't going
> to get this to happen on film.

Rawlings' reputation among editors and directors is well established, having
edited *Alien*, *Chariots of Fire* and *Blade Runner* (Ridley Scott, 1982). Direc-
tor/editor Stuart Baird, who has had a long working relationship with Terry
Rawlings, believes that much of the credit for the success of *Chariots of Fire* is
owed to Rawlings' editing together with the musical score by Vangelis.

Terry Rawlings at a film trim bin

Inspiration during post-production, however, can come not just from editors, directors or composers, but from beyond the cutting room. Antony Gibbs described the source of ideas for the optical effects at the beginning of *Tom Jones*:

Obviously Tony [Richardson] was going to shoot it in some wacky way, which he did, and I put it together. And then we discovered in the back of Humphries' [film laboratory] Optical Books all these weird opticals – the flips, the fans, and I thought these would be fun, and Tony said 'Yes', so I rang up Humphries and said, 'Listen, we want to use some of these opticals', and they said, 'Oh, you can't use those. We haven't used them since 1924.' Anyway, we made them re-do all the mattes, and we put these in. Tony suggested the little iris to say 'he's the baddie' and so it romped along from there, and we put in a lot more voiceover, and then at the beginning of the picture we had this prologue – you know, where the baby is found, and initially it ran about five minutes. I got it down to about three minutes, and it was just too long, and Tony said, 'We've got to do something about it, because I mean, you're the editor ...' and we talked about it and I cut it down a bit more, took another fifteen seconds out of it here and there ...

Tony, Vanessa [Redgrave] and myself would go out in the evenings, have fun, and talk about the movie, and future movies and so on ... We were driving down Wardour Street in a traffic jam, and Vanessa said, 'Why don't you cut it like a silent movie.' And Tony and I looked at each other [*laugh*], 'God yes, why hadn't we thought of that.' And you know, the five-minute scene which had become two and three-quarter minutes, suddenly became one and a half, which is what it should have been. And it was Vanessa.

The stylistic inspiration for the beginning of *Tom Jones* would in all likelihood be attributed to its director Tony Richardson, but the complexity of film production will often allow an unimaginably diverse range of creative inputs. Conversations in cabs, film laboratory liaison, chance and what is discovered during the physical act of cutting itself may often result in new creative perspectives.

FROM ROUGH CUT TO FINE CUT

The initial stages of editing typically take place during principal photography, the standard six- to eight-week period when the film is being shot. A print is taken, usually on a daily basis, from the original camera negative, and the synchronised sound and picture 'rushes' provide the basis for the cutting copy which goes through a number of editing stages before reaching a fine cut approved by director and producer. The film's individual sequences are constructed from shots photographed from a number of different camera set-ups, usually ranging from a master shot to individual closer shots, which are then combined – or 'articulated' according to Mick Audsley – into a coherent shape by the editor.

The fine cut, usually finished within twelve to sixteen weeks of the completion of principal photography, then has mixed sound and music tracks added while the original film negative is matched to the cutting copy. A fresh print is then struck which is fully graded in the laboratory to ensure the required photographic consistency and quality. This final combined sound and picture release print will include optical effects such as dissolves, freeze-frames, wipes and titles.[1] The organisation of the soundtracks now usually lies outside the jurisdiction of the film's picture editor, who may nevertheless express strong opinions on the placing of specific sound effects and overall sound texture (for the emergence of the role of sound editor, see Chapter 3). There is not the scope in this book to write a separate section on the work of the sound or dubbing editor, although there is a growing critical recognition of how much this aspect of post-production contributes to enriching the final film.[2] Mike Le-Mare, sound editor of *The Boat* (Wolfgang Petersen, 1981), and Richard Hymns, who worked on

Saving Private Ryan (Steven Spielberg, 1998), are among those who have established formidable reputations in this field, and a number of highly regarded film editors like Terry Rawlings claim that a sound-editing background has helped their picture editing by developing a feeling for the pacing and timing of cuts.

For the editing cycle to begin only on completion of shooting would be unusual, but there are directors who wish to work alongside the editor continu-ously. For example, director Ken Loach and editor Jonathan Morris, who have worked as a team since 1986, aim to jointly construct a first cut nine weeks after the end of filming, and spend a further five weeks fine cutting. There is no distinction between the editor's first cut and the director's fine cut on a Ken Loach film. Typically, however, editing runs in parallel with shooting so that a first assembly or rough cut of the complete picture in story continuity can be shown to the director shortly after completion of principal photography.

Editors take individual approaches to making their first assembly. Tariq Anwar prefers to use temporary music to indicate mood and effect, even at this very early stage:

How we translate the director's wishes in first assembly and sometimes re-interpret them may distinguish our differing styles in that some editors – myself included – like to present a cut as close to a fine cut as possible, with temp music and effects. Others prefer to show something looser and are reluctant to use music because it may give a false impression of the cut.

Lesley Walker, whose credits include *Shadowlands* (Richard Attenborough, 1993) and *Nicholas Nickleby* (Douglas McGrath, 2002), sees film editing as working through a series of layers, from a first assembly which she produces within a week of the production coming off the floor, through to a rough cut two weeks later, and then on to producing a fine cut within the following five to eight weeks. Unlike Tariq Anwar, her approach to the initial edit is spartan: 'I never put in music very early. I keep it fairly bleak. This is your first layer, and the other ones are only going to enhance it.' In film editing, unlike computer-based editing, removed frames or sequences need to be hung in a trim bin or filed away by an assistant editor. Restoring removed material may be time-consuming, another reason why Lesley Walker has tended to cut long when editing on film: 'I do not cut very tight on a first assembly, because some things get lost. But I will work out a pattern of editing ... in essence it will be long and have everything in it.'

Peter Tanner, who cut *Kind Hearts and Coronets* (Robert Hamer, 1949) and *The Cruel Sea* (Charles Frend, 1953), mapped out a tight cut from the very beginning, working against the more conventional approach of an initial loose or rough edit, and in so doing made an early narrative assessment of the film:

> I do go for a fairly tight cut right at the start. I don't like rough cuts as such. Your first cut is very important, because it's the whole feel of the thing. What you do afterwards is just busying it up – a refinement. Maybe you change one or two things, and then the director sees it and he may want to change a few things.

Tanner's early creative rather than mechanical involvement in constructing the film demonstrates how important the editor's role is in transforming the raw rushes material from the outset of cutting. Russell Lloyd also liked to put his own stamp on the first, editor's cut, which suited the working methods of director John Huston, for whom Lloyd edited many films:

> When I've done the first cut, I've always done it for myself – to hell with the director, you know. I mean the director may say things. John [Huston] was very easy. You have to understand that John didn't like to be in the cutting process, he liked to be quite away from it. You'd run the picture with him, and you'd come to a sequence and go through it and he would say, 'Oh I think you'd better go through that again.' That's the only thing he would say. He would never say, 'I want a close-up there.' He didn't like to just bend everybody to his way, he liked to see what somebody else brings to it.

In practice, most directors will allow an editor a degree of interpretation in constructing the first cut, and some editors prefer not to involve the director until after this has been screened. John Bloom endorses Lesley Walker's idea of the first cut as being a pattern or blueprint for the finished edit. He also provides an insight into the way in which the editor's perception of the material begins to influence the final shape of the film:

> As far as I'm concerned, I'm sort of giving him [the director] my ideas. I hope that they will work. This is on the best level of friendship where you get on with somebody very well and can express yourself, and so forth, but eventually I expect the film to be merely a blueprint, and to carry on from there.

Tony Lawson agrees that it is important at this early stage to 'take a view, not to just top and tail rushes', and states in plain terms that 'the first job is to put it together, and the second job is to make it work'.

Mick Audsley considers that the first cut transforms the rushes into a version of the film reflecting the writer's and director's original intentions:

You want the first cut to be an articulated version of the film. I've never quite understood this thing about what a 'loose cut' was at each particular stage, because for me to read a scene rhythmically and for the pieces to mesh together and to be saying all sorts of things, it's got to be cut. If it's a first cut I feel I have an obligation to realise all of what is written on the page at that moment, because people have spent years to get it that far, and it's been shot, which is a huge effort. I feel obliged to present that on the screen at least once, within reason. So my first goal when it's been shot is to honour everything that's been shot, to try and understand it and it's an irony to me that an assembly, or 'editor's cut' as it's known, is not really an editor's cut in my view, it's a *writer's* cut. It's what the director shot in his obligation to shoot the pages he's given, or has decided on, or collaborated in.

The obligation to present this version 'at least once', in Audsley's words, suggests that the first cut (which may be up to 50 per cent longer than the fine cut) marks the beginning of an editorial journey in which the film undergoes some significant further changes in both content and structure, before the negative is finally cut. The time spent in close proximity to the material over a considerable period of time can produce what Audsley has referred to as 'film blindness'. For Terry Rawlings the freshness of the editor's first cut provides a valuable benchmark against which the final cut is measured:

The first cut of any film is the editor's, no one else's really. The one *you* present to everybody, practically – unless the director's on your neck every night. But mostly they haven't got the time. You present the film. It's your version of the film. And from then on you start working on it together, and getting it to what the director really wants. But that first cut is usually one of the best. It's far too long probably, the story may not work completely well, but usually the first cut is a very interesting version. Your first thoughts are so often right. During the course of the editing process you'll try other things. But it's amazing how many times you come back to what you first thought.

ENHANCING SCRIPT

Most editors agree that a film is more than just a photographic version of the script. They would also agree, however, that the original script is usually a reliable guide to the film's eventual quality. Although the script may evolve in post-production, it is unlikely that unpromising material can be completely transformed by editing alone. At the beginning of his career Tony Lawson, whose credits include *Bad Timing* and *The Good Thief* (Neil Jordan, 2002), thought that he could take any project and make it work editorially but now accepts that 'a script that is solid is a prerequisite'. Lawson tries to get involved at the writing stage and make suggestions if he feels they are required. For Antony Gibbs, the screenwriter is the under-recognised 'cog' in the creative process: 'For me the most important aspect of film-making is the script. If you've got a lousy script, nobody can fix it. Editors and directors, we're all as good as the scripts we work on.'

Tom Priestley considers the script to be only one of several important elements: 'It's certainly true that the stronger the script, the stronger the cast, the better the cinematographer – the easier the job is for the editor. You can't make bad material good.' But he also notes that the film's final form is not entirely predetermined by its original script: 'The cliché about sculpture, that the sculptor merely finds the statue which is waiting in the stone, applies equally to editing' (quoted in Sharples Jr, 1977, p. 24). The uncut rushes therefore constitute the raw material that will need to be worked on during editing to reveal the film's final shape. The eventual relationship between the shooting script and the film's fine cut (referred to by a number of editors as 'the final draft') may be distant.

Tony Lawson in Dublin, 1999 (Reproduced by kind permission of Frank Fennell Photography, Dublin)

It is difficult for those not directly involved in the editing process to have a full understanding of the journey taken between viewing rushes and screening the final print. Tariq Anwar echoes Stuart Baird's earlier observation about the apparent inevitability of what is screened:

> In story terms the film that's screened or televised is assumed by reviewers and audiences to have always been that way. The fact that scenes may have been deleted and rearranged will not be apparent. The fact that shots have been re-framed, re-graded or digitally enhanced will also go unnoticed. Maybe an actor's performance is improved through judicious cutting or in post-synching, or a point made more clear by editing for overlaid ADR [automatic dialogue replacement] lines.

These improvements to a film's overall effect are significantly dependent on the technical and creative skills of the editor. A highly developed sensitivity to the nuances and timing of performance, a feeling for dramatic construction and story structure ('requiring an understanding of the curve', as Lesley Walker describes it), would be expected of a creative feature film editor. John Bloom, who won an Oscar for his editing of *Gandhi* (Richard Attenborough, 1982), was initially drawn to film-making through a love of theatre, and came into editing via the script department. But the notion that editing is essentially a process of realising a pre-existing script was not reflected in his long experience of the cutting rooms:

> I've always had this nightmare that you're going to start on a film and it's going to be shot and edited in such a way that there's nothing for you to do – just literally put it together and that'll be it, and I think a lot of directors I've worked with, apart from Karel Reisz, really believed that in their hearts. And then comes this terrible shock when they find the film isn't working.

Bloom's experience, shared by Karel Reisz, was that to edit was to re-write the film in the cutting room:

> So in a way, almost every film one's ever worked on *does* take a very seriously different direction from the script. I mean I can't think of anything I've done that [hasn't] really. If you looked at the original shooting script and you looked at the film you would say, 'Well wait a minute, what happened?' Because in simply trying to make things work – often brought about by over-length – it really does end up with you having to do restructuring in order to make up for it.

Bloom cites the example of *The First Wives Club* (Hugh Wilson, 1996) where a leading actor's part and his affair with the Goldie Hawn character was deleted:

> The film couldn't stand, didn't want, another relationship. You just didn't want to be away from the central three for any length of time and concentrate on anybody with another character, except for brief moments. So the J. S. character had to go. I just tried it, and just completely lost the character one day, and showed it.

Clearly such decisions would need the approval of director and producer, but an editor of Bloom's standing would be expected to take a position on story structure and if necessary initiate or suggest modifications to the original script.

The role may also require the editor to act as a custodian of what was originally written, and Bloom argued for the removal of additional sequences directed by Richard Lester in his production of *The Ritz* (1976), an adaptation of a stage play brought over from New York. Lester had added 'lots of business, and little comedic moments' in an attempt to open the play out:

> He required lots of persuasion to take them out, and he finally agreed, but I always felt he was a bit embittered in a way about it. I remember him once, when his credit came up – 'A Richard Lester film' – and he said, 'Oh it's a John Bloom film'. You know, he wanted to bring something of himself to it – very much a sort of scatty type of madcap comedy – but the comedic moments just didn't work. They got in the way . . . they weren't that well done, I suppose, so you took those things out and the film seemed to flow a lot better. Yes, it wasn't as particularly cinematic, but it never was going to be, and the other things didn't make it cinematic.

Bloom's suggestions were not always accepted, however. On *Gandhi* he urged director Richard Attenborough to make a cut of fifteen minutes to tighten up the structure which 'would have jumped forward the action somewhat', but Attenborough was adamant and in retrospect Bloom considers the director to have been right in retaining the sequence, given the epic length of the film.

Jonathan Morris found himself in the reverse position of having to argue for the reinstatment of a flashback sequence originally scripted and shot for *My Name Is Joe* (1998), which was taken out of the film by director Ken Loach, partly on the suggestion of actor Iciar Bollain, partner of the film's writer Paul Laverty. The flashback graphically depicts reformed alcoholic Joe (Peter Mullan) making a vicious drunken attack on his former girlfriend, Rhona (Carol Pyper Rafferty). The sequence was carefully shot to inter-cut with a scene in the present, where Joe explains his reasons for giving up drinking to his new girlfriend Sarah (Louise Goodall). The alternating shots between Joe and Sarah

Jonathan Morris, Ken Loach's regular collaborator, editing a documentary in 2000

match the screen space of Joe and Rhona, relating both women to him in past and present. The problems of shifting time within a sequence caused some unease with Loach and Bollaín, according to Morris:

> Social realism shouldn't use flashbacks, it is not 'arty' film-making and so I think that was in the back of Ken's mind. He's an icon for social realism, and yet he's got this flashback in there, a flashback within a sequence. I think it worried him slightly, and when Iciar said she wasn't keen on it, it may have been for similar reasons, and that's why it went out.

The deletion of the flashback with Joe and Rhona concerned Morris:

> I said we've got to put them back, because the whole power of it is seeing him as he was, otherwise we never saw him as a drunk. And there's a sequence towards the end of the film, where he grabs Louise Goodall, his girlfriend in the film, he grabs her at the wall, and she says, 'Are you going to hit me, too?'

For Morris, this sequence with Louise Goodall achieved its full pathos only within the context of Joe's previously violent and abusive life, and Morris successfully argued for the reinstatement of the deleted flashback.

Mick Audsley finds that the conventional practice of overlapping editing and shooting allows a valuable editorial input into the production process, and he describes the dialogue that took place with director Stephen Frears on *High Fidelity* (2000):

> It was a lot of fun, because there we were considering the writing as we went along and it was kind of shaping itself, so the conversations were interesting. If I thought there was a beat missing or a scene was redundant, we could find ways of shooting something to short-circuit it and head off problems. But we were having that conversation while the film was being shot, on a daily basis. And mostly that's happened with all the directors I've worked with.

A crucial function for Audsley is to assess how the film components work as the material arrives in the cutting room, and to make vital decisions about whether additional covering shots are required:

> A good director handles the film tempo well. You don't want to be cutting something just because it took so long to walk across the room. You want the shots to be able to compress it, or want an editorial way of leaving it out. That's crucial. Often we have these conversations on the phone: 'Should we provide something that allows us to take that out at a later date if we need to' – and we say, 'Yes, let's have a shot that allows us to skip that bit quicker.' To me that's the job, you've got to make the film and understand how it works as building blocks, dramatically . . . it's wrapped up in the relationship between the writing and the editing or the movement of the film forwards. That's what you're dealing with all the time – what is the first shot of the scene, what advances the story, what is its meaning when placed against the last shot of the previous scene? I'm asking myself those questions about the dramatic structure all the time.

Jim Clark had a long and productive working relationship with director John Schlesinger. The opening sequence of *Darling* (1965), as originally scripted and shot, did not work at the editing stage, and Clark and Schlesinger planned a new opening sequence over dinner one evening, and gave their version to writer Troy Kennedy Martin to develop in a re-write. Schlesinger valued Clark sufficiently as a collaborator to fly him out to the United States to advise on the post-production of *Midnight Cowboy* (1969) which, according to Clark, had run into problems during editing: 'We all knew John had a great picture there, but the structure had eluded him.'

The transposition of narrative from script to unedited rushes is the first stage in the production process. The film may then take a different conceptual direction, either by reworking the existing shot material, or by adding new elements, as Tom Priestley found on *Leo the Last* (John Boorman, 1970):

The script is a version of that story on paper. The filming process is re-writing it on film, so in a sense you then do it backwards. I mean having re-written it on film, editing is then making that into the form in which it functions effectively. As to how far it changes, it depends – you know there's actually no rule. One of my films, *Leo the Last*, from the first cut we cut hours' worth of material out, then added a lot of songs which were not in the original concept at all.

Priestley considers that the film develops a life and momentum of its own during shooting and editing, and making it work effectively may mean departing from what was originally written, and ignoring cutting points and timings suggested in the marked-up script:

In a sense what you're doing is you're allowing something to come to life, and it happens, I think, with writers, too. They start writing and suddenly a character will want to do something they'd never thought of, but it's just in the nature of that character to do it … I can take any text, and I could mark it up with a pencil at the cutting points, a dialogue scene, and it would all make perfect sense and would seem good; and you could work with the film and not actually use a single one of those cutting points because the film's telling you something different … Any conversation or any scene is more than just a lot of dialogue strung together. I mean nothing is more boring than a scene that is cut strictly: 'I speak', cut – 'you speak', cut – 'I speak', cut – because there's no subtext allowed for, and then it's just a game of ping-pong, if you like.

As the edit progresses the editor's perspective usually shifts from an exclusive concern with detail to a deepening engagement with the final structure of the film. In Tony Lawson's words:

That's what I think editing is in a way. When you first assemble the scene, you worry about frames, you worry about one shot to another, and then once you've got that and you forget that you've worried about that section, you start to see a rather more general view of it. And you start to worry about bigger things, scenes and juxtaposition of scenes, as opposed to juxtaposition of shots.

Creative editors are intimately involved in determining the film's final structure, as Mick Audsley explains:

You're having a constant conversation in your head about the long-term goal of editing film as well as the short term. That for me is the fun of it. I still enjoy sticking the scenes together, but it's making the movie work that I'm really keen about.

ENHANCING PERFORMANCE

Some editors prefer to come to a production 'cold' – that is, to stay well away from the set during shooting, and to dispense with the script at an early stage, so as to approach the filmed material with as much objectivity as possible. Tom Priestley mentioned the importance of preserving 'creative doubt', that the editor particularly should bring 'no baggage' to post-production. Other editors visit the set during filming, hoping to gain a better understanding of the director's intentions, as well as developing an insight into how sequences may cut together and perhaps advising on tricky questions of shot coverage. It would be unusual, however, for an editor to communicate any feelings about performance on set, since this is the director's domain. An editor's evaluation starts in the cutting room, and comments relating to performance are frequently discussed with the director by telephone during shooting. Monitoring performance begins while reviewing the rushes (or 'dailies' as they are called in America), which, in John Bloom's case, reflects his early interest in the theatre:

> That is, I think, one of my main jobs, to be watching and seeing if the
> performances are, in my terms at least, working; if, in simple terms, I feel they're

John Bloom (r) with Richard Attenborough on the set of *A Chorus Line* in 1985 (Photograph by Alan Pappé from *A Chorus Line* special photography presentation book. Reproduced by kind permission of SB International, London)

going a bit over the top, they're straining too hard, or maybe they're not lively enough. Something that can be controlled, shall we say – apart from the unfortunate thing of having a miscast actor. I certainly feel that's absolutely a part of what I should be doing, and drawing the director's attention to.

The careful monitoring of performance during production is also part of Mick Audsley's approach in his working relationship with director Stephen Frears:

> That conversation while we're still shooting is absolutely crucial because that, in a way, is where so much of the work is done … So on a daily basis you can express your concerns, certainly about performances. With Stephen, it's not whether they are good or bad performances, but what do we think is appropriate to make this film tick. And that can be very difficult. Artists come in and they are pushing one particular way and it just takes time.

Performances may have to be reined in by the director on set and in post-production by the editor. They can also be fabricated by judicious cutting. Lesley Walker has pointed out a contemporary difficulty of getting reaction shots, particularly with some actors trained in the method school:

> There are certain actors and actresses, once they've done their line, will not have anything here, in the face … Debra Winger is wonderful at it, and she's there all the time. I mean she's totally in role, [Anthony] Hopkins is the same. Johnny Depp, fabulous at it. Benicio Del Toro who was in *Fear and Loathing in Las Vegas* [Terry Gilliam, 1998], he too, but he's a method actor … You get it in the end, but that's a totally made-up performance in the cutting room, because in one scene in *Fear and Loathing* there are ten takes of him in one scene. I've used a line from this one and two from that one, a word from that one, because that's the way he performs.

John Bloom mentions some of the tricks of the trade, which include using reaction shots to tighten performance and adding pace to a scene by cutting away from problems in one actor's delivery of a line, and sometimes changing statements into questions:

> Cutting for reaction shots when you need either to tighten up performance, tighten up the dialogue, make it flow better, and in flowing maybe taking out a word or even changing a syllable, or half a syllable … Something where a line should be a question mark, where somehow the actor has managed each time to deliver it as a statement, then you go through all the various takes and find one where there was an upward inflection.

Many of the editors interviewed talked about how intervention in the cutting room had saved or improved performance. Bloom, for example, had to use the startled expression of an actor at the sound of a clapperboard in *The Last Valley* (James Clavell, 1971) to get a surprised reaction shot which the actor had previously refused to give. He also cited the example of a well-known Hollywood actor whose performance on set required additional work in post-production:

> She just wasn't hitting it really, I suppose, and certainly by [using] various tricks of the trade, by obviously culling together the very best that you can find, and then at the end of it to come up with a performance of which people say, 'Gosh, [she] has never been as good', which many people did, well I was thrilled by that.

One of Britain's outstanding editors was Jack Harris, who cut for David Lean. Jim Clark, who worked as an assistant to Harris (and considers him to have been his mentor), recounts how Harris carefully moulded a performance by Marilyn Monroe:

> I've always said that dialogue films are far more difficult to cut than action films, because dialogue involves nuances of characterisation, and very often, if the actor isn't particularly good, or if the performance isn't great, you can do an enormous amount of what Jack Harris always called 'love cutting', and I've 'love cut' many actors. It means liking the actor enough to help improve the performance because, for example, when we did *The Prince and the Showgirl* [Laurence Olivier, 1957] all those years ago, Jack was forever love cutting Marilyn, who was very short-sighted and would bump into things quite a bit, and her performance would change every take. And very often it was a matter of how you use the best bits – one bit from one take, and one bit from another – and knit them all together by adroit cutaways. I think you've got to like your actors, because you come to live with them and they become living, breathing creatures on your machine. But you've also got to be very aware of performance pitch, and you've got to be able to pass comments to the director without actually causing him to feel that you're dumping on him.

It is one thing to assist a professional actor by judicious editing, but quite another to rise to the challenge of creating characterisation from non-professional actors. For Antony Gibbs this was one problem among a number that beset the editing of *Performance*:

> The biggest, biggest problem I had on that picture was making the non-actors work ... To get a performance out of them required pretty flighty scissors to do it. And

I've always thought to myself, whatever anybody else thought about *Performance*, the fact that people seem to accept them as actors is a tribute to my scissors.[3]

Many actors appreciate the power of editing to shape performance. Kathleen Turner has remarked on her need to return to the theatre to tune and refresh her acting skills: 'You can forget how much a camera and a good editor can do for you. You need to be on stage where nobody can fix it to be sure of your work' (quoted in Charity, 1999, p. 27). As a film editor, John Bloom considers that his primary responsibility is clear: 'The most important part of my job is protecting and making performances work, because without performances you're not going to have anything which is believable.'

MAKING IT WORK

Editing is difficult to convey because much of its visual impact eludes written description. The following, however, is an attempt to reveal some of the approaches and techniques employed.

CUTTING MONTAGE

A film script will give only a cursory suggestion of shot structure, and for montage sequences the film editor often has an almost infinite number of cutting options. Lesley Walker has described an approach to montage that underlines the huge range of shot choices in cutting a crowd sequence, in *Cry Freedom* (Richard Attenborough, 1987) for example, a method she learned when working as an assistant editor to John Bloom:

> I normally go through every take, and I will pick – it's something that Bloom used to do actually – pick the best bits out of each take and hang them in the bin. In film days I'd have a peg that will be, say, 'The Funeral', and then I'll have 'Faces' and then I'll join them all together without actually looking, just join them and work on it from there ... If there's a face that is interesting, and it's only three feet, I'll take that out. So I take the interesting stuff out of the big rolls, and then assemble it in any way I feel like, depending on the mood of the day, and work on it from there.

Though this may appear somewhat random, it allows the editor to reduce the sheer amount of material available (often shot on a ratio of twenty to one for drama and, in a few cases, as much as a hundred to one) and to examine unexpected shot juxtapositions, while providing a structure that imposes some thematic continuity. Clearly the choice and running order of the shots would be reviewed as she works through the sequence, but this method of defining shot themes allows a start to be made on constructing a montage.

DRAMATIC TIMING AND CUTTING COMEDY

Many editors find cutting dialogue more challenging than cutting action, music and montage. Many of the transitional moments that constitute a film's dramatic development come from dialogue delivery and reaction, and accuracy of timing is paramount. There are conventions to help the editor, which may or may not be observed. Rarely are level or 'straight' picture and dialogue cuts made from the delivery of one actor's lines to the succeeding lines from another. As Edward Dmytryk points out, the flow of dialogue editing mimics human consciousness: in everyday conversation the sense of a statement is usually implicit before that statement is concluded. This also holds true in editing (1984, p. 56). The editor will cut away from the speaker's delivery in picture only (usually on the last word) to the listener before the reply, so anticipating the response. Level cutting of picture and sound between lines of dialogue will jar and slow the pace, making the exchanges seem mechanical (although this choppy technique may be employed for a staccato effect in an interrogation scene, for example). The technique of 'anticipatory' dialogue editing may be used to inject additional pace into a scene, and some of the energy of Tony Lawson's finely judged cutting of *The Butcher Boy* results from this method. In the first scene between the priest and the two boys at the fountain, for example, Lawson cuts early from the delivery of the characters' lines in vision, increasing the overlaps between speaker and listener, which gives the exchanges added momentum. The technique of splitting picture and sound tracks, of favouring picture before sound to anticipate the next point where they are fully synchronous, is reversed by Lawson in the following scene where he prelaps the sound of the television set as a link from the fountain to the living room.

Rather than cutting early in vision, there are occasions when the editor may instead hold the picture of the first speaker over the beginning of the second speaker's reaction line, delaying the cut. Walter Murch has summarised the reasons for cutting 'early' and 'late' in dialogue exchanges:

> ... by cutting away from a certain character *before* he finishes speaking, I might encourage the audience to think only about the face value of what he said. On the other hand, if I linger on the character *after* he finishes speaking, I allow the audience to see, from the expression in his eyes, that he is probably not telling the truth, and they will think differently about him and what he said (1995, p. 67).

In editing comedy, however, John Bloom gives an example where standard dramatic timing (that is, anticipating the reaction) had constrained the humorous impact in much of Mae West's *My Little Chickadee* (Edward Cline, 1940):

The way in which you approach comedy is just that much different, in terms of allowing for a laugh line. Mae West always claimed that the film was ruined in the editing because she said her comedy doesn't come from the line, it comes from the look *after* the line. And the way they had edited that film was in fact to get the comedy out of the line, and after it was delivered they would cut away to the reaction.

Bloom maintains that the editing should have been against expectation, by holding the shot on her in order to maximise the comedic moment instead of 'banging' to a reaction shot:

> What you get is out of the slow burn. So that after she delivers the line, you have to stay on her, stay on that character to see it develop; maybe play incoming lines if you need the pacing, prelapping and so forth, but what you *can't* do is go bang, bang [and cut] away. So in comedy one is forced into a slightly different style – to get your laughs and then to hone the laughs down.

Lesley Walker, while not claiming to use this technique herself, recounts how a previous generation of editors applied a rule of thumb to timing reaction shots, using a formula that was fast and effective:

> Some old-time editors, in fact very good old-time editors used – not necessarily in dialogue, but certainly in reaction shots – to measure the film rather like a piece of material from the nose to the end of the arm, and say 'that's two seconds' or whatever, and cut it in. And nine times out of ten they were totally correct.

EDITING AND CONTINUITY

The dominant editing style, first established in the early twentieth century, maintains continuity from shot to shot within scenes, ensuring a smooth flow of cuts to propel the narrative (see Chapter 5). Single camera set-ups require that action is overlapped on wide and close shots, allowing the editor to cut between them, with physical movement to cue the edits. But the established convention of matching action and observing continuity across cuts is not always possible, nor is it necessarily aesthetically or dramatically desirable. Edward Dmytryk has argued the necessity of cutting for 'proper values' rather than for accurate matches, and that dramatic demands take precedence over seamless continuity edits, 'regardless of a bad action or position match' (1984, p. 44). Certainly Tom Priestley is sceptical about the importance of routinely observing continuity and recalls the challenges of editing the river scenes in *Deliverance* (John Boorman, 1972), shot under extremely difficult conditions by cinematographer Vilmos Zsigmond:

I don't believe in continuity. I don't think it's important. I think the only continuity is the continuity of emotion. If it feels right, then it is right. The first rapids scene in *Deliverance* ... some of the stuff on the river, they just picked it off. Ronny Cox, in one take he has a hat on, and in some he doesn't. I've run it as a single scene for audience after audience and I've said, 'There's a deliberate mistake in this.' And it's about one person in five hundred who spots it. Most people say something else because it doesn't matter, it's part of the whole that's working.

Priestley further illustrates how selecting a different camera angle can disguise continuity errors:

In *Isadora* I did a cut where somebody raises a glass to his lips, and cut close and he's got it in his other hand. It doesn't matter, the idea's the same; because as soon as you've changed the camera angle, then you are looking at it in a different way.

He goes on to challenge the convention of continuity editing, where matched action cutting can restrict the opportunity to change pace and emphasis:

I think the notion that there's a kind of standard cut – that you should cut on movement – I don't believe in that. I think it's much better to allow the movement to happen, and ideally you cut in the pause between movement. If you strictly followed natural time, it's slightly duller, because some things you want to see more of ... That's the element of cheating, it's not slavishly repeating everyday life. You're going for the heightened experience.

In the cutting room, new connections between shots may be discovered, enhancing the dramatic potential of the material. In a dialogue scene at the end of *Eureka* (Nicolas Roeg, 1983) Tony Lawson uses physical movement as a cutting cue to underscore the uneasy parting encounter, rather than being solely bound by the interplay of dialogue:

Rutger Hauer and Theresa Russell are having dinner on the veranda draped in black, after the death of Jack McCann. I cut the scene using hand movements as the key, in the hope that at least you'd feel they weren't comfortable with each other. And they were trying to find things to do, rather than just talk to each other . . . you follow the action that's within the material, rather than the dialogue.

Like Priestley, Lawson also recognises the constraints imposed by editing convention, and contrasts this with the creative freedom offered by dynamic discontinuity cutting:

I've always appreciated what I consider 'the American cut' and it is throwing continuity out of the window. You can see the result of it now in the high-paced American action movies where they just don't bother with continuity – for shock value. You see somebody pull their fist back and the next thing it's connected with the chin. You don't see the throwing of the fist.

REPETITION, PAUSE AND PUNCTUATION

Tom Priestley's editing of *Deliverance* was well advanced by the end of principal photography, assisted by director John Boorman's decision to shoot the film in sequence. The celebrated 'duelling banjos' scene between the city guitarist (Ronny Cox) and the banjo-playing hillbilly (Hoyt J. Pollard) was shot to playback, and the albino boy's inability to play the banjo was overcome by using a musician hidden behind him, extending his arm around the boy to do the left-hand fingering. Priestley's editing of this scene needed to disguise this problem as well as interweaving the dialogue and action of the onlookers, without disrupting the developing momentum of the banjo/guitar duel. 'A tricky thing, as I'm sure you know, is when you've got a piece of music and you have other activities going on, of incorporating that in the time scale, of getting the rhythm of that right.' In structuring the scene, Priestley decided that the musical climax occurred too swiftly, and decided to duplicate some of the music footage to extend the *pas de deux* of the two musicians before the eventual stand-off:

It becomes a kind of ballet, you see. It goes beyond reality. I repeated this section, because I felt that, having that long, slow build up, without it the climax was too short. So in order to accommodate all the material, I just repeated a section of the music. Nobody worried about that.

An editor's sense of timing and punctuation needs to be both musical and dramatic. Antony Gibbs remembers a tribute from writer Harold Pinter: 'Pinter once said, "Tony, you put in pauses where even I didn't think about it", in *The Birthday Party* [William Friedkin, 1968].' Gibbs uses this approach in longer dialogue scenes to punctuate for emphasis where possible, so that a lengthy dialogue scene, for example, becomes effectively two shorter sequences:

You just need to stop it with a couple of cross-cuts, or something like that, and start again. Cut back to the master scene, for a pause or something like that while somebody pours a drink, lights a cigarette – and smack in again, and you can emphasise something quite interestingly, if you find the right place to make the pause.

In *Ronin* Gibbs employs this technique in a long dialogue scene where five mercenaries are seated round a table receiving instructions. He inserts unpredictable cutaways to disrupt the flow:

> I tried cutting it so that the rhythms were rather strange . . . I was trying to make people think 'Is he a goodie or a baddie, and who's he?' I was trying to make a tremor around the whole thing; the unease of the whole thing. I think it worked to some degree.

After working together on *Performance*, Nicolas Roeg and Antony Gibbs collaborated on *Walkabout* (1971), shot in Australia (co-edited with Alan Pattillo). Roeg, together with camera operator Mike Molloy, shot numerous inserts of outback wildlife, including lizards, scorpions, ants and porcupines, anticipating that Gibbs could weave them into the film's structure:

> [Roeg] shot all these tiny pieces of strange little creatures wandering around, and he said, 'Tony, we've got to put these into the picture', and I said, 'Oh God, we don't want a Disney movie, where somebody says "Oh look" and you cut to an animal.' And he said, 'Find some way', and I sat down, and I used them as punctuation marks, in many cases very significant because they would relate to the scene that had just finished, or the one that was just about to start. A lot of fun.

Gibbs found ingenious and poetic ways of incorporating these punctuating shots. They are used to signify transitions, for example in location, from city to desert and from desert to mountain; in time, from day to night; and in mood and atmosphere. Occasionally they also serve to avoid the monotony of cutting directly between similar outback shots, for example, two shots of the Volkswagen driving away and towards camera near the beginning of the film. Shots of a scuttling porcupine link vertical and lateral movements where Jenny Agutter moves between sand dunes, and the porcupine rolling in the sand humorously anticipates the brother's tumbling towards camera. Elsewhere, a yellow-hooded reptile at the water's edge provides a dramatic transition to a yellow, reddening sunset sky. Gibbs' characteristic use of pause can be seen as the aborigine hunts for food: freeze-frames are used to denote his stillness, in the moment before making a kill. Gibbs' editing, the deeply atmospheric soundtracks and the visual literacy of Roeg's direction in *Walkabout* combine to produce uniquely cinematic textures rarely exceeded in British film-making. It remains one of Gibbs' favourite films.

THE DREAM REPAIR MAN AND DOCTORING THE FILM

At an early and less auspicious stage in his editing career Jim Clark was glad to leave the cutting rooms and go out to direct documentaries,

> which put me in touch with life … I was living life vicariously through a Moviola, and as I used to say, 'I was the dream repair man' – that was my job. I used to sit there, repairing other people's dreams.

His talents as a creative editor eventually led to a contract as an executive alongside David Puttnam, who was running Columbia Pictures in Hollywood. Clark's ability to repair films that were not working enhanced his reputation as a film post-production doctor:

> I was forever touching up the corpses of the films that were wheeled into me, films which we had perhaps had nothing to do with … So the directors were always terribly pleased to see me, because they thought I could come and breathe some life into their movies.

But rather than doctoring, Clark often felt that he was officiating at a post-mortem:

Jim Clark during the editing of *The World Is Not Enough* in 1999 (© 1999 Danjaq LLC and United Artists Corporation. All rights reserved)

Well, mortician seemed to me to be more apt, because most of the corpses were actually dead. You can resuscitate and there are examples of films that have started life being total disasters, that have been re-cut and fixed. I don't think there are that many, because once a film has got away it's very hard to bring it back. You can touch it up – you can apply rouge and make-up, and put a nice track on it, and pretty it up – and you can get away with it. And all the things that we did for Columbia all got released in one form or another, mostly to video. But at least they got shown.

Stuart Baird is more positive about the transformation that can be made by film doctors, and describes the role in the following terms:

Really a film doctor is somebody who comes in and re-edits a picture, that's essentially the job. He's only brought in when the picture hasn't previewed well, or the director and the editor haven't been able to get the story down or tell the story in the length of time ... My job is to make that material work better. And I enjoy doing it because I think a real film editor is a director as well.

Here, the common assumption that a director is effectively the film editor is neatly inverted by Baird. He is careful to emphasise that his Hollywood doctoring work takes place on mainstream commercial projects, rather than on 'auteur category' films. However, it may be worth reflecting why good editors command very considerable fees as film doctors – in Baird's case on *Mission: Impossible II* rumoured to have been $750,000 for three weeks' work (Morris, 2000, p. 7) – if editorial skills are so readily possessed by studio executives and directors. Lesley Walker's particular understanding of 'the dramatic arc' has brought her into the role of film doctor several times, but on each occasion she has only accepted it 'because the director wanted it. I would never doctor a film if the director wasn't involved.' One film that needed restructuring was at a very advanced stage (the negative had already been cut) and realising that there was insufficient coverage, she decided to work with cut material rather than going back to original rushes.

For those editors who do take on doctoring work, the role is professionally sensitive, as Anne Coates points out:

Sometimes a film has been perfectly well cut, actually, [but] they'll get in an older editor to look at it, kind of a doctor job [because] producers don't have confidence in a young editor. I've done that a couple of times and said, 'Well, I think it's perfectly well cut. I think that the editor has done a really nice job, and you really need to re-take the end, because it doesn't make any sense, and there's no editor

Stuart Baird, Los Angeles, 2003

that's going to make any sense of it.' Some editors don't do that, they just go in
and doctor it up.

Years of experience and a distinguished track record do not always guarantee
respectful treatment by producers and directors. Anne Coates recounted the
case of a highly regarded senior editor who had been 'doctored' on two occasions in Hollywood, and had once been replaced without even being informed
by the director, 'so it doesn't always pay off if you're an older editor, they don't
necessarily trust you'.

SOME EDITING ANALOGIES

Many editors agreed that the process was very difficult to convey in words. John
Bloom remembered a line from a Lena Horne song and suggested that film editing was as intangible as the way a singer performs: 'You just sort of stand there,
and just sort of do it.' Jim Clark acknowledged that 'film editing is not a very
easy craft to discuss,' while Tony Lawson noted that 'discussing editing is really
tough'. Mick Audsley outlined the wider problem of understanding the role and
the art of the editor, and remarked on the language specific to film that he had
learned as a young editor from director Bill Douglas:

Even film-makers, other departments, still find it hard. I do myself. The surprise
when you move a scene, which is exactly the same, to a different place and witness
how differently you perceive it. The nuances of perception, the relationship to
sound and so on, which is fundamental to the architecture and building of films,
are a mystery to most people and often quite hard to get across, even to somebody
who's a part of that ... The bang you get from a cut and the meaning or the look
when it's in the right place, *should* be indescribable. I was lucky in that Bill Douglas
taught me all that. He had this instinctive understanding about the way shots
should go together and also wanting to communicate, not through words but
through images or through images and sound, not necessarily dialogue. He
surrounded himself with people devoted to this language, and that is the root of
cinema: $a + b = x$, and not c.

Given the elusive nature of their craft, a number of editors volunteered analo-
gies in an attempt to clarify their work and their different approaches to it.

TERRY RAWLINGS

I've had this funny analogy about film editing and I say that first of all it's like
building a house, it's like building the best house you've ever built. First of all you
need a fantastic blueprint, you need an architect to give you the right drawings.
And then the director goes off and supplies all the building bricks and the bits and
pieces, and he gives it to you, and you're the builder. The editor builds the house.
And then the director comes back and we decorate it.

DAVID GLADWELL

I think there are two ways of looking at [editing]. If you look at it as sculpture, you
would actually start with a very long rough cut and whittle it down, but equally ...
you can talk about it as a modeller and building something up. If you're carving a
head you start with a block of stone which might be five hours long and you've got
to cut this stone down to an hour and a half. And that's what you do, just chisel
away. Alternatively, you could start with the armature of ten minutes and build up,
until it becomes an hour and a half.

MICK AUDSLEY

There's an analogy with painting – what if I heightened certain colours? But unlike
painting or sculpting, which are one-to-one activities, the truth about film editing is
that it is collaboration and it's criticism coming at you all the time. You have to
accept it as the terms of the job in my view. Because we're dealing with expensive
cinema that has got to reach an audience, you've got an obligation to try and satisfy
the people who are paying for it. In the back of your mind, unlike the painter, you

don't have the freedom to use the splashy, unbelievably pink line that you want, without thinking, 'Will this work in the whole scheme of things involved in getting people to go and see the film and recoup the cost of making it?'

JIM CLARK

I used to say that film editing was very much like knitting a sweater with a pattern in it. That you would knit it according to the pattern book and you would finish it and you'd look at it and would say, 'Well, I don't like that bit there, and this bit doesn't seem to work too well, and do we need that?' Then you would take it all down, you'd unknit it, and put it together again, and form a new pattern, of which you'd say, 'That's nice, I like that much better than I liked the other.' In other words, what you've done is re-write the script, and that's what we do all the time. What we do is the last version of the script, and it's a tremendously exciting job, I must say. It's one I've never personally grown tired of, even when I'm working on stuff which isn't going together too well, and the arms and legs are all in the wrong place.

JOHN BLOOM

The end part of a film, when you're in post-production, it's rather like an air traffic controller, you know, everything has to go right until something goes wrong, in which case it's a disaster, but nobody pays too much attention to what air traffic controllers do every day. We're the same in the cutting rooms – particularly in the latter end of post-production, when you're waiting for opticals. If it's a bad optical it's going to look terrible, and the film will suffer, but it should be perfect. All these technical aspects should be perfect. Now, if it isn't, they say, 'Oh my God, that optical is terrible, what are you going to do about it?' So the air traffic control simile is really what it's about in terms of editing generally now. Trying not to have the big accident, trying to keep an even keel, trying somehow to preserve the integrity of the film and not simply turn it into what is so often seen as a piece of commerce.

EDITING AND FILM STYLE

The style of a film is generally attributed to the director, although writers like Thomas Schatz (1988) have argued that the Hollywood studios also imposed a house style on their productions. The editors interviewed are divided on the question of whether the style emanates from the director or producer, is determined by genre such as comedy, or whether editors themselves bring a particular visual character to their work. For John Bloom, an editor's style is partly determined by genre, modulated by detailed editorial preferences, but essentially influenced by the way in which the film has been shot:

I mean, if you're doing comedy or if you're doing drama, your style just changes. My style suits whatever I am working on. I suppose one can only say there are certain things that editors will develop as a style. I mean some editors, for instance, really hate to start a line on a character. They prefer to simply overlay a little bit of the incoming/outgoing lines so that you're into the character. I like to overlay quite a lot of the latter end of a line over the reaction. I find that a director's style will dictate – I mean the way he shoots. Some will shoot very simply, sort of meat and potatoes: master, over-shoulder, close-up and so forth. You're forced into a kind of pattern of cutting. Others will be very freewheeling and give you masses of material in which you've got to find your way and simply make it work, just find the best moments to do it.

Style, for Tariq Anwar, consists of personal preferences and dislikes that inform his general approach to cutting, and like a number of other editors – including Jim Clark – he singled out the style associated with Oliver Stone as an influence to avoid:

> I wouldn't say I have any rules but I do have dislikes, like arbitrarily cutting in the middle of a word (telephone conversations) or having an unbalanced or untidy exchange of dialogue – unless deliberately trying to create an unsettling effect. I don't particularly like relentless cutting – *Natural Born Killers* [Oliver Stone, 1994] – whip pans and unsteady camera in dialogue scenes, or contemporary techniques used in period pictures. I do like jumping in and out of shots, cutting to temporary music and discovering scene transitions that haven't been scripted or directed.

In a review of *Petulia* (1968) directed by Richard Lester, Tony Rayns credits cinematographer Nicolas Roeg with developing a visual and narrative style on that film which was to be carried forward to *Performance*:

> Did Nic Roeg have a hand in directing *Petulia*? He's credited as the cinematographer, and the visual style is unmistakably his, but the film's 'Roegian' currents run deeper than that. There's the splintered narrative, full of cuts back and forward through time … Overall, though, the film leads into *Performance* much more than it harks back to *Help!* and *The Knack* (1997, p. 624).

Tony Lawson's and Tariq Anwar's earlier observations are reinforced here, that, apart from the director, the cinematographer's input is most tangible to the film reviewer. If the roles of directing and cinematography can be combined, then the auteurist critic can argue an even more impressive case in terms of visual consistency. In the above review of *Petulia*, the film's structure – the final responsibility of director and editor – is primarily attributed to a cinematographer who would in due course direct. In detecting a stylistic signature common to *Petulia* and *Performance*, however, Tony Rayns may well be correct, since both films were edited by Antony Gibbs. The importance of *Petulia* in Gibbs' creative development as an editor was clearly articulated by him:

> In some ways *Performance* does come out of *Petulia*, in terms of editing. When I did *Petulia*, the script called for a number of flashbacks, and it was very 1960s – in fact, I find it now one of the most dated of the pictures I've ever done. It doesn't really stand up today I don't think, but as a piece of innovative editing I think it does. We shot it in Sausalito and San Francisco and Richard Lester said to me, 'We have to find a style for this picture,' – which he said on every movie we worked on – 'I really don't want to see it until you've found a style.' So I said 'OK', and it was some weeks after shooting, and I was fooling around and I put it together as it was shot, and, as I said, it had all these flashbacks. Richard, bless him, just left me alone to produce a cut that had some different style to it, and I suddenly thought of flash forwards. And I spoke to him about it and he said, 'Oh, what a great idea, wonderful. Do quick flash forwards,' and I said, 'Richard, you can have quick flashes of flashbacks, but you could never have quick flashes of flash forwards, you've got to allow people to be able to register the image.' It did give the picture style, that's for sure, and it also gave it an interesting sort of form, because what happened was it was like two wedges with the thin ends together. In other words we started off with flash forwards, which, as the film progressed, diminished and then, from – I don't know – halfway on, the wedge of the flashbacks started, and the flash forwards finished. I could not have cut *Performance* without having cut *Petulia*, and given *Performance* a lot of the style that it had.

The National Film Theatre programme notes for October/November 1999 describe *Petulia* as being 'in danger of becoming another acknowledged masterpiece by the director … this film's subtle use of time-shifting is still breathtaking' (p. 9). This review unfortunately omits any reference to the editor, which underlines the problem of assessing how significant the editorial contribution may have been, structurally and stylistically. Gibbs has remarked that an editor's style is a subtle form of 'handwriting' which impresses itself on the film, and although this is familiar to the individual editor, it is usually indecipherable by anyone else.

Terry Rawlings' 'trademark' may be more discernible, and consists of using long dissolves, which initially could only be done in American film laboratories:

> In the first *Alien*, when they're getting up in the morning, I wanted it to be like a
> flower opening, just coming out of each other, coming out of themselves. I was
> doing twelve-foot dissolves and the [UK] labs couldn't do A and B here for those
> [see Glossary].

Having persuaded British laboratories to equip for long and complex A and B
roll film opticals, Rawlings was able to take his experiments with long dissolves
a stage further when he utilised them in some of the race sequences in *Chariots
of Fire* and later in *Yentl* (Barbra Streisand, 1983).

When discussing style, film critics and scholars have an obligation to deepen
their understanding of the entire production process, including editing, rather
than default to a position which foregrounds only the director – or, if in doubt,
the cinematographer. Tony Lawson has commented on what he sees as an eva-
sion of responsibility:

> Critics talk about film without knowing what they're talking about. Everyone can
> have an opinion about a film in a personal sense, but if you start to talk about the
> process of film-making then you must at least understand, even at a basic level,
> what people do.

ESTABLISHING RHYTHM AND PACE

In an article entitled 'The Care and Feeding of Auteurs', critic Andrew Sarris
outlined his criteria for selecting pantheon directors:

> I have argued over the years that great directors do not have to write every line of
> dialogue in their scripts, or indeed any line of dialogue in their scripts. The
> placement of camera, the rhythms of editing, even the casting are parts of the
> process of writing for the screen (1993, p. 66).

In any production context Sarris' assertions are widely problematic. The
responsibility for establishing rhythm and pace is a function of editing, although
this will be influenced by how material is shot and directed. The extent to which
the cutting process is either initiated – or approved – by the director will be discussed later, but it is executed by the film editor. Mick Audsley has described
the inseparability of rhythm from editing:

> What is tricky to get across to people is that when you see material you see
> potential in it and there's a feeling you get of something that shows up in these tiny
> little fragments, and if you orchestrate them – 'rhythm' as we would say – you start
> to find an excitement which is purely a film experience and it doesn't exist in

dramatic terms: it's the syntax, the nuts and bolts of film. And that's deeply hidden in the root of editing, and that attracts me.

Tony Lawson considers the determination of pace to be the most important contribution he makes to the films he has edited. The momentum of *The Butcher Boy* 'had quite a lot to do with what I did'. He values the creative space given to him by director Neil Jordan:

> I don't mean to say that he's not interested and not there a lot of the time, because he is, but he doesn't say, 'Do this, do that.' It's all by inference – you know – cajole,whatever. So yes, I would say that I had quite a lot of responsibility for the way that work moves along.

To illustrate this, Lawson describes in greater detail how he paced the cutting of a key scene, by using voiceover to tighten the underlying dialogue, creating an elaborate interplay between picture and sound:

> After the party ends, there's an argument that takes place, and within the scene there's some voiceover. So I cut the scene knowing that I was actually going to overlay the voiceover, and drown out half the dialogue, and you know, that gives a tremendous pace, because you're watching something that's physically violent, and it's an argument . . . and you're listening not to what they're saying, but to a character's point of view of what he's seeing. And it gives a terrific kick.

Acknowledging Lawson's contribution to this film emphasises collaboration as the cornerstone of effective film-making.

CRAFT AND COLLABORATION

In a review of *Unfaithful* (Adrian Lyne, 2002) Philip French, a critic particularly alert to the realities of film production, wondered why 'splendid British cinematographer' Peter Biziou and 'great British editor Anne V. Coates' were working in Hollywood when they were needed in the UK (2002, p. 7). Apart from the generally parlous state of British production, the reasons for the continuing presence in Hollywood of so many leading British technicians are their high status, and the fees they can command. Anne Coates believes that their reputations resulted from the long craft apprenticeships whereby British technicians worked their way up in more challenging environments than could be replicated in film schools. The gradual decline of British cinema output meant that much of the training for higher-end film production took place in public service broadcasting. This training investment by British broadcasters appears to be nearing its end, however, due to the inexorable process of budget cuts and the replacement of staff jobs by freelance labour. Whether the transference of training from UK broadcasting to metropolitan post-production facilities and higher educational media departments will develop the same regard for the craft elements of film production is open to question.

The marketing of the director as a kind of Hollywood star as reflected in popular film journalism has reinforced the image of the artistically self-sufficient director, serviced by technical grades. Many directors, however, readily admit to the crucial contribution made by key production crew. Stephen Frears, director of *Dangerous Liaisons,* described his relationship with his team of collaborators:

> I don't think I have any sense of how the film will look. I can't pretend that my films are more visual than they are ... I tend to rely on the people around me, they know far more than I do – especially the team on *Dangerous Liaisons*. What the cameraman, set designer, costume designer and so on, have to say about their subjects is infinitely more interesting than what I have to say. I concentrate on the bits which I can do – creating conditions in which the actors can work (quoted in Hacker and Price, 1991, p. 172).

A director may well possess a particular expertise, but Frears' belief that he is a part of a team more accurately reflects the conditions of film-making.

Ken Loach has talked about the significance of collaboration on the films he has directed:

> The contributions of the people you work with have to fit into a central template. It has to knit together to become a personal work, while still not less than the sum of many diverse talents. In particular, the cameraman, designer and editor are really crucial in combining to make what appears to be a very personal, separate individual statement and approach (quoted in Hacker and Price, 1991, p. 297).

Loach's long-time collaborator, editor Jonathan Morris, commented on the above quotation, and pointed to a poster in his cutting room:

> 'A film directed by Ken Loach' it says up there ... But it will never have 'a film by Ken Loach' because, as he always says, it's a collaborative situation ... And so he'll never have 'un film de' like some of these guys who make one film in their life, you know. It's a cheek really. It's not like a painting, it really isn't. I mean Ken is the first one to acknowledge it. But, of course, the man who acknowledges it most is the man who probably contributes more than most other directors.

The cult of the director, Tariq Anwar believes, may have misled some of the young hopefuls set on a career path in the media, who fail to realise that craft and collaboration are indispensable to film-making: 'Directing is the most sought-after profession in the industry and yet it's the one least requiring of craft skills. That's why there are so many young "wannabes" with no experience being given the opportunity.' From his vantage point as a film doctor, Baird considers that the cult of the director has created a number of problems for the younger and less experienced: 'A lot of directors, younger directors, get themselves into all sorts of problems because they think they're supposed to know everything, and they know – well, how can they know everything?'

An inexperienced director, for example, may show a preference for overcutting, a trait shared with trainee editors. This practice has been accentuated by the introduction of computer-based editing systems and John Bloom worries that there is a resulting decline in coherence: 'Films are not working because narrative strength is getting lost. Older editors have a much better sense of narrative thrust.' Bloom's observation is borne out by the continuing demand for experienced editors in both the UK and Hollywood, because they provide producers with a degree of quality control. Whether the old system of long and arduous apprenticeships is the most effective way of training editors is questioned by some. Jonathan Morris, who spent seven years as an assistant before being allowed to make a single edit, articulated a widespread insecurity that has always existed in the cutting rooms: 'Every assistant who becomes an editor becomes a rival for the next job.' But the continued existence of an editorial culture depends on the transmission of skills from editor to assistant, although this may be threatened by changes in post-production practice (see Chapter 6).

THE QUESTION OF VISION

In critical analyses of the careers of directors, the existence of a discernible style, or a unifying vision across the body of their work is sought as crucial evidence of auteur status.[4] Tony Lawson has given much thought to the responsibility of the editor in the production process, and how that meshes with notions of directorial inspiration:

> Helping the director to achieve a 'version' of the film that he wants – avoiding the word 'vision'. That's not being a button-pusher, but interpreting his desires in a creative and practical way. I've always believed that film is a director's medium, he is the one who takes the criticism and the praise, it's with him that 'The Buck Stops' . . . The editor should work towards bringing the director's wishes to the screen, and when the editor disagrees, to encourage, persuade, an alternative approach.

However, for Lawson creative interpretation implies taking an editorial view of the material being worked – 'putting your stamp on things' – and he feels that the word 'version' better describes the results of working through drafts of the cut by director and film editor. He recalls his experience of working with Stanley Kubrick: 'Stanley was not a perfectionist; he didn't have a vision. He was tirelessly exploring by trial and error until he came upon something that for him was the correct way.' The final cut of *Barry Lyndon*, which Lawson worked on for two years, bore little relationship to its original script which 'read like *Tom Jones.* It was bawdy, it was fast. The film's got absolutely nothing to do with that.'

For Lawson, 'the idea that somebody has a vision that comes perfectly formed and is translated into the finished film' is belied by the compromises and practical difficulties that beset film-making. Lawson believes that the mass of speculative comment surrounding Kubrick was stimulated by the director's reluctance to discuss his work:

> Because of his silence, he's been credited with an enormous number of motives that people have given him, as it were. He has not dispelled them or contradicted them or agreed with them. He's just remained silent. That's partly why I suspect these great theories have evolved about him.

Lawson also worked with Sam Peckinpah, co-editing *Straw Dogs* (1971) with Roger Spottiswoode and Paul Davies, *Cross of Iron* with Michael Ellis and Murray Jordan. Although many critics have attempted to classify Peckinpah's films in terms of their style, Lawson considers that Peckinpah's work is distinguished rather by a set of concerns. He quotes the example of *Junior Bonner* (1972):

> It's a wonderful, fairly slow-paced film, not excessively edited in terms of cuts per minute. So I think I would probably characterise Sam's films – not quite, I think, in editing terms, though that's remarkable – but more in terms of what actually interested him. And they were all very human stories, all loners, people struggling against modernity or things like that.

A director's use of a recurring theme need not exclude creative suggestions from the crew. Lawson has no doubt that Peckinpah relished the interaction with editors, and was open to valuable ideas that they could bring to his projects:

> He [Peckinpah] wanted to be part of the team, he wanted that social atmosphere to pervade the entire time. It wasn't obsessive in that he wanted to make the edits himself in any way, but he wanted to be around, he wanted to enjoy whatever it was that was going on at the time.

Mick Audsley cultivates an atmosphere that encourages reflection and communication between editor and director, away from the enormous pressures that occur during shooting:

> I've always wanted the cutting rooms to be a safe place, like home, where it's safe
> for anybody – me, the director – to say exactly what you think. Because it's very
> hard, people can easily delude themselves. There's so much riding up there, and we
> all kid ourselves and we also make dreadful mistakes . . . So the cutting room
> during shooting and certainly during post-production should be the place where we
> can be frank with each other.

The evaluation of each other's work by director and editor underscores the collaborative nature of film production. The film that emerges is likely to be a fruitful combination of creative inputs. For Audsley, although the overriding conception may come from the director, one of the most important responsibilities of the editor is to gauge how the audience will respond to the film. This informs the choices he makes during cutting, and even influences the selection of his assistant editors:

> If I can I like to involve them as I am showing things, just to get a feedback . . .
> They will laugh at some of the choices and ask why didn't you use *that* bit, and I
> want to know that. I like to surround myself with people who I trust in that way.
> It's a collaborative process and if I'm representative as head of department for the
> audience, my first audience is the people working literally in the room with me.

Ideally the editor's view of the final cut should correspond with that of the director, but the exhausting post-production schedule often has to bear the strain of a rapidly reducing budget. This calls for particular stamina, with the editor needing to retain a strong personal conviction about the direction the film is taking, according to Audsley:

> It's the journey and trying to pick your way through the route, chop down this
> jungle on the way to get to the clearing. That's what makes it fun. You have to have
> a vision of your own as an editor of what you think the film should be . . . you
> adjust it on the way but I think you both want to be making the same film . . .
> otherwise you are in deep trouble in the cutting room and that will become
> evident.

Tensions between editor and director may well arise, however, and John Bloom's occasional 'battleground' encounters in the cutting rooms are echoed by Tony

Lawson's recollections of the 'good fight' that can take place there. Bloom explained that his working relationship with a director is governed by his overriding commitment to do what is best for the film: 'I start with the view that the director is paramount. But as the film develops, you find too many times that the director doesn't actually have a vision.' Bloom will already have developed a sense of what the film should be as he makes his first cut: 'And I feel I have to fight to get my vision across, not for ego, but for the film.' As the editing of the film continues, Bloom will then be in a position to work more productively with the director, knowing that they are progressing from the best first cut that he could have achieved. If the original approach to the edit falters, then a new one will be argued. Anne Coates sets out wanting to share a director's sense of how the film should develop in post-production:

> Directors should be in control. They should be the person whose vision you are helping to achieve. But by helping to achieve it you don't have to slavishly do what they want ... I mean you should always be working for what's best for the film, in your opinion.

THE EDITOR/DIRECTOR RELATIONSHIP

No discussion of the final responsibility for the way a film is presented to its audience can take place without attempting to understand the nature of the relationship between editor and director. While it is certainly true that there are some directors who would want to dominate the edit – an example given by Antony Gibbs was director William Friedkin – an experienced editor expects to be creatively involved. When an editor's creativity is restricted, the working atmosphere may be difficult, as Tariq Anwar discovered when taking over the editing of *American Beauty* from Christopher Greenburg. Director Sam Mendes had already developed a particular way of working:

> He wanted to be present at every decision-making process, which I found inhibiting. In the end he reluctantly gave me time to myself to play, but his desire to exercise control of everything led to an oppressive atmosphere. I can't imagine what pleasure established editors get out of working for the likes of James Cameron and Oliver Stone, Academy Awards or not!

Clearly directors should be able to recognise what they want when they see it, whether or not they are able to produce that editorial result themselves, as Antony Gibbs pointed out in relation to Tony Richardson: 'He had no idea of the basics of the mechanics of film editing, and didn't even pretend that he wanted to know. He just knew what he saw up on the screen.'

For the relationship to work creatively, it is essential that the director trusts the judgment of the editor. Although some directors may wish to spend long hours in the cutting room,[5] many editors such as Antony Gibbs and Terry Rawlings prefer to work alone, showing various stages of the cut to the director when they are completed. Once a productive working relationship becomes established, directors may feel able to leave the final post-production stages in the hands of an editor, allowing them to start work on new projects, as was the case with Richardson and Gibbs:

> The marvellous thing for me was that he would go off and leave me, and I finished *Tom Jones* completely. I mean I dubbed it completely. He was there for the music recording, of course, but he was away doing *Luther* or something somewhere, and I dubbed *Tom Jones* and ran it for him and I had three alterations in one reel of the twelve. Of the twelve reels there was only one that he changed. We knew each other so well. We knew what we were doing.

A two-hour picture like *Tom Jones* will contain thousands of picture and sound edits, and for Richardson to have requested only three alterations suggests an extremely close working relationship. Similarly, Anne Coates oversaw the final stages of *Erin Brockovich* (2000) as Steven Soderbergh was setting up his next project, while Peter Tanner struck a particular rapport with director John Irvin: 'We thought very much the same way. Otherwise he wouldn't have left without sometimes seeing even the first cut.'

For a younger editor, establishing a degree of trust with a new director can be daunting. This would be particularly so with a director who had himself been a distinguished editor, as the young John Bloom found with Anthony Harvey while cutting *The Lion in Winter* (1968):

> I realised what was happening was that if I'd cut the film exactly as he thought it should be, it was wonderful. If it was different, then from his point of view it was dreadful ... So I said, 'Tony, if you know exactly what it should be, there's no point in having me. I mean why not just have an assistant or an apprentice, and basically, you know, sit over them and tell them what you want to do. If you want to use an editor the way an editor should be used, then at least allow me to contribute ... And if you don't do that, then as I've said, you may just as well get somebody, get a pair of hands and carry on from there.' And he was terrific, Tony, and he accepted that, and actually from that time on we had a marvellous relationship.

Senior editors are loath to be used just as a 'pair of hands'. Antony Gibbs contrasts the productive partnerships he enjoyed in the UK in the 1960s[6] with the current climate of Hollywood, where certain directors expect to control all aspects of production, including editing. Gibbs points out that these directors generally choose not to employ him. Tony Lawson rarely experiences that kind of non-collaborative relationship and suggests that it is eventually detrimental to the best interests of the film:

> You do get used as a pair of hands, a button-pusher. Now I realise that if that happens, you abdicate your responsibility. It can be very destructive from a personal point of view, and might harm the film.

Tariq Anwar echoes Bloom on the importance of maintaining a creative role within the partnership, and has noted how an editor's comments may be sought, even prior to any contractual engagement, where the initial job interview often has a hidden agenda:

> Interviews are like 'vivas' where one's grasp of the script or book (if it's an adaptation) is questioned. One's 'take' is of paramount importance. It's no good just saying, 'It's a great script, I want to do it and I need the work.' One has to strike a balance between sycophancy and criticism . . . If one were to be cynical, the purpose of these events is not only to hire someone suitable, but also to get free input on scripts from some of the best people to give it.

Stuart Baird has noted that the long-established partnership of director and editor constitutes a 'symbiotic relationship, joined at the hip' – and indeed one of the first appointments made on a feature film production would be that of editor. Baird is acutely aware of how his editing experience informs his own work as a director, and as a post-production consultant:

> Because I'm a director who's been an editor I have a very specific idea of how I want to edit. Not many directors, in my experience, do have that. They're only too pleased to have someone present them with the material that works in any way at all, but I know it can work in a dozen different ways. Unless you've been an editor, unless you've done it, you don't understand the difference you can make.

A cost-benefit analysis of post-production might conclude that either a director or an editor is creatively redundant, and the two roles should be amalgamated. In practice there are very few editor/directors who can combine the roles on the same film, quite apart from the logistical problems. Baird, however, considers that many directors do claim to edit their own films:

A lot of directors would consider that they do. A lot of directors will have a very good editor who will do it all; then they will go in for a couple of days, do some tweaks and will say, in his mind, that he's cut the film. We all delude ourselves.

Since the director does not physically edit the material, and is therefore reliant on the skills of the editor, it becomes apparent that the role of the director in post-production is not necessarily to initiate the cutting of the film, but may often be more one of approval. John Bloom lists reasons why directors rarely edit their films:

Not every director is a good editor. That's number one. So you're going to eliminate quite a few who just don't have good editing ideas ... They know how to produce the basic material, but you know they haven't got much [more] they can offer. Technically: obviously not merely the question of buttons, and so forth, but actually the ability to build up the scene. Exigency: I mean frankly nowadays there wouldn't be time for that. There are very few people who could effectively say, 'I'll cut it when we've finished shooting,' because you have to be that much further advanced.

Bloom considers his time editing with Karel Reisz to have been creatively one of his most productive periods. He says that Reisz possessed an overall conception of what he wanted to achieve, but they still worked in a dialectical relationship, which required each other to defend their editing ideas. On an occasion when Bloom was unable to cut for Reisz, he recommended another editor:

Karel had met him, and he said, 'I met M., and he's very nice. I might like to take him on but tell me, will he give me a good fight?' And that, for me, epitomises what I think is the best of film editing. It's that fight, you know, you get in there with a director, and from that moment onwards during the director's cut, it's you making the director justify what he's doing, or to unjustify what you're doing ... Of course it's always the film that matters. It's not your egos, but unfortunately it often becomes a thing of egos, and depending who you're working with, it becomes very personal.

Every relationship between editor and director is different, although it is more often than not a partnership. Mathematical approximations of the ratio between the director's cutting decisions and those of the editor can never be conclusive, but they do at least indicate the levels of editorial contribution during post-production. American editor John D. Dunning, who edited for William Wyler and

Anthony Mann, estimated that 'if an editor does his cut well, the chances are 75 per cent of it is his cut' (quoted in Oldham, 1992, p. 268). Working as a first-time editor after a long and often difficult apprenticeship as an assistant with Reginald Mills, Noreen Ackland talked about her contribution to *Peeping Tom* (1960), directed by Michael Powell, who was well aware of Ackland's initial nervousness:

> I showed him the sequence of the opening, where the body is carried out, and he said: 'That's interesting, it's not the way I saw it, but leave it, because it's perfect.' And from then on I had confidence. But he never touched it, not a frame. He didn't touch much at all, actually. I would say almost 80 per cent [was my work] because there was only one sequence that we worked on a little bit, and that was the studio sequence – the shooting, the actual shooting with Esmond Knight, and that was not well shot. He hadn't planned it properly. He did it quickly, and it was jolly hard work to get it right. And that was the only thing that we worked on. All the scenes in the dark room, you know, where he was playing back, it was nearly 100 per cent the first cut.

Richard Best estimates that the final director's cut assimilates on average 75 per cent of the editor's first cut, which is often unsupervised by the director. The standard ten-week period between first and final cut may produce fine tuning, or a radical re-cutting of the editor's first attempt, but Best considers this 75 per cent approximation to hold true over his long career.

Tony Lawson considers that if the editor/director relationship is working, 'when it's good it's 50 per cent, say, me and 50 per cent because the director wants it different'. Perhaps for Lawson this reciprocity during post-production is evidence of how a balanced creative partnership between editor and director will eventually benefit the film. Lawson maintains that 'whether the director or the editor drives the cut is different every time', and this would be determined by personalities, experience, and the wider production context – including pressures from producers and distributors. The speed and flexibility of electronic editing systems over traditional methods of film editing has meant that changes dictated by the studios can now be achieved with greater technical facility.

The esteemed 'director's cut' that the directors' guilds have struggled to institute seems to be endorsed by film editors insofar as it should ideally represent the cut achieved by the creative partnership of editor and director, rather than one imposed by the film studios. The cut is deemed to be the director's, who has to represent this combination of collective inputs from the designer, writer, camera and sound departments, actors and editor. Even in situations where there have been disagreements between director and editor, John Bloom is still acutely aware of who takes final responsibility:

Now I have to say that there's that moment when you have to run the film for the studio, or to the audience, and you suddenly realise you can take a back seat. It's the director who actually has to take it on the nose, and really answer for it. Depending on the person, if they've given you the support and so forth, and have gone along with your ideas, you feel suddenly very responsible for the fact that they're having to defend this.

The valued creative partnership between director and editor – and the final cut achieved by them – is in Bloom's view 'so reliant on a director who has the strength to fight off the studios'.

Because of his long career which spans Ealing Studios, Hollywood and the Goldcrest films, Jim Clark has often taken on the role of a 'father confessor', acting as a post-production consultant, advising on scripts and working with younger directors, where his level of experience acts as 'built-in insurance'. Where there are disagreements between director and editor, he adopts a subtle approach: 'You don't want to overstep the mark, and yet you want somehow to impress upon the director that there is another way. Usually trying to make him believe in the end that it was his idea.' Clark was happy to make the transition from the more cumbersome method of physically cutting film to digital editing, which facilitated a synthesis between the director's and editor's versions:

Now that we're working digitally the whole thing becomes so much easier. You no longer have to send out a reel to be duped overnight so that you can re-cut it. You can do it instantly, so that if there's any contention, it's now very easy to say, 'Right, we'll do your version now', and you re-cut it, and you show it. Then you say, 'And, of course, there is this other version here, which I happen to have up my sleeve', and you run that as well. And very often what happens is that you use a bit of this, a bit of that, and you create a third version, which is the director's and yours, amalgamated and adjusted.

Popular film culture in the United States generally takes a broader interest in the craft of film-making, and editors like Thelma Schoonmaker, Walter Murch and Dede Allen have a much higher profile than their counterparts in Britain. Director Arthur Penn, whose work with editor Dede Allen produced *Bonnie and Clyde* (1967), had this to say about the chemistry that takes place in post-production:

The relationship between director and editor is one of those phenomena where you really are just craftsmen, and then sometimes a little spark of magic happens, and it turns out to be art. It's probably independent of both persons. Something in the collaboration creates a point of view that is maybe a little larger than both individually (quoted in Sherman, 1988, p. 248).

Throughout its history British cinema has produced powerful director–editor partnerships, but exclusive concern with the director has overshadowed the vital contribution made by numerous distinguished editors.

NOTES

All unattributed quotations from editors are drawn from the interviews conducted for this book.

1. The past decade has seen extensive changes in film post-production technology, with much of the laborious physical cutting of film and manipulation to produce special effects transferred to computer systems like Lightworks and Avid. The impact that new technology has had on working practices will be discussed in Chapter 6.

2. Sound editing is the subject of a book by Vincent LoBrutto (1994). For a discussion of sound design see

3. Gibbs claims not to have been consulted during the research for Colin MacCabe's monograph on *Performance* (1998), although he is the film's credited editor (together with Brian Smedley-Aston). The discussion of the film's editing excludes Gibbs' contribution.

4. Auteur-structuralism argued that the director may be unaware of the meanings implicit in the body of his or her work; that the 'vision' constructed by the critics, and the thematic and stylistic consistencies revealed are the result of critical interpretation rather than conscious intention on the part of the director.

5. Working with John Schlesinger in the 1960s was Jim Clark's first experience of a continuing directorial presence in the cutting room, a practice that became more widespread with the advent of Steenbeck flatbed editing tables and the growth of independent production – see chapters 4 and 6.

6. Gibbs recalls: 'I was lucky to work with three people who left me alone – Richardson, Lester and Roeg – to give them my version, if you like, of what they'd shot' (quoted in Combs, 1999, p. 62).

3

Aspects of British Editing from the Beginnings to the 1950s

THE EMERGENCE OF BRITISH FEATURE FILM EDITING

Editors did not begin to appear on British film credits until the later 1910s. Prior to this editing skills were acknowledged within film-making circles, but the notion of 'the editor' as a distinct and separate role within the production process was not yet fully established. Mabel Clark, for example, joined Cecil Hepworth's studio and laboratory at Walton-on-Thames shortly after the summer of 1899, and is described in his autobiography as a 'cutting expert' (1951, p. 42). Clark contributed her expertise to the enormously successful *Rescued by Rover* (Lewin Fitzhamon for Cecil Hepworth, 1905). Her responsibilities, however, extended beyond editing. According to Fitzhamon: 'May became film cutter and cashier and actress and general utility' (quoted in Gifford, 1986, p. 316). This combination of duties was an aspect of the artisanal mode of production characteristic of this early period. Each member of Hepworth's small staff at Walton-on-Thames performed multiple functions. Each phase of production, from shooting to developing, was carried out within the grounds of his family home.

Over the next twenty years the production sector of the British film industry transformed from an artisanal into a properly industrial concern. Specialised roles began to be more clearly defined. Film historian Rachael Low says of film terminology during this period of transition that in an 'unpremeditated way the word "editor" emerged from an uneasy shuffling of the functions of editing the script, writing the titles, sticking the film together, and doctoring an unsatisfactory film with scissors and cement' (1997a, p. 268). The design of newly constructed film studios, with separate cutting rooms, assumed a clear division of labour as the norm. The Stoll Studios at Cricklewood, modelled on American precedents, were one of the largest and most modern British studios in the 1920s. As Low notes, Stoll 'was one of the first British companies to employ specialised film editors, among them Billy Williams, Challis Sanderson, Leslie Brittain and Sam Simmons' (1997a, p. 269). These editors were some of the first to receive credits on British films.

The gradual industrialisation of British film production did not completely eradicate the earlier practice of moving between different roles. Even at Stoll some directors, such as George Ridgwell, did their own editing. Conversely, some production workers who eventually specialised as editors gained experience during the 1920s of a variety of roles. David Lean moved around different departments at Gaumont-British, as did Alfred Roome at British and Dominions and British International Pictures. Roome worked in the property department, as a camera assistant, and in the cutting rooms. He describes the atmosphere in these studios as 'vague and easygoing . . . we were all sort of enthusiasts in those early days'. This wide and varied experience served Lean and Roome well in their later careers as director and senior editor respectively. The unionisation of production workers in the 1930s addressed a fundamental issue: the extremely long hours 'enthusiasts' were expected to work. Defining production workers' terms and conditions of employment more clearly also led to less mobility between different departments.

Alma Reville's career emerged from the movement between departments and the combination of roles possible during the earlier years of the British studio system. She edited producer Michael Balcon's first big success *Woman to Woman* (Graham Cutts, 1923) and became an important member of the Gainsborough production team that set the tone for British film production from the mid-1920s onwards. *Woman to Woman* was praised for matching American standards of professionalism. Previously, Reville had worked at Famous Players-Lasky's Islington Studios, which eventually became the home of Gainsborough productions. There she received a thorough grounding in American production methods. Film historian John Russell Taylor offers an account of Reville's career leading up to this assignment:

> She was [*Woman to Woman*'s] editor, combining the job . . . with that of continuity girl on set . . . she would keep careful note of what was shot with what intention, and then afterwards she would have a clearer idea than anyone else (except hopefully the director) of how it all fitted together. Alma had gone into the film industry early, at the age of sixteen, first of all in the very humble capacity of a rewind girl in the editing room at Twickenham Studio . . . but had already progressed to the point of having, herself, edited several major British pictures (1978, p. 47).

Recent historical work on Alfred Hitchcock's British films (Barr, 1999) has emphasised the importance of his collaborators and the adventurous yet pro-fessional production context Gainsborough provided in the early years of his career. Alfred Roome worked alongside Hitchcock and Reville on several films at British International Pictures at Elstree towards the end of the 1920s. In Roome's view Reville's input was definitely creative: 'Alma did a lot [of cutting] herself', as well as supervising scripts. She was able to perform various functions because she had moved around different departments in her already extensive film career before specialising as an editor. To draw attention to Reville's contribution is to take nothing away from Hitchcock's achievements. What it demonstrates is the contribution editors can make within an essentially collaborative medium. This continued to be central even as production contexts and technologies changed during subsequent decades.

THE COMING OF SOUND
TRANSITION

An important dimension of editing was lost in the transition to sound. Prior to the coming of sound, editors had to consider exactly when to insert and how long to hold continuity and spoken dialogue titles. Alfred Roome recalls that during his time as an assistant working on silent films 'the editor used to mark … where the titles had to go and my job was to cut them in … he used to … allow three feet for the first word, then two words a foot after that, for reading time'. Decisions about how frequently to use titles, and how prolix they should be, could dramatically alter the pacing of a film. When Ivor Montagu was assigned to re-edit *The Lodger* (1926), he eliminated many of the titles in the 'cluttered' (1980, p. 190) first cut of what became a breakthrough film for director Alfred Hitchcock.

There was a brief period when titles and spoken dialogue might coexist on certain projects. Some transitional films, most famously *Blackmail* (Alfred Hitchcock, 1929), were produced in silent and sound versions. *Rich and Strange* (Alfred Hitchcock, 1931) contained gag titles as well as recorded dialogue. Silent and sound versions were also made of *The Crooked Billet* (Adrian Brunel, 1929/30), the first film Ian Dalrymple was credited with editing. Brunel offered advice on how editors faced with possible silent and sound versions could hedge their bets:

> When inserting spoken titles into the print of your film, you should cut out all the speaking shown in the picture, with the exception of a fraction shown at the beginning and at the end of each speech, but when cutting your negative I would advise you to preserve all your cut-outs in case you decide to post-synchronise recorded dialogue in another edition of your film (1933, p. 115).

On some early British sound productions motorised cameras were insulated to prevent unwanted noise being picked up by sound recording equipment.

This rendered the cameras immobile, but filming a scene simultaneously from different camera positions allowed additional coverage for editing. *Rookery Nook* (Tom Walls, 1930), the first of the Aldwych farces to be filmed by Herbert Wilcox's British and Dominions Film Corporation at Elstree, was shot like this. In some early British sound films the novelty of hearing dialogue temporarily became more important than establishing a dynamic editing rhythm. As film historian Rachael Low puts it: 'A typical passage would cut to the speaker before he spoke, hold the shot while he delivered his lines carefully and slowly, hold it further to show him having finished and then cut away' (1997b, p. 86). The tendency in some films of this period to privilege sound over other considerations is demonstrated by Leslie Norman's editing of *Maid of the Mountains* (Lupino Lane, 1932). To get an extra laugh he cut a reaction shot of a man eating a banana into a comedian's song. The shot caused such laughter during the film's trial run that the song lyrics were drowned out. The shot was subsequently removed.

Technological constraint was not the only factor affecting editing during the transitional period. Brunel had high hopes for the multi-camera set-up comedy revue film *Elstree Calling* he directed in 1930:

> When [A. C.] Hammond, the chief editor, saw the rushes and the results of the camerawork with our five or six cameras, he told me that I had got the effect of twenty-five cameras, that it would take him about eight weeks to cut, but that it would be epoch-making (1949, p. 159).

John Maxwell, the studio chief at British International Pictures, was more concerned that the humour and integrity of the popular star performances featured in the film should be preserved intact. He insisted, '*every* shot should be funny *by itself*' (quoted in Brunel, 1949, p. 160). Hitchcock was brought in to direct some re-shoots and editors Hammond and Emile de Ruelle were instructed to have the film ready in a week. In the short term Maxwell was vindicated because *Elstree Calling* proved to be a box-office success.

Despite this unhappy experience Brunel nevertheless argued that, in the longer term, the continuing importance of editing and editors was acknowledged by producers and 'the basis of the moving pictorial art was in part revived' (1949, p. 156). This is highlighted in an essay published in 1933 by Ian Dalrymple, who learned to edit at the small film-doctoring firm Brunel and Ivor Montagu ran in the 1920s. Dalrymple insisted that 'until the speed, *tempo*, or what you will is infused into the assembled material, the film is something dull and lifeless' (1933, p. 170). More specifically, he argued:

It is not necessary for every perambulation around every room to be shown in detail. Hold the shot you are leaving just so long as it carries analytic interest, then sharp into the next shot into which the artists move, following the movement and creating a joint *tempo* between the two shots, by picking up that shot only at such points as meets your own requirements, irrespective of true movements in detail. Watch a Lubitsch picture and you will realise his wonderful economy of movement. Where the movement is not in itself a thing to feast on, he takes the artists out of one shot into the next, or out of one set into the next, or out of a set into a totally different location with a marvellous economy, so that the amount of movement he gives becomes almost a shorthand symbol, quite acceptable to the audience, of the total movement (pp. 174–5).

Dalrymple's enthusiasm for the potential of editing to elegantly compress actual movement echoes one of the ideas contained in the 1929 English translation by Ivor Montagu of Soviet director Vsevolod Pudovkin's book *Film Technique*. Pudovkin discusses how editing can 'eliminate all points of interval, and thus concentrate the action in time to the highest degree ... not only separate incidents, but even the movement of a single person' (1958, pp. 84–5). After the coming of sound some film theorists, including Pudovkin, were initially concerned that dialogue, 'synchronis[ed] exactly with the movement on the screen', might result in stylistic 'inertia' (Eisenstein, Pudovkin and Alexandrov, 1988, p. 234). Dalrymple's essay contains traces of Pudovkin's ideas but is more positive about editing after the coming of sound.

Working for Michael Balcon at Gaumont-British, Dalrymple edited a number of musicals and comedies such as *Sunshine Susie* (Victor Saville, 1931) and *There Goes the Bride* (Albert de Courville, 1932).[1] The musical is a film genre specific to the sound era where the type of editing described by Dalrymple could be given relatively free rein. In *Evergreen* (Victor Saville, 1934), Dalrymple's editing creates some uniquely cinematic movements. When Jessie Matthews dances, he holds shots containing her more graceful gestures but eliminates some intermediate actions. Transporting actors 'out of one set into the next ... with a marvellous economy' also occurs, for example at the end of the film's first sequence when music hall star Harriet Green (Jessie Matthews) gives a farewell speech to her adoring audience. Dalrymple employs the unusual device of dissolving from the middle of this speech into the middle of another speech she makes at a dinner celebrating her impending marriage. *Evergreen* also boasts a montage sequence for the production number 'Springtime in Your Heart' that transports Harriet rapidly through sets representing different locations and historical periods. By the time this film was produced the transitional period of British film production adjusting to sound was clearly over.

NEW ROUTINES AND RHYTHMS

Sound technology brought about changes in editing routines and practices, and some editors responded imaginatively to these new developments. Thorold Dickinson travelled to America to study sound technique in 1929 and was involved in spearheading a more flexible approach to editing sound film at Elstree in early 1930. He recalls how with a multi-camera set-up the sound negative produced by a separate sound recording machine 'was never edited and re-recording was unknown. When we got the rush prints the next morning, we just matched the positive image with the sound, cutting from camera strip to camera strip. Nobody dared to put scissors into the soundtrack.' Then, rather than being presented with a sacrosanct 1,000-foot roll of sound negative, 'this apparatus came in, where you turned over one camera as in a silent film and each shot had its own soundtrack . . . I thought, well, what fun, this is much better, you can alter the timing and everything now' (quoted in Richards, 1984, pp. 28–9). Similarly, David Lean describes the situation at the start of his career when he was working in various junior roles at Gaumont-British:

> They were doing a film . . . *The Night Porter* [1930] . . . It was directed by Sewell
> Collins . . . I'd wheedled my way into his cutting room, keeping the cuts and
> handing him bits of films. Sewell Collins hadn't the foggiest idea how to
> synchronise sound and picture. There was only one person in the studio who could
> cut and synchronise sound and picture, and he was called John Seabourne who cut
> the Gaumont Sound News. Seabourne said to Collins, 'I can spare you an hour.'
> Thank God, Collins was completely unmechanical, and at the end of the hour he
> was as blank as he had been at the beginning. But I had picked up the idea of it
> and how it worked.
>
>   Synchronisation was very crude. You had to hold the film together tightly in your
> hand, and move it laboriously, sprocket by sprocket, foot by foot, through your
> fingers and make marks with a grease pencil every so often.
>
>   The fact that I cut *The Night Porter* with Sewell Collins gained me the position of
> being a kind of director's help in the cutting room, because lots of them found it
> very difficult. It *was* very difficult, too. But I managed to get the hang of it, and
> then, gradually, synchronisers came in which kept sound and picture level (quoted
> in Brownlow, 1997, p. 61).

A year later Dan Birt, who worked on *Tell England* (Anthony Asquith, Geoffrey Barkas, 1931), refers to the use of synchronisers at the British Instructional Films studio at Welwyn (Birt, 1931).[2] Two years later Michael Hankinson, a supervising editor for the British and Dominions Film Corporation at Elstree, described a relatively standardised routine (Hankinson, 1933). This routine was more time-consuming than the previous one of handling silent film alone. Rushes of the previous day's work were delivered from the laboratory and had to be synchronised before any editing could be done. Hankinson describes two methods of achieving synchronisation. The exact frame where the arm and base of a clapperboard meet were matched with the corresponding modulation on the soundtrack. Alternatively start marks were simultaneously punched in the soundtrack and the film in the camera. Some studios were reported to have numbering machines that put one consecutive number along the margin of every foot shot and every foot of soundtrack to maintain synchronisation throughout the editing process. Other pieces of equipment Hankinson considered standard by 1933 were synchronisers and sound-and-action-head Moviolas. One editor and one assistant editor were described as the typical allocation for an average film.

The new technology altered the way editors worked with their material or required a particular dexterity with the machinery in order to impose a preferred rhythm. Charles Frend, an editor at Gaumont-British in the 1930s, agreed with the widely held view that 'system as well as equipment is of great importance because without system there cannot be speed', and that 'the whole crux of the Cutter's endeavour is to try to make his hands catch up with his brain' (1945, p. 57). Speed is tied up with the economic imperative of keeping the film on schedule but there is also the aesthetic imperative to maintain 'the feeling of rhythm he has been trying to acquire' (p. 62). In ideal circumstances a good working rhythm translates into a deftly structured, well-paced film. When sound arrived, this could be jeopardised. As Lean recalls, 'it slowed everything down. The soundtrack became a tyrant. Having to lace up and run track and picture together. Bloody cumbersome. You need a rhythm to edit well' (quoted in Brownlow, 1997, p. 84).

Lean responded by taking advice from Merrill White, the American editor he worked with at British and Dominions. White had more experience of sound than any British editor at this time, having worked extensively at Paramount on musicals with Rouben Mamoulian and Ernst Lubitsch. White suggested that editing could be expedited by learning the dialogue by heart and lip-reading actors. This allowed Lean the option of working on a Moviola designed for picture only and allowed him 'to throw the film about with the old abandon' (quoted in Brownlow, 1997, p. 84). Being able to 'read', that is, recognise the source of the modulations on a soundtrack was another craft skill some editors acquired after the coming of sound in order to develop and maintain a good working rhythm. Lean prided himself on his ability to do this, whereas Frend admitted he found it more difficult.

Individual editors utilised and adapted to the new technology in different ways, but basic underlying considerations changed. Well-edited individual films would have their own specific rhythms but British editors also began to find new ways of conceptualising the rhythm of sound film in general. Sidney Cole agreed with Frend and Lean that 'the physical process of cutting is a matter of establishing a rhythm throughout a sequence and, indeed, throughout a picture'. What was axiomatic now was that this rhythm should be founded upon an interaction between sound and image where 'the completely parallel cut of sound and action should be the exception, rather than the rule'. Cole offers a tangible illustration:

> If you were to wind through on the synchroniser an average reel of a cutting copy of mine, you would find that the sound and picture cuts were throughout staggered in relation to each other by anything from one frame to several feet. This of course makes for tautness – the eye and the ear of the spectator are, as it were, in harmonious competition, always tending to be fractionally ahead of each other; but more importantly, it enables the film to reach the audience on two planes at once, the ear taking in one thing, while the eye takes in another with exciting possibilities very often of dramatic effect (1944, pp. 8–9).

A body of practical knowledge about editing dialogue accumulated during the 1930s. Already in 1933 Dalrymple was advising prospective editors on conventional methods for cutting dialogue in a manner that would move the narrative along as fluidly as possible: 'cut sharp on the last word of a sentence, possibly while the modulations are still in evidence, unless it is particularly desired to preserve a glance on the face of the speaker after he has spoken.' Advice on dealing with script deficiencies was also offered: 'If the dialogue is too verbose and the same idea is achieved in half the words, do the dialogue writer's work and cut it for him.' Similarly with the verbal aspects of performance:

> If dialogue is wrongly timed and so conflicts with a good cut, or if the cut is made difficult by actors speaking too quickly one to another, it is often possible to amend this by stopping the track at the cut and inserting blank film (1933, pp. 173–4).

Cole, on the other hand, cites examples where dialogue and performances gave him rich material to generate an editing rhythm from. In *Gaslight* (Thorold Dickinson, 1940),

> there were many scenes between Anton Walbrook and Diana Wynyard in which it was important for the atmosphere aimed at, to decide not only in the middle of which *sentence* the visual cut from one to the other should occur, but in the middle of which *word* (1944, p. 9).

More generally, he concludes by pointing out that,

> in my own practice, I always make every endeavour to preserve the tempo and
> character of a good performance ... such performances may dictate the whole
> approach of the editor. Leslie Howard's performance did this throughout the
> whole of *Pimpernel Smith* [Leslie Howard, 1941] for instance (1944, p. 15).

Recalling his editing of *Pygmalion* (Anthony Asquith and Leslie Howard, 1938)
Lean corroborates Cole's assessment. Howard would

> go at one of [George Bernard] Shaw's long speeches with a real attack and speed
> ... Wonderful nerve and verve ... He was so good at reactions ... You could have
> played practically the whole shot on his close-up, running the dialogue of the other
> people on him (quoted in Brownlow, 1997, p. 124).

From the coming of sound until the 1940s most British editors were also directly
involved in editing sound as well as dialogue. Thorold Dickinson recalled of his
time at Ealing when Basil Dean ran the studio: 'There were no "sound" or "dubbing editors" in those days' (quoted in Belfrage, n.d., p. 65). On *Sing As We Go*
(1934), director Basil Dean gave Dickinson carte blanche with regard to both
sound and picture editing. Reginald Beck's inventiveness similarly extended
across both areas when he edited *The Stars Look Down* (Carol Reed, 1939):

> We practically ran out of money, and I hadn't finished editing. There was a scene of
> a mining disaster and the sound crew had not shot me any effects. In the film there
> is seen some rushing water, flooding the mine, with tunnels collapsing, and pit-
> props smashing, everything. And I had to devise sound effects for all that lot. For
> the pit-props smashing I went through all the takes and used the clapper-board
> modulation at the beginning of each take, manipulating several together to produce
> the sound of rending wood (quoted in Belfrage, n.d., pp. 118–19).

Beck's account makes clear that editing sound effects was his responsibility. This
began to change during the war. Ralph Kemplen describes the gradual emergence of separate sound editors and the economic rationale that led to this
further division of labour:

> When I left feature films during the war all Editors did their own bits of dubbing
> ... When I came back Harry Miller had established himself at Denham ... it had
> become obvious that the average Editor was bored with a film by the time he'd
> finished cutting it; not only was he not very good at dubbing it but he did a

slipshod job to finish it quickly so time was wasted. But Harry specialised and was very good at it. So much time was saved in the dubbing theatre by him and he was so productive ... the Producers could see money saved by him. Naturally, it built from the point where Harry couldn't do every picture, so from there it grew (quoted in Musgrave, 1979, p. 15).

Unlike Beck, who covered both areas in *The Stars Look Down*, Harry Miller and Fergus McDonell divided sound and picture editing between them on *Odd Man Out* (1947), the first post-war feature directed by Carol Reed. Sound editors were familiar figures within the British film industry by the mid-1940s, but not every film had one. Charles Frend, in a paper delivered in 1945, noted that after a final cut had been arrived at, sound editing 'is usually carried out by specialists, although in some cases the poor Cutter has to see the film through dubbing also' (1945, p. 57). Teddy Darvas, who worked as an assistant editor at London Films in the late 1940s and 50s, recalls that only bigger productions had credited sound editors. For John Glen, working on inexpensive Group 3 productions such as *John and Julie* (William Fairchild, 1955), 'the assistant editor was generally responsible for the soundtrack of the film as well' (2001, p. 28). Yet by this time, with the emergence of renowned specialists such as Winston Ryder, it had become possible to build a career exclusively as a sound editor.

QUOTA QUICKIES

Films subsequently called 'quota quickies' became a distinctive part of the British scene between the 1927 and 1938 Cinematograph Acts. The first Act established incremental quotas for the distribution and exhibition of British films. One aspect of the industrial definition of 'British' was that 75 per cent of labour costs, not including the star's or producer's salary, should be paid to British citizens. A 'film' was defined as anything over 3,000 feet (approximately thirty-three minutes) in length. American distributors responded to the Act by financing and distributing quota quickies. These were cheap, quickly produced films, put together either by British subsidiaries of the major Hollywood studios or small British companies commissioned by American distributors. Minimum cost provisions in the 1938 Act encouraged the production of fewer, more expensive films, but for much of the 1930s low-budget features constituted a large part of the British film industry's output.

These parameters could cut down the creative options available to editors. Shooting ratios were likely to be tightly controlled. For example, special permission had to be sought from the producer if a director wished to shoot more than three takes on quickies filmed for Paramount at the British and Dominions studios during the mid-1930s. Time allotted to production and post-production schedules was limited. Payment could be difficult to obtain. Sidney Cole cites a strategy he and some other quickie editors resorted to 'when the financial situation became difficult, which was to take the cutting copy home under my arm every night until they paid up'. Adrian Brunel, who directed several quickies, praised the efforts of editors working under these circumstances but lamented their career prospects:

> The greatest genius in the world could not achieve much with a quickie, because his material is limited and his time is limited. I know some brilliant fellows who achieve miracles, but not perfection, for perfect editing requires considerable time and infinite patience – and time they are never allowed ... As a result the editor's work is usually criticised, and a quickie editor has to remain a quickie editor (n.d.[a]).

Brunel was particularly sensitive to the quickie editor's plight because the contract for *The Prison Breaker*, a quota film he directed in 1936, had stipulated that for every foot less than the 6,000 feet the distributor had been guaranteed, one pound would be charged against the production team. Consequently,

> the so-called finished film was full of those blemishes which a patient editor can whittle out, if he has the time ... To have cut the film, say five minutes, might have made it an acceptable little film of 64 minutes running time, instead of a rather terrible film lasting 69 minutes – but such a cut would have eliminated most of the producer's profits (1949, p. 167).

Brunel emphasised that even for experienced editors these conditions often proved 'just too tough for them'. Yet he conceded that because of the increased volume of production 'many technicians and artists got continuity of employment for the first time and became expert performers in their various fields, a number of them graduating to big production' (p. 166). Editors graduating from quickies included Thorold Dickinson, Sidney Cole, Leslie Norman, Peter Tanner and Richard Best. Towards the end of the 1930s Fox and some other American studios committed to more serious investment in British production as the quota percentage gradually increased. With the 1927 Act due to expire after ten years, the possibility of more stringent legislation loomed on the horizon. In this context it made economic and diplomatic sense to produce films that, although low-budget, exceeded the minimum legal requirements. Fox renovated the Wembley studios and sent Peter Tanner to study editing in America for several months in 1938 as part of a training scheme agreed with the Association of Cinematograph Technicians (ACT). Richard Best similarly gained a thorough training by working as an assistant to Lister Laurence and Reginald Beck on quickies produced at Pinewood and Denham. He regarded quota production as a good starting-ground for new entrants to the industry like himself.

Film historian Linda Wood has pointed out that the generally pejorative term 'quota quickie' has been used to describe what was actually 'a wide and complex continuum within the low-cost spectrum' (2001, p. 55). Some Hollywood majors were willing to invest more into their quota productions than others, and with some independent quota producers a certain amount of latitude was possible. Adrian Brunel praised producer Paul Soskin for allowing him and editor Michael Hankinson an unusual 'six to eight weeks' work on the editing' to complete the higher-than-average budget quota comedy *While Parents Sleep* (1935) for United Artists at British and Dominions' Elstree studios (1949, p. 175). British and Dominions operated a policy of producing higher-budget prestige as well as quota productions, and Hankinson worked on both. Thorold Dickinson's experience under Basil Dean's regime at Ealing was similar. He moved between films such as the relatively expensive *Sing As We Go* and the modestly budgeted *The Silent Passenger* (Reginald Denham, 1935) for an independent producer renting studio space at Ealing. Producer Julius Hagen's quota productions were released under the Real Art banner whereas his more expensive films went out as Twickenham Film Productions. In the early 1930s resident editor Jack Harris alternated between the two.

Jack Harris' experience at Twickenham is indicative of what could be achieved by an editor within the constraints imposed by quota production. Hagen's company was always less well capitalised than major British producers such as Alexander Korda's London Films. Production schedules and working hours were oppressive. David Lean, loaned to Twickenham to edit the Real Art quickie *The Ghost Camera* (Bernard Vorhaus, 1933), considered Hagen a slave-driver. Film historian Linda Wood (1998, p. 43), on the other hand, notes that Hagen assembled a core production team, including Harris, who stayed with him until the company collapsed. Hagen worked his crews incredibly hard but paid his key people well. Harris was one of the most highly paid British editors in the mid-1930s. His dedication to editing under pressure was such that by the mid-1930s new arrivals in the industry such as Richard Best regarded him as the best British editor after Lean. Discussing Twickenham Film Productions' *The Last Journey* (Bernard Vorhaus, 1935), film historian Geoff Brown highlights its rapid editing and deft cross-cutting between people outside and passengers on board a train speeding out of control. 'Shots last only one, two or three seconds. Vorhaus and his editor Jack Harris . . . make us breathless as we try to keep pace' (Brown, 1998, p. 192).

Jack Harris and other ambitious editors and technicians in the 1930s searched for ways to collectively raise the standards of the quota productions they worked on. Bernard Vorhaus praised the crews at Twickenham because 'if they saw a director was trying to make something good and not just churn out footage they responded marvellously' (quoted in Wood, 1998, pp. 55–6). In situations where such collective enthusiasm did not exist, and the editor felt the material delivered to him or her was very poor, the only option was to attempt a rescue operation. Sidney Cole tried this with *The Avenging Hand* (W. Victor Hanbury, 1936): 'I just decided to cross-cut everything in sight in order to try and make it look more interesting.' The result was unsuccessful, and Cole received

> one of my worst editing notices in the trade press, *Kinematograph Weekly* I suppose … It said that the story of this film started off as being pretty hard to follow and the editing made it totally incomprehensible. I always thought that was one of the nicest reviews I ever received.

Cole could laugh this off because his mentor, Thorold Dickinson, engaged him soon afterwards to edit *The High Command* (1937), his first film as director. Yet if *The High Command* represents the kind of break into better films that many quota quickie editors hoped for, *The Avenging Hand* is a reminder of the kind of intractable material that was closer to the norm.

EDITING IN THE BRITISH STUDIO SYSTEM

Between the 1930s and 50s there was a periodically unstable but nevertheless relatively enduring British studio system. In the 1930s it encompassed major production companies such as Gaumont-British, British International Pictures and London Films. In the 1940s and 50s it included the Associated British Picture Corporation (ABPC) and Rank with its constellation of affiliated production companies such as Gainsborough and Ealing. Certain generalisations can be made about how the editing process operated within the broad context of the British studio system. There was a definite hierarchy, with the ultimate objective being, in Charles Frend's words, to 'present a version of the picture which meets with the satisfaction of the Associate Producer … Director [and] executives of the company' (1945, p. 57). The production process did, however, allow the editor to make a creative contribution. He or she could do so collaboratively, at screenings and discussions as the film progressed from rough cut to fine cut stage (see Chapter 2), and also individually, for example before shooting had finished.

Richard Best, who edited at ABPC between the late 1940s and 60s, emphasises that within the studio system directors 'never, never' came into the cutting rooms to involve themselves in the minutiae of the editing process. This was because of the very clear division of labour. After viewing the rushes together 'it was your cut from then on' until the screening of the rough or first cut. Best always tried to 'do as much as I can in the time I've got' up to the screening of his first cut, because this was the period in which he could most fully exercise his individual creativity. Prior to this screening Best might show the director major sequences he had cut, in order to confirm their thinking was on the same wavelength. Obviously the editor's work had, in Charles Frend's phrase, to 'meet with the satisfaction' of the producer and director, but satisfaction could often be obtained by eliminating weaknesses in the material, editing it in particularly effective ways, and coming up with new ideas. The editor's creative autonomy within this context should not be overestimated, but neither should the director's. As Hugh Stewart put it, based upon his experience at Gaumont-British and London Films: 'In a properly made studio film there was a definite limit to the creative work of the editor, but the same could be said about direction' (1948, p. 201).

Within this general framework there were variations according to the working methods of, and personal and power relationships between, particular directors and editors. Frend, for example, edited three films directed by Hitchcock: *Secret Agent* (1936), *Sabotage* (1936) and *Young and Innocent* (1937). His comparison between two types of director was clearly informed by this experience: 'A good Director will shoot sparingly but will be very clear as to how he wants his material cut. A less experienced man will shoot masses of material, throw it at the Cutter and hope for the best' (1945, p. 56). By the mid-1930s Hitchcock had, in the words of his former editor and then associate producer Ivor Montagu, attained 'technical mastery and assurance'. He was able to 'visualise the cutting afterwards' while shooting, and 'knew so well what he was going to do that he could draw the exact tiny fraction of background which was all he would need built, because he knew what would be in the shot' (1980, p. 192). The editors of the first and last entries in Hitchcock's 1930s thriller cycle felt that this precise approach to direction made their task very straightforward. For Hugh Stewart *The Man Who Knew Too Much* (1934) was 'one of the best films he had ever cut ... It joined together with the neatness of a jig-saw puzzle' (1948, p. 201). Similarly, Hitchcock's economical approach to shooting resulted in Alfred Roome applying only 'some final trimming up here and there' (quoted in McFarlane, 1997, p. 498) to *The Lady Vanishes* (1938). However, Sidney Cole, who worked uncredited on *Jamaica Inn* (Alfred Hitchcock, 1939), expressed a dissenting view:

> I am told that he always shoots very sparingly, taking only the angle on a scene which he thinks he needs, and only overlapping the end of it with the action at the beginning of the next angle to the minimum necessary to enable a cut between the

two to be made at all. Occasionally this has landed his editor in almost insoluble difficulties, because shooting in this way postulates that everything will work out 100 per cent accurately. A certain latitude is nearly always advisable to allow for unforeseen accidents or for a change of intention at the editing stage. If we consider the shooting in the studio as the raw material for the scissors of the editor, some allowance for waste is permissible. In making a coat, the tailor does not try to work with the exact number of square inches of material that can be measured in the completed garment. If, on the other hand, he were to demand many times that amount, that would be the other extreme ... The best practice in film as in tailoring, lies between the two (1944, p. 6).

Hitchcock's method of providing very limited coverage occupied the more extreme end of the spectrum. Certainly, most editors preferred directors who shot with reasonable economy and gave them some indication in the material of what their intentions were. Masses of coverage would significantly increase an editor's workload. On the other hand, as Cole points out, sufficient coverage to give editors a range of options was usually appreciated.

Insofar as producers were concerned, their relationship to editors and the nature of their involvement with the creative process could vary depending upon their management style, the particularity of a studio's hierarchy, and the types of film being made. Alexander Korda at London Films in the 1930s loomed imposingly over editors as well as directors. It was quite common for directors to be changed midway through production and for several editors to be assigned to his more ambitious productions. At Gainsborough in the 1930s and 40s senior editor Alfred Roome interacted as much with producers Ted Black and Sydney Box as he did with directors. This was partly because Gainsborough typically produced less prestigious films than those directed, for example, by Hitchcock. Ordinary directors at Gainsborough therefore had less clout than Hitchcock did during his mid- to late 1930s British heyday. The experience of editors such as Peter Tanner offers another perspective from which to assess the Ealing 'team spirit' as well as the division between creative and technical grades that Michael Balcon, like other studio chiefs, presided over. The following case studies of London Films, Gainsborough and Ealing explore typicality and variation in procedures and working relationships across the British studio system.

LONDON FILMS

Alexander Korda's employment of foreign production personnel was vigorously debated in the 1930s. In some cases, as film historian Tim Bergfelder has noted, this debate was 'infused in varying degrees with xenophobia and ... anti-Semitism' directed towards European Jews (1996, p. 32). However, in Korda's editing department the senior figures were initially imported from Hollywood, where he had worked before setting up in Britain. His American editors included Harold Young, William Hornbeck, Jack Dennis and Francis Lyon. At London Films young British assistants such as Stephen Harrison, Charles Crichton, Russell Lloyd and Robert Hamer were attached to and able to learn from these Hollywood editors. One reason for this was that work permits could be obtained more easily if it could be claimed that foreign nationals were being brought over to train British technicians.

On the whole young British editors seem to have thrived in London Films' culturally diverse environment. Like many British editors, Crichton greatly admired Hornbeck. One lesson he learned from him was that 'matching doesn't matter' in sequences where 'continuity of thought is more essential'. Because of his directorial experience and involvement in the actual film-making process, Korda could also be a useful source of knowledge for British editors gradually working their way up the industry ladder. Crichton remembers that:

> When I became one of the editors on *Things to Come* [William Cameron Menzies, 1936], I showed him a rough cut of a sequence showing London under attack from the air. (This was before the war.) The sequence was full of violence, gunfire, bombs, people running for their lives ... Alex said, 'Charlie, you have made a bloody mess of this. It should be that everyone is standing there worried, waiting because they know something is going to happen, and you haven't put that in the cut at all.' And I said, 'But the director didn't shoot such a scene.' So he said, 'You are a bloody fool, Charlie! You take the bits before he has said 'Action!' and you take the bits after he has said 'Cut!' and you put them together and you make a marvellous sequence. What's wrong with you?' ... I was beginning to learn that a script is not the Bible, it is not a blueprint which must be followed precisely, word for word, to the very last detail (quoted in McFarlane, 1997, p. 152).

The volatility sometimes generated by Korda's close involvement with many London Films productions in the 1930s created opportunities as well as difficulties for editors. Former editor Harold Young completed the direction of *The Scarlet Pimpernel* (1934) after Korda sacked the film's first director Rowland V. Brown. *Elephant Boy* (Robert Flaherty, Zoltan Korda, 1937) posed a daunting editorial challenge. William Hornbeck and Charles Crichton had to integrate an enormous amount of documentary footage with other material shot by Zoltan Korda and American director Monta Bell. Crichton remembers how 'things were so chaotic in those days'. After Flaherty's footage had been shot,

Alex was rewriting the story all the time ... I had a big long cutting room with two doors. Flaherty would put his nose in and say, 'Charlie I am the director of this picture, don't take any notice of those other two ... Then Zolly would come in just like a cuckoo clock and say, 'Charlie, Flaherty doesn't know what he is doing.' That went on and it was a nightmare.

Given these circumstances, one reason for the film's considerable box-office and moderate critical success was Hornbeck and Crichton's contribution. They provided a stabilising factor, with their valuable previous experience of integrating spectacular, exotic documentary material into a rudimentary narrative structure on the similarly troubled *Sanders of the River* (Zoltan Korda, 1935).

Montage sequences were an important part of the sheen of sophistication and modernity Korda's productions sought to project. The early *Wedding Rehearsal* (Alexander Korda, 1933), edited by Harold Young, opens with a montage of newspaper headlines and printing presses. More elaborate montage sequences occur in *Sanders of the River* and *The Four Feathers* (Zoltan Korda, 1939), the latter edited by Hornbeck and Henry Cornelius. Rather than follow the usual practice of scoring after editing, *Things to Come* features montage sequences edited to complement passages of Arthur Bliss' music for the film. All of these later montage sequences were at least nominally supervised by Hornbeck, and they provided opportunities for young British features editors to edit primarily for 'continuity of thought' rather than conventional matching. In many cases the guiding 'thought' is Western civilisation under threat, either through a devastating future war as in *Things to Come* or through native revolts against the British Empire in *Sanders of the River* and *The Four Feathers* (Stollery, 2000, pp. 201–2). The newly built, ultra-modern Denham laboratories helped facilitate these increasingly sophisticated montage sequences.

The Lion Has Wings (Michael Powell, Brian Desmond Hurst, Adrian Brunel, 1939), one of London Films' last major productions prior to Korda's departure for Hollywood, can justifiably be called an editors' film. It builds upon two trends editors had been developing at London Films since the mid-1930s: the integration of documentary or newsreel footage with material shot in the studio, and ambitious montage sequences. Russell Lloyd confirms that during his time at London Films, 'in a rush three editors might work on a picture'. Five were involved on *The Lion Has Wings*: Cornelius, Hornbeck and Charles Frend (credited), Hugh Stewart and Derek Twist (uncredited). The associate producer was ex-editor Ian Dalrymple. He claimed that 'William Hornbeck and I compiled [the] rude opening sequence denigrating Nazism' (1982, p. 210). It employs the simple but effective device of conflicting the direction of movement from shot to shot to make pointed contrasts between Nazism and an idealised British way of life. In later montage sequences dissolves and superimpositions of dramatic newspaper headlines over images of devastation trace the spread of military conflict across 1930s Europe. A series of wipes pave the way for footage from an earlier London Films feature *Fire over England* (William K. Howard, 1937), signalling a transition back in time to when England was menaced by the Spanish Armada. As in *Things to Come* and *The Four Feathers* these sequences are among the most dynamic in the film, and are concerned with fundamental threats to Britain as the apex of Western civilisation.

In the later 1940s, London Films was reconstituted but operated differently from its pre-war incarnation. Korda was less actively involved in production, partly because he was responsible for administering a sizeable National Film Finance Corporation loan. The American editors who predominated at London Films in the 1930s had dispersed. Korda bought Russell Lloyd's contract from Two Cities in order to lean on the expertise of one of the many now well-qualified British editors who had worked for him in the past. In addition to editing *A Man about the House* (Leslie Arliss, 1947) and *Anna Karenina* (Julien Duvivier, 1948) Lloyd advised on other productions: 'I was not supervising editor but Korda liked to have me at times just to look at things with him.' An advisory rather than supervisory role was appropriate because London Films in the post-war period brought in several of the independent production units that had emerged during the war as part of Rank's Independent Producers initiative. These units usually included their own editors whose primary allegiance was to the directors they worked with. Reginald Mills was first and foremost a member of Michael Powell and Emeric Pressburger's Archers production team; Thelma Connell during this period was more closely associated with Frank Launder and Sidney Gilliat than she was with London Films per se. Gainsborough and Ealing studios, however, continued to operate along more traditional lines.

GAINSBOROUGH IN THE 1930s AND 1940s

In the 1930s the Gaumont-British studios at Lime Grove Shepherd's Bush handled the most expensive productions, whereas the company's other production arm, the Gainsborough studios at Islington, concentrated on films aimed primarily at the domestic market. Gainsborough proved to be more economically viable over the longer term. It was a studio where, throughout the 1930s and 40s, an impressive continuity of employment was possible. Senior editor R. E. Dearing was there for approximately fifteen years. Alfred Roome stayed for an equally long period after a brief stint at Gaumont-British. He valued Gainsborough's 'family' atmosphere and interacted particularly well with studio chiefs Ted Black (1936–43) and later Sydney Box (1946–50). Under Black's regime Gainsborough was orientated towards a relatively high volume of genre film-making, and directors were typically less prominent than producers and senior editors during post-production. During Black's time at Gainsborough the usual routine, according to Roome, was for the editor 'to do the rough cut as [the director] wanted it and then he just disappears and Ted Black and Bob Dearing took over from there'. Carol Reed, who began his directing career at Gainsborough, was rather aggrieved by the fact that 'very often I wasn't even invited to see the editing' (quoted in Wapshott, 1990, p. 115).

Rather than being seen as completely interchangeable, Roome felt that when Black assigned editors and other technicians to productions at Gainsborough 'possibly a bit of personality' was taken into account. Having worked on several Tom Walls films Roome was already established as a comedy specialist. Comedy was a major component of Gainsborough's 1930s production programme, and Roome was teamed with director Marcel Varnel on a number of Will Hay comedies from *Oh, Mr Porter!* (1937) through to *Ask a Policeman* (1939). Varnel was liked by and generally worked well with editors. Sidney Cole remembered him from their early collaborations *Freedom of the Seas* (1934) and *Dance Band* (1935) as a theatre director who, on moving into film, 'told the company he was working for that before he started directing he wanted to spend a few weeks in the cutting rooms to see how films were put together'. Consequently he understood 'what an editor could contribute to a film'. Roome recalls that Varnel would sometimes ask him for advice on the Hay films. Varnel, Roome and Gainsborough staff cinematographers such as Arthur Crabtree developed a dynamic approach to the later Hay films, with 'more cuts and more close-ups and general camera movement'. Roome also devoted considerable attention to the all-important issue of performance. Hay's style, derived from music hall, posed him some problems:

> His double takes were famous, delayed reactions to something, and the only trouble, from a cutting point of view, was he used a strange device of a sniff, which worked very well on the stage, but could be overdone from a film point of view. So that he used to either sniff before saying something, or say something and then sniff, and so that half the time I was cutting these sniffs out, which made it a bit different.

The Second World War brought many changes for editors. Film editing was a reserved occupation only for those over thirty years old. Younger British editors such as Russell Lloyd, Richard Best, Frank Clarke and Peter Tanner were called up or volunteered for military service and they worked primarily on documentaries during this period. Different opportunities arose for slightly older editors who continued working in features. Roome, in his early thirties when war broke out, was conscious that 'people were sort of moving around ... people were being called up and one thing and another'. This moving around enabled the emergence not only of new directors and new approaches to film-making but also an expanded role for Roome. During the War several Gainsborough screenwriters got their first chance to direct. Roome became an increasingly visible, respected presence on the studio floor as well as in the cutting rooms: 'I often used to get a message, would I, quick, come down on the floor, they've got themselves in a muddle or something.'

Roome provided reliable support for several Gainsborough directors' early films. He recalls that when Val Guest, previously a screenwriter on many of the Will Hay comedies, came to direct *Miss London Ltd* (1943), 'I was really given the job of holding his hand properly there and I helped a great deal with the actual direction of that one, setting up the camera and so forth.' Roome also proved useful during the production of *Millions Like Us* (Frank Launder, Sidney Gilliat, 1943) and *Waterloo Road* (Sidney Gilliat, 1944). According to him, Sidney Gilliat was a director who

> knew what he wanted from the artists and how they should say it. What he wasn't sure was how to put it together, to get from one shot to another and that sort of thing, which is what I was ... largely doing.

Moreover on *Millions Like Us* Roome, unlike Launder and Gilliat, already had experience of incorporating documentary footage into a fictional narrative through his editing of *Bank Holiday* (Carol Reed, 1938). Roome's contribution to the pooling of expertise and the nurturing of new directorial talent at Gainsborough during the War was clearly a significant one.

Roome's star rose even higher when Sydney Box took control of production at Gainsborough. Box 'was very receptive' to Roome.

> He liked listening to people. He would take their ideas and digest them, possibly turn them round in a different way, but he'd often use it, and he seemed to like some of the ideas I had about things, and so I was ... in and out of his office a great deal.

In the post-war period Roome forged a good working relationship with Ken Annakin. For *Holiday Camp* (1947), Annakin's first film as director, Box asked Roome to adopt a now familiar role, 'to be on the floor as much as possible to give Ken a hand, as he'd never done a feature before. He actually didn't need much sorting out, because he was naturally a film man.' *Holiday Camp*'s utilisation of documentary footage within a fictional narrative followed in the tradition

Frank Clarke editing for the Army Film Unit during the Second World War

of Roome's earlier work on *Bank Holiday* and *Millions Like Us*. Annakin and Roome later extended this practice in their 1950s Empire films produced by Rank. *The Planter's Wife* (1952), set in Malaya but mostly shot at Pinewood and in Sri Lanka, 'was interesting to work on because it meant splicing together the studio stuff with the location footage'. With *Nor the Moon by Night* (1958), set in Africa, 'matching studio and location footage [could] be a problem with colour but the laboratory very often sorts that out'.

With his status reflected by an associate producer credit, Roome was also deployed as a supervising editor and film doctor during Gainsborough's final years. In this capacity he tried hard to make something of a film whose shooting ratio was excessive: 'I actually re-cut *The Bad Lord Byron* [1949], which was so bad the first time. It wasn't the editor's fault; the director, David MacDonald, had just let it run, pages of stuff without any cuts. I did all sorts of tricks with it – bits of Byron's poetry, travel shots – but it was an un-savable film' (quoted in McFarlane, 1997, p. 499). With the British film industry undergoing a major crisis in the late 1940s, due to a failed and costly attempt to penetrate the American market, the Rank Organisation instituted an economy drive and

Gainsborough productions were terminated in 1950. In Roome's case his reputation was sufficiently established for him to be moved over immediately to Pinewood where he continued to edit into the mid-1970s. What changed for him when Gainsborough wound down was that 'nearly all the contracts the studios could get rid of, they did, and I lost my contract at that time and became an "independent labourer"' (quoted in McFarlane, 1997, p. 500). With important exceptions, such as Ealing in the 1950s and Hammer in the 1950s and 60s, the era of continuous contracts with one British studio or production company was beginning to draw to a close.

EALING STUDIOS IN THE 1940s AND 1950s

Michael Balcon was noted for his role as a catalyst for film projects and the assembling of dynamic creative teams rather than for getting deeply involved in the production process. Sidney Cole's recollection of Balcon at Ealing in the 1940s and early 50s is that 'he would see the rushes every day. Beyond that he didn't interfere – not at all in the editing. He backed his judgment of us by letting us get on with the job' (quoted in McFarlane, 1997, p. 137). Peter Tanner corroborates this: 'Balcon ... didn't make cutting suggestions ... unless it was something, a sequence or something he disliked.' Three recurring dislikes, according to Tanner, were blood, studio rain and studio-built banisters that might move during a scene. The only other point at which Balcon could be involved in specific editing decisions was if the BBFC (British Board of Film Censors) raised objections to a completed film. Tanner recalls a discussion between Balcon, the BBFC secretary and himself as editor of *Kind Hearts and Coronets*. Despite having already gone through the usual procedure of script vetting, the censor had compiled a list of fifteen to twenty objections to the finished film. Shots featuring a stag's head, symbolising cuckoldry, given by Louis Mazzini (Dennis Price) as a wedding present to Sibella (Joan Greenwood) and Lionel (John Penrose), were excised. The long shot of a punt propelled by Louis falling over a weir with his first victims in it was saved.

The most senior member of the Ealing team specifically and closely involved with editing in the 1940s and early 50s was Sidney Cole. Having worked on various features and documentaries he joined Ealing in 1942 as a supervising editor. He was a key contributor to the emergent Ealing style of film-making. Films he supervised included *The Bells Go Down* (Basil Dearden, 1943) and *For Those in Peril* (Charles Crichton, 1944). *The Bells Go Down* integrates documentary footage of Blitz firefighting into a fictional narrative. Cole took sole editing credit on *Went the Day Well?* (Alberto Cavalcanti, 1943), but his broader contribution to editing at Ealing cannot be identified by credits alone. Typically he would 'look at the rushes and discuss the approach to the editing. Sometimes take a sequence and do the final cut oneself. Generally overseeing everything that went on ... Sometimes although supervising editor, you would occasionally edit a film yourself.' Subsequently, from 1944 to 1952, he was credited as an associate producer or producer, but would often be involved in editing, for example on *Dead of Night* (Alberto Cavalcanti, Charles Crichton, Basil Dearden, Robert Hamer, 1945). When asked which role he preferred, Cole emphasised Ealing's co-operative spirit and explained:

> It is difficult to answer your question because, as associate producer or producer, I feel one of the most important things is to be there all through the editing process, including the dubbing stage, to the final print. So I suppose I would have to say I like being a producer, because then I am involved in the scripting and the editing as well, even if I am not billed as scriptwriter or editor (quoted in McFarlane, 1997, p. 137).

One example of Ealing's co-operative spirit is the post-production of *Whisky Galore* (Alexander Mackendrick, 1949). Cole was involved and Crichton did a lot of uncredited editing on this film. Tanner recalls, 'we all had a hand'; he helped edit the sequence in which bottles are taken off the wrecked ship. Team spirit notwithstanding, working relationships within the production process were organised along relatively hierarchical lines. As film historian John Ellis argues, 'Ealing's team still preserved the normal relations of production of any studio: a top echelon of creative artists and a large number of employees whose effect over the shape of projects was very limited' (1990, p. 358). For those outside this 'top echelon' Ealing could seem a rigidly hierarchical environment. Jim Clark, who began his career at Ealing as an assistant editor on *The Titfield Thunderbolt* (Charles Crichton, 1953), confirms: 'there was a definite team spirit and they were very proud of it.' He was less enamoured of the

> class system operating in the studio as well ... It split itself very easily into the two public houses across Ealing Green. There was the Red Lion, which was out of bounds, basically, to anyone who was not in the hierarchy. So if you were not a writer or director or producer you didn't go in there and if you did go in there you were sort of frowned upon or not spoken to, and you learned these lessons very quickly. The 'lads', us lot, used to go over to the Queen Victoria, which was the other pub.

Clark's memory of his work at Ealing is that 'when I was an assistant, I didn't really get that much involved in the creative process ... You're always so busy servicing the editor, and looking after the rushes, and doing the numbering and whatever.' This was a fairly typical assistant's routine for this period. For those fortunate enough to graduate from assistant to fully fledged editor while at Ealing a different perspective was possible. Bernard Gribble, who gained his first editing credit on *Another Shore* (Charles Crichton, 1948), states clearly: 'I wasn't part, shall we say, of the creative process there when films were in the gestation period. It was really the writers, Michael Balcon, the producers and the directors. The editors were really just assigned to the shows.' Once an editor had been assigned, however, 'you were part of a team, and your input was certainly wanted'.

Peter Tanner's position within the relations of production at Ealing makes an interesting case study. He was afforded 'quite a bit' of creative responsibility by the directors he worked with, while also 'learning from them', given that most Ealing directors were ex-editors. He tended to avoid the most obvious expression of the social division between creative as opposed to technical grades by not visiting either the Queen Victoria or the Red Lion after work. Occasionally, however, he would go with director Charles Frend to the Red Lion, where Sidney Cole also drank. Recommended to Balcon by editor Michael Truman, Tanner joined Ealing in 1947. He had edited documentaries during the Second World War, and 'Balcon wanted somebody who had a documentary background, particularly for *Scott of the Antarctic* [Charles Frend,

Bernard Gribble at a Moviola,
Ealing Studios, 1946

1948] which was the first of my pictures, and that was treated in a documentary way.'

Tanner was subsequently assigned to several films with a strong documentary element, including *The Blue Lamp* (Basil Dearden, 1950), *Pool of London* (Basil Dearden, 1951) and *The Cruel Sea*. His first contribution to *Secret People* (Thorold Dickinson, 1952) involved selecting material for a montage sequence representing the 1937 Paris Exhibition. Lindsay Anderson recorded:

> [Peter] accompanies Thorold to the Bonded Film Store (where film is held by the Customs until duty has been paid) to view the Exhibition material which has arrived from Paris ... At Peter's side his assistant notes the shots which director and editor agree should be printed up. With duty payable at 5d. a foot, it is important that wastage be kept to a minimum (1952, p. 29).

On *The Cruel Sea*, Tanner's integration of documentary and fictional material ultimately 'seemed to work out well', although it involved spending

> a lot of time which I could ill afford going through library material to get all that actual stuff of the Russian convoys and then trying to match up, it was easier of course being black and white, but matching up the sea and that sort of thing, it didn't always match very well.

Tanner was interested in stylistic innovation, for example, the one-frame cuts used to augment an explosion in *The Cruel Sea*. He experimented with eliminating fades and dissolves in *Kind Hearts and Coronets* and *The Blue Lamp*. Sound bridges are also used to good effect in *The Blue Lamp*. Sounds of telephone lines being connected and telegrams arriving bridge a series of sharp, rapid cuts, helping to create a feeling of urgency and teamwork as the Metropolitan police move into action after PC Dixon (Jack Warner) has been shot. This was a practice Tanner experimented with across several films in different genres during this period; 'even in *Scott* I did one or two'. The consummate example is *Kind Hearts and Coronets*, when Edith d'Ascoyne (Valerie Hobson) realises her husband Henry (Alec Guinness) has just been blown up. Tanner later wrote:

> Immediately after [Edith's exclamation] 'Henry' on the soundtrack there is a deep sonorous church bell. In the middle of this bell sound we direct cut to a long shot of the funeral cortège outside the church. By eliminating the conventional dissolve and using the sound device to get us into the next sequence, we not only get a smooth and natural transition, but also a certain laugh (1960, p. 889).

Peter Tanner at Ealing Studios during the 1950s

Tanner unreservedly enjoyed the wittiness of *Kind Hearts and Coronets*' script and his collaboration with Hamer. He was quietly amused by Balcon's discomfort with the finished film. Tanner relished the freedom Dennis Price's rough voiceover, recorded before editing began, gave him to experiment. The first part of the extended flashback visualising Louis Mazzini's memoirs moves quickly, often using direct cuts, from events occurring before Louis' birth through to his adulthood. Dissolves are often used for specific emotional and conceptual effects, rather than just as a conventional linking device. They connect several quite similar shots of Louis working as an assistant in a drapery store, accentuating the monotony of the humiliating job his reduced circumstances have forced him to take. Earlier, Louis' voiceover narrates his mother's traumatic and scandalous banishment from her ancestral home. The voiceover explains how she eloped with his father and 'exchanged the medieval splendour of Chalfont Castle' – cut – 'for the modern conveniences of number 73 Balaclava Avenue SW9'. The direct cut between shots of these locations is made all the more abrasive because preceding shots have been linked by dissolves.

The timing and pace of *Kind Hearts and Coronets*, within sequences and across the film as a whole, is expertly modulated. Spatial and temporal freedom and the speed of the first part of the extended flashback is counterbalanced by sequences where, in Tanner's phrase, 'deliberately leisurely' editing helps create suspense and comedy. In one of these Louis, Edith (Valerie Hobson) and Henry d'Ascoyne (Alec Guinness) spend a day together. What his companions do not know is that Louis has planted explosives in the garden shed where Henry hides alcohol. As Tanner puts it, 'the audience already knows what is probably going to happen'. To extend the suspense 'leisurely cutting, dwelling on each shot' predominates as Louis and the film's spectator wait impatiently for Henry to visit his shed.

Film historian Charles Barr has described *Kind Hearts and Coronets*' style as one 'built on the tension between the formal surface and what we, and Louis, know to be going on behind that surface' (1993, p. 124). In the sequence where Henry is blown up after entering his shed this tension is established by playing off 'leisurely' shots, detailing the niceties of social intercourse, against Louis' murderously vengeful intentions, wittily reiterated in his voiceover. On the crucial issue of timing the editing in this sequence, Tanner wrote, 'it is the editor's job, as well as the director's, to know just how long this time shall be' (1960, p. 888). Robert Hamer was aware that *Kind Hearts and Coronets* became the yardstick against which other films he directed were found wanting: 'Friends ... look at my other films and say, "good, brilliant, superb" but not, of course, so "good, brilliant, superb" as *Kind Hearts and Coronets*' (quoted in McFarlane, 1997, p. 271). One reason for *Kind Hearts*' uniqueness within Hamer's oeuvre is that it was the only film he collaborated with Peter Tanner on.

EDITING AND DIRECTING: CROSSOVER AND CRAFT SKILLS
The aspiration to become a director is by no means common to all editors, although many editors have made a successful transition. Indeed, editing has been considered at certain times to be the most valuable training for directing. For Sidney Cole, one historical factor explaining why a number of British editors became directors during the 1930s and earlier part of the 40s was:

> The older among them certainly learned a great deal about how *not* to make pictures by working on quota pictures in the bad old days of British films.
>
> In those days ... it was a not uncommon experience of editors to be called in, rather like Harley Street specialists, to revamp a film which had become the despair of the studio and to suggest a new ending or beginning or middle. After a few such experiences, the editor began to wonder why the company didn't save time and money by calling him in beforehand to direct the picture properly. The same wonder seems finally to have occurred to the industry generally (1944, p. 11).

Editors this applies to include Thorold Dickinson, David Lean and Leslie Norman. Dickinson's first credit as director was *The High Command*, filmed on location and at Basil Dean's Ealing Studios where he had been editing for some years. Having turned down offers to direct quota quickies, Lean shared his first directing credit with Noel Coward on the prestige project *In Which We Serve* (1942). After several years as an editor of Warner Bros.–First National's quota productions, Norman's progress towards direction included some second unit work on *They Drive by Night* (Arthur Woods, 1939) and a co-directing credit on *Too Dangerous to Live* (co-director Anthony Hankey, 1939). Norman's features directing career was interrupted by being called up during the Second World War, but he eventually made the transition in the mid-1950s. Russell Lloyd, on the other hand, felt that war service thwarted his aspirations to direct: 'Charlie Crichton became a director, Bob Hamer became a director ... The same thing might have happened to me but I was in the navy.' Other editors not called up because of their age found themselves presented with new opportunities.

During the Second World War, Charles Frend as well as Crichton and Hamer moved from editing to direction under Michael Balcon's leadership at Ealing Studios. By the late 1940s the core directing team at Ealing had been consolidated, so although the policy of promoting certain editors to director continued, later appointees were less prolific. During Balcon's second decade as studio chief ex-editors Henry Cornelius, Michael Truman and Seth Holt directed one Ealing film each: *Passport to Pimlico* (1949), *Touch and Go* (1955) and *Nowhere to Go* (1958) respectively. Leslie Norman, who began at Ealing as supervising editor on *The Overlanders* (Harry Watt, 1946), finally moved into direction with *The Night My Number Came Up* (1955), *The Shiralee* (1957) and *Dunkirk* (1958). Norman suggested that Balcon favoured graduates as directors: 'I had a council-school education, hadn't been to university and Mick Balcon was a real academic snob – anyone who had a degree *must* be good, he thought. So that slowed me down' (quoted in McFarlane, 1997, p. 440).

Other British studios occasionally gave editors who wanted it the opportunity to direct. Towards the end of his long tenure at Gainsborough Alfred Roome co-directed *My Brother's Keeper* (1948) and *It's Not Cricket* (1949) with Roy Rich. His colleague Terence Fisher took advantage of the informal training scheme at Rank's Highbury Studios to build a career, from 1948 onwards, as a director of modestly budgeted genre films. The British film industry, however, underwent a major production crisis in the late 1940s, and Russell Lloyd's attempt at moving into direction reveals some of the impact this had on individual careers. Julien Duvivier praised Lloyd's second unit direction on *Anna Karenina*. Lloyd's next assignment was co-directing another London Films production, *The Last Days of Dolwyn* (1949), with Emlyn Williams, who was primarily a man of the theatre. The division of labour was similar to Lean's and Coward's on *In Which We Serve*:

> Emlyn used to talk to the people who were going to be in the scene and then I would decide where the camera went and what they did and all that stuff ... if I felt the way they were saying things was not quite right I would do that as well.

After this Lloyd tried to set up a solo directing project, but because of the production crisis this was 'a very inopportune moment ... so I thought I'd better go back to cutting where I was more or less sure of getting a job'.

Further crises within the industry during the 1950s and the increasing shift towards independent production also broke up older patterns of career progression. Geoffrey Foot hoped that after second unit direction on films such as *One Good Turn* (John Paddy Carstairs, 1954), and editing films such as *Blue Murder at St Trinian's* (Frank Launder, 1957), he could move into direction:

> I would have liked to have directed ... at one stage, I thought it was going to come off. Launder and Gilliat were going to promote a subject ... We got very excited about it and then of course it died ... I think it was one of those vacuums that occur every now and then in the film business.

Seth Holt was one of the last editors to benefit from the traditional pattern of promotion to direction within a relatively stable studio context. His erratic progress compared to predecessors who had followed a similar route can be partly related to the period in which he made his transition. *Nowhere to Go* was one of the last films Ealing produced before closing down. In a context where, for example, Rank announced redundancies and the postponement of some productions in early 1958, Holt traded on his greater experience as an editor to secure work on independent productions such as *Saturday Night and Sunday Morning* (1960). Hammer, the company he resumed his directing career with, was unusual in providing consistency of production and a traditional studio structure in an industry where employment patterns were changing. Clive Donner, another ex-editor who moved into direction in the late 1950s, found after directing two features that television initially provided more regular employment for an inexperienced director than the film industry could.

Many editors who became directors looked back on their editorial experience as excellent training. Terence Fisher claimed, 'most of what I learned filmwise was in the cutting rooms. That gives you a great sense of the pattern of a film, the overall rhythm. This dramatic rhythm is the basis of technique, of style' (quoted in Dixon, 1991, p. 9). Russell Lloyd's view is that editors, compared to scriptwriters or stars, can make good directors because, 'like David Lean, I suppose, they know more about [technicalities] than anybody, by just looking at it they know what's good lighting. At least they can say to a [cinematographer] what they'd like in the way of light.' Lean is the person most often cited in such discussions. In an essay written a few years after he made the transition he listed several reasons why he thought editing was good training for direction. He argues that the director must have a thorough working knowledge of what the crew and the technology they operate can provide: 'he must have authority, and he can only have that authority if he has a general knowledge of his craft'. This was a major component of Lean's reputation within the industry. More specifically, 'the film editor or cutter is a second director'. Both are fundamentally 'concerned with the dramatic presentation of a scene and the performance given by the actors in that scene. They are both story-tellers. They both decide what the audience has got to look at – and when' (1947, pp. 27–8). Unsurprisingly, other editors who became directors, including Donner and Stuart Baird, make the same comparison.

Despite these areas of overlap, there are important differences between particular craft skills essential to each role. In David Gladwell's opinion assistant direction is more useful preparation for direction than editing, because it provides experience of working with actors and a crew on the studio floor or on location. Many editors wanting to direct have sought work in this capacity before making the transition. Sidney Cole suggests a clear demarcation when he states the director 'deals with *people*', whereas the editor 'deals with *celluloid*' (1947, pp. 152–3). Lean was less categorical but conceded that, although recognising good performance was a vital editing skill, directing actors was not an easy task for an ex-editor. As an editor, 'by watching the actor's mistakes you will see what *not* to do. You will also see *what* to do, but that always looks so very, very easy when it is done properly and believe me it is very, very difficult' (1947, p. 30).

Alfred Roome, finally, extrapolated from his own experience when assessing the directing skills of Britain's best-known ex-editor:

> I would quote a heresy and say that some, not all, but some of David Lean's pictures show that he started off as an editor, and they can be too mechanically perfect. Just sometimes it shows, you know? Because I found that when I tried directing. It's not at all easy. You can do the parts you know, which was, I could edit the picture, I could stick it together, but it somehow had lost a bit of warmth or humanity or something ... Because you were being too perfect, or trying to be.

Roome did not continue directing, partly because he was 'not too keen on dealing with the foibles of actors', and he was glad to return to the cutting rooms.

Some editors working in contexts where the opportunity to direct might have been available had they pushed for it, for example, Peter Tanner at Ealing, decided not to pursue this route. They found more than enough creative challenge and fulfilment in the cutting rooms.

NOTES

All unattributed quotations in this chapter are drawn from BECTU History Project interviews, apart from the quotations from Richard Best, Bernard Gribble, Russell Lloyd and Peter Tanner, which are drawn from the interviews conducted for this book.

1. Film historian Tim Bergfelder argues that, with their emphasis on surface and style, and narratives typically concerned with masquerades or crossing social boundaries, films such as *Sunshine Susie* and *There Goes the Bride* tend to display 'social, national and gender identities ... in a state of flux' (1997, p. 43). Dalrymple's preference for editing that moves characters gracefully and easily through space is well suited to the concerns Bergfelder identifies.

2. Birt (1931, p. 205) identifies the clapperboard method as RCA's, the hole-punch methods as Western Electric's, and adds that Tobis-Klangfilm, the system installed at the British Instructional Films studios, provided continuous numbering on the edge of the film.

4

Aspects of British Editing from the 1950s Onwards

Freelancing became the normal mode of employment for British film editors in the latter part of the twentieth century. Rather than being assigned projects from the production schedule of the studio they worked for, editors were increasingly employed on a film by film basis. Some editors worked as freelancers in the earlier period, but this was less common than it later became. The gradual decline of the British studio system in the post-war period led to freelancing becoming the norm. As Colin Belfrage puts it: 'Most film technicians, who had become used to working under contract, never again were "contracted" employees, instead they became . . . casualised labourers' (n.d., pp. 184–5). Continuity of employment became even less certain than it had previously been but successful careers became more diverse.

Editors' assessments of these changes differ. Bernard Gribble established himself as an editor at Ealing before going freelance in 1953. He embraced the change:

> Working staff you were assigned to a film. I'm sure there were situations where if a director wanted you, he'd have you, but the studio wouldn't put you aside for months to wait for him. So one felt part of the furniture. If you're hired to do a film freelance you really feel that you're earning your money . . . I've never regretted it.

Jim Clark's experience of the Ealing ethos during the same period was 'once you were there you didn't leave unless you were forced out. It was fifty-two weeks a year, full employment, they were working on wonderful films, had a great reputation, we were all lucky to be there.' Clark, with some trepidation, left full employment at Ealing for the uncertainties of freelancing. Like many leading British editors from the 1950s onwards his career was thereafter varied, sometimes precarious, and often rewarding. He subsequently worked on American-financed productions such as Universal's *Charade* (Stanley Donen, 1963), British productions such as *Darling*, and later worked in Hollywood itself.

Three major employment contexts for British editors in the post-war period have been Hollywood in Britain, British productions and Hollywood itself. For the purposes of this discussion Hollywood in Britain covers the range from films produced by British-based subsidiaries of Hollywood studios to Hollywood-financed projects that hire British studio space or post-production facilities and personnel on a more ad hoc basis. It also includes films directed by exiled or expatriate Americans. The British films discussed here are ones that have been identified as particularly significant by virtue of subject matter, stylistic inno-vation or critical acclaim. The examples considered are the British New Wave films of the late 1950s and early 60s, the youth-orientated films of the later 1960s, and Goldcrest productions of the early 1980s.

Obviously there are large areas of overlap between these categories: British productions can also be Hollywood-financed, and although Hollywood-financed projects tend to have higher budgets than British ones this is not always the case. Some editors have worked primarily in one category; others have crossed between them. Therefore the discussion that follows uses these categories not to demarcate rigid divisions but to map some of the different kinds of projects British editors have been involved in from the 1950s onwards. Moreover, this chapter is not in any way an exhaustive account of British editing during this period; its aim is to discuss general trends and representative examples rather than every significant piece of work. Given the increasing fragmentation of British production since the 1980s, the more recent work of some important editors currently working in Britain is explored in the filmographies at the end of the book.

HOLLYWOOD IN BRITAIN

British subsidiaries of Hollywood studios provided a new source of employment for British editors in the earlier part of the post-war period. As film historian Robert Murphy points out, the pattern of American investment in film produc-tion in Britain differed from the pre-war period: 'In contrast to the quota quickie days of the 30s, the predominant trend of the 50s was to make big-budget pic-tures which would appeal to American as well as British audiences' (1986, p. 62). This shift of emphasis was partly the result of the post-war balance-of-payments problem that forced the British government to restrict the earnings American companies could take out of the country. Many American-financed productions also received financial aid from the Production Fund, derived from the Eady levy on box-office takings established in 1950 to support films legally registered as 'British'. For a film to qualify as 'British' a significant proportion of British technical personnel had to be employed on the production. Conse-quently editors including Jim Clark, Tony Lawson and Terry Rawlings began their careers or got significant breaks working on big-budget American-financed films produced in Britain.

The cultural 'Britishness' of these films, or lack of it, has been a matter for debate inside and outside the industry. However, in addition to providing relatively stable employment for some editors during a period when the British studio system was contracting, American-financed productions helped to internationalise their professional experience and expand the scope of their responsibilities in several different ways. Freddie Wilson, appointed 'Executive Editor' of Universal's British and European operations in the late 1960s, recalled: 'The work involved co-ordinating all post-production work on their films in Europe and keeping Universal City fully informed of progress, particularly during the post-production period' (1979, p. 12). Frank Clarke, supervising editor at MGM-British during the 1950s and 60s, worked on several major films showcasing important Hollywood stars such as Clark Gable and Ava Gardner that were directed by the likes of John Ford and George Cukor. Clarke's contribution to these films involved travelling across the Atlantic to work in Hollywood:

> I would do a rough cut or assembly and then take it to America ... Whenever they were doing an American film over here – a British production but really American-controlled – we would order two prints. We would order a print for rushes to go to America and have another print here that I would work on. So when I took over a rough cut of the film to America they had complete takes of that as well so we could do alterations over there.

Clarke would typically edit the American as well as British versions of the MGM-British films he worked on, but in Hollywood he was ghosted by an American editor because of union regulations. The practice of flying him over on a regular basis highlights a recognition on the studio's part of the value that can be added to a film when a skilled editor is allowed to work continuously on a project and on any alternative versions. At the same time the 'two prints' system was clearly designed to maximise head office's control over geographically distant projects. For example, on *Bhowani Junction* (1956), one of Clarke's MGM-British assignments, director George Cukor was involved in a stage play during post-production. The 'erotic implications' of this romance between an Anglo-Indian woman and a white British officer in India on the verge of independence were 'trimmed back' at the studio's behest to placate anticipated hostile responses from certain American audiences to representations of interracial sex (McGilligan, 1991, p. 245).

Richard Best worked occasionally on Anglo-American film productions for Fox between the late 1940s and 60s. He felt the oppressive degree of long-distance control exercised by Hollywood-based producers outweighed the

Frank Clarke at a Steenbeck editing machine in the 1960s while supervising editor at MGM-British

higher pay and status working on such productions could bring. The second set of rushes from *Britannia Mews* (Jean Negulesco, 1949), for example, was edited in Hollywood under Darryl Zanuck's supervision into the final release version of the film. Zanuck, as film historian Win Sharples Jr points out, is 'frequently cited as the [Hollywood] producer who best understood editing, and who rigorously and consistently controlled the editing on all his pictures' (1977, p. 7). In the case of *Britannia Mews* Best was effectively the British ghost for a film edited in America. This and other similar experiences, for example, on *The Most Dangerous Man in the World* (J. Lee Thompson, 1969), also financed by Fox, led Best to conclude there was 'no pleasure in it' and 'I was able to give much more input to indigenous films'.

Foreign capital injected into the British film industry by Anglo-American film production contributed to infrastructural modernisation. ABPC's tie-up with Warner Bros. from the late 1940s onwards, for example, helped finance the reconstruction of their Elstree Studios. By common consent the most impressive development during this period was MGM-British's expansion of the Borehamwood complex. This boasted ten spacious sound stages and state of the

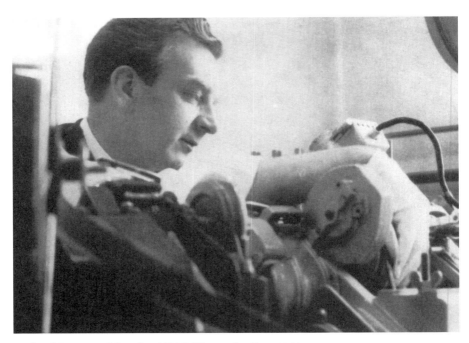

Richard Best at a Moviola, ABPC Elstree Studios, 1960

art editing facilities. For many British editors this technological legacy is not to be underestimated. Stuart Baird argues:

> MGM had opened a studio here after the war ... Under the aegis of the American film industry we'd built up this fantastic, solid support base of editors, art directors, cameramen, construction people, fantastic because we'd been making huge pictures. Rome had as well but England really was the home from home for the American film industry ... In many ways by the 1960s and 70s the equipment that we were using was often better, more modern, more up to date than Hollywood because Hollywood still had the residues of the studio system and they had all this old equipment from then and they weren't renewing like in England ... Our crews were smaller, our wages were smaller, it was a big advantage financially for America to make pictures here, but it gave us a great training ground.

Baird's general point is valid but his early career was in some respects unusual. He worked as an assistant director for Lindsay Anderson on the Paramount-financed *If* ... (1968) and then on various American-financed films directed by Ken Russell from *Women in Love* (1969) to *Valentino* (1977). Baird's career began at the very end of the peak period of American-financed production in Britain but continued to flourish in its aftermath thanks to his close association with Russell, then Britain's most prominent director. During 1969–70 a massive contraction of American investment affected many technicians within the British film industry. The biggest setback was the closure of the MGM-British Borehamwood Studio. Its equipment was transferred for use in subsequent EMI-MGM British-based productions such as *The Boy Friend* (Ken Russell, 1972), which Baird worked on as assistant to editor Michael Bradsell. For many other British technicians consistent work in features proved difficult to secure during this period. Gerry Hambling, for example, dropped out of features for seven years to work on commercials before returning to edit *Bugsy Malone* (1976) for former commercials director Alan Parker. Jonathan Morris moved from working as an assistant editor on feature films to working for television. Although the pay was less, it provided more continuity of employment. Frank Clarke found his feature film editing career abruptly terminated after nearly twenty years at MGM-British when the Borehamwood Studio closed down.

The most enduring strand of Anglo-American film production to survive the late 1960s downturn is the Bond franchise. The series has given several British editors the opportunity to experiment with action editing. John Glen, editor of several Bond films in the late 1960s and 70s, was full of admiration for the contributions his predecessor Peter Hunt had made to the series, both in terms of its overall style and in relation to specific sequences. On *Thunderball* (Terence Young, 1965), for example:

> They were breaking new ground by setting so much of the important action underwater, and I don't think Terence realised until too late that everything would slow down to such a degree. The film would have run the risk of grinding to a virtual standstill had it not been for some damage limitation in the cutting rooms. Peter Hunt speeded up a lot of the underwater action by editing a lot of the sequences at double speed, removing alternate frames (2001, p. 44).

At the beginning of the 1980s producer Albert Broccoli wanted *For Your Eyes Only* (John Glen, 1981) to return to a more conventional thriller format and move away from the fantastical elements prevalent in preceding Bond films such as *Moonraker* (Lewis Gilbert, 1979). One of the ways new director Glen and editor John Grover fulfilled this request was through deft editing. As one critic noted: 'For example, when Bond [Roger Moore] watches Krieger [John Wyman] at the shooting range we feel each bullet hit harder than the previous one; intercutting each shot with Bond's reaction heightens the realisation that he is going to be dealing with a professional killer' (Rivers, 2001, p. 121). In *GoldenEye* (Martin Campbell, 1995), which revived the series in the mid-1990s, Terry Rawlings improvised some tension-heightening editing to facilitate one of

Bond's escapes from his captors. A series of rapid cuts alternate between a pen twirling in Bond's hand and reaction shots of the people around him. This gives Bond the opening he needs to use the pen as a weapon and break free.

GoldenEye also had a more serious task to perform, namely to establish a perspective on the new Bond's sexual politics. A key moment in this respect is when M (Judi Dench) expresses her low opinion of Bond's apparent sexism. For Rawlings, playing M's dialogue over reaction shots was the only way to answer the questions this sequence posed:

> That was really dressing him down and putting him on the carpet. Who do you want to see? You don't want to see the person who is dressing you down, you want to see the person who is being dressed down. How is it affecting them?

GoldenEye neither endorses nor rejects M's criticisms, partly because Pierce Brosnan's impassive performance style makes his reaction to her ambiguous. Bond films have given those British editors who have worked on them an opportunity to help elaborate some of the most iconic star images in world cinema. Rawlings was well aware of the new personae director Martin Campbell wished to construct, which the selection of takes should support. He recalls Campbell's discussions with Brosnan: 'I want you to do nothing and you'll be perfect for Bond ... I don't want you to do Roger Moore with the expressions because that was Roger ... I want you to be absolutely still.'

Although often overlooked when British cinema is discussed in primarily cultural terms, Hollywood in Britain has been a fact of British editors' working lives for more than half a century. The degree of British editors' creative input into Hollywood-financed productions in Britain has varied considerably according to how studio hierarchies operate at any given time, the scale of any particular project, and the sensibilities, track records of, and relationships between the individuals involved.

At one end of the spectrum is Richard Best, who felt the long-distance control exercised by Hollywood studios stifled his creativity. Frank Clarke, on the other hand, worked happily and efficiently as a supervising editor for MGM-British. Nonetheless as a senior permanent staff member identified with the studio he sometimes found himself in the uncomfortable position of 'working partly with the director and partly with the producer and they had conflicting ideas and you had to be in between'. Similarly, on the Bond films some British editors have found opportunities for creative experiment, albeit within the clearly defined parameters of this long-running series.

At the other end of the spectrum to Richard Best's experience is Stuart Baird's assessment of how some independent-minded British directors, such as Tony

Richardson and Ken Russell in the 1960s and 70s, managed to access Hollywood funding while remaining true to 'an attitude which wasn't hidebound by the old studio system'. In his view,

> we were at the outskirts of the empire, when we were making films in England, you didn't have the studio bosses breathing down your neck, until they saw the damn thing ... whereas in Hollywood they were working in the studios and they were having to show their rushes every day.

The desire for more creative autonomy was also one of the reasons why several American directors emigrated from Hollywood to Britain during this period.

EXILES AND EXPATRIATES

Some British editors from the 1950s onwards found creative satisfaction and a degree of insulation from the vagaries of freelancing through long-term collaborations with American directors working in Britain. These directors were there to work with independent production companies, because they were exiled from Hollywood as a result of the blacklist, or because they chose residence abroad for other reasons. Ralph Kemplen was the first British editor to collaborate with John Huston on independent productions for Sam Spiegel's Horizon Pictures and the Woolf brothers' Romulus Films. Kemplen's and Huston's collaboration began with *The African Queen* (1952) followed by *Beat the Devil* (1953) and *Moulin Rouge* (1953). They reunited in the 1960s for three more films. Kemplen believed the desire of American émigré directors for creative independence led to some mutually beneficial partnerships with British editors. Contrasting his and Huston's work together with the latter's conflicts with MGM over *The Red Badge of Courage* (1951) Kemplen suggested:

> I think for a time in Britain editors were given more scope than in Hollywood, because in the 50s and 60s many of the best directors came here to get away from the older system where the producer took over a film after a first cut and played hell with it (quoted in Musgrave, 1979, p. 17).

Russell Lloyd enjoyed an even more sustained collaboration with Huston. They worked on eleven films together. The first, *Moby Dick* (1956), involved Lloyd filling some narrative gaps during post-production by commissioning miniatures to match live action footage. The last was *The Man Who Would Be King* (1975). Like Kemplen, Lloyd had a wealth of experience behind him when he teamed up with Huston. Similar ideas about editing cemented their relationship. Lloyd found that 'some of the things that I had found out in cutting suited John'. With regard to working methods he agreed with Huston that coverage should be kept to a minimum for efficient and cost-effective productions. There was no need to shoot a master shot throughout a scene if a broad sense of where the likely cutting points were had already been established. Huston and Lloyd settled into a preference for particular options within a broadly classical style:

> He would do an opening shot, usually of some distinction, then maybe you'd go into favouring shots over one shoulder and then the other, and then you'd have close-ups for the same thing. There was always enough [coverage] but not too much, so that part was easy. But when you went from the favouring shot to the close-up, he would never want you to go back to the favouring shot. He said that the whole thing should build so that, mechanically, you also got closer, to build up the emotion (quoted in McFarlane, 1997, pp. 369–70).

Most British editors during this period welcomed this type of economy of shooting because it kept the amount of footage they had to sort through to a manageable level. For Lloyd it provided a clear initial sense of direction without encroaching on his autonomy. Stylistically, Lloyd liked to play dialogue over

Russell Lloyd (l) with Joel McCrea during the making of *Rough Shoot* in 1952

reaction shots and was inclined towards what he describes as a 'smooth', classical style of editing that carefully matched movements between shots and favoured fades and dissolves to indicate the passing of time. Lloyd felt and Huston agreed that spectacular action should, for the sake of realism, be presented where possible in its entirety rather than in a series of shots. At the end of *The Man Who Would Be King*, for example, discredited king Danny (Sean Connery) falls to his death off a drawbridge in a single shot.

Flexibility and openness to what editors can contribute characterises several of the long-term working relationships between British editors and directors during the post-war period. Reginald Mills, another experienced British editor, teamed up with blacklisted American director Joseph Losey for six films between the mid-1950s and mid-60s. Losey's preference, consciously modelled upon that of European auteur directors such as Ingmar Bergman, was to build up a regular group of talented collaborators. Mills, unlike Lloyd, was an advocate of eliminating fades and dissolves altogether, something he achieved in *The Servant* (Joseph Losey, 1963). Film critic Alexander Walker argues that cinematographer Douglas Slocombe's carefully staged long takes 'enabled the "logic" of the relationships to be maintained unbroken' (1974, p. 213). This is augmented by Mills' avoidance of fades and dissolves. There are no visible pauses in the claustrophobic, gradually intensifying relationship between feckless aristocrat Tony (James Fox) and insidious manservant Hugo Barrett (Dirk Bogarde).

Editing also counterbalances the stateliness of *The Servant*'s frequently slow, complex camera movements through sharp cuts from relative stillness to rapid movement. The opening sequence, for example, ends with a shot lasting approximately two and a half minutes. The transition to the next sequence is through a sharp cut on a very slight movement of Barrett's head and eyes to a shot in a club full of movement. People dance in foreground close-up and a waiter in the background carries flaming meat on a skewer towards the camera. Later in the film a relatively placid shot lasting nearly a minute of Barrett serving Tony a meal is cut in a similarly abrupt manner on a slight movement of Barrett lifting a tray. The next shot is of Barrett waiting on a station platform as a train rushes in. The train brings Tony's new maid Vera (Sarah Miles) into the narrative. Her presence, engineered by Barrett, profoundly unsettles Tony's domestic routines. In this instance a calculatedly abrupt cut serves a thematic purpose in addition to sustaining narrative pace.

Reginald Beck, who subsequently edited for Losey, established the longest-running collaboration between a British editor and an American émigré director. They worked together on sixteen films between the 1950s and 80s. Beck praised Losey's meticulousness:

> Joe's characteristic was that he was very particular about getting the script to resemble what he thought the picture ought to look like. Once the script was written, he never deviated, so all you had to do was read the script and digest all the problems attached to it (quoted in Eyles, 1985, p. 39).

The precise 'digestion' and resolution of the ensuing 'problems' was Beck's province. In *Accident* (1967), a sequence involving Oxford don Stephen (Dirk Bogarde), his wife Rosalind (Vivien Merchant), and his colleague's wife Laura (Ann Firbank), inter-cuts between two different times as well as two different places. Beck's editing makes the parallels between the two situations clear and convincingly establishes continuities across time and space.

Losey was unsure about whether his intentions for this sequence could be realised. Only after Beck had edited it was he sure:

> I shot it in such a way that it could have been perfectly chronological. But since I was the producer of the film, when Harold [Pinter] and I and the editor, Reginald Beck, decided it had worked, then it was never touched and left as it was intended (quoted in Ciment, 1985, pp. 267–8).

Thus Losey's preference for pre-planning was also tempered by the knowledge that trusted collaborators could contribute to the successful improvisation of certain sequences. The actors for *Accident*'s narrative of physical and mind games were cast to contrast Stephen's coolly intellectual manipulation with rival don Charley's (Stanley Baker's) athleticism. The tennis match they play in the film was, Losey recalled, 'improvised out of the characters' physical attributes', shot 'entirely free' by cinematographer Gerry Fisher, and 'done in the cutting room after that' (p. 271).

Beginning with Anthony Harvey on *Lolita* (1962), Stanley Kubrick collaborated with a number of British editors during his long residence in Britain. Harvey considered working with Kubrick one of the most important influences on his own development as a film-maker, but some editors avoided working with Kubrick because of his reputation as a director determined to completely control every aspect of a production and thereby stifle collaborators. Tony Lawson's account of the experience, early in his career, of working on *Barry Lyndon* confirms some of these suspicions but also highlights more subtle aspects of their relationship. During the film's extended post-production Kubrick definitely aspired to be the editor of the film and was 'there the entire time, nothing happens unless he's there'. Nonetheless Lawson raised questions he would raise with any director regarding editing decisions: 'Why aren't you doing that? Why don't you do this?' His conclusion is: 'I did take part, I did have some sort of influence and who's to say if it had been somebody else it might have been, still a Stanley Kubrick film, but it probably would have been different.'

THE BRITISH NEW WAVE

The British New Wave began with *Look Back in Anger* (1958) and *Room at the Top* (1959). These films launched Tony Richardson and Jack Clayton as leading new British directors and initiated what some commentators described as a revolution in British cinema. Publicity surrounding Woodfall, the independent production company responsible for several New Wave films, emphasised the principle of artistic control. Producer Harry Saltzman argued that a precondition for making groundbreaking, 'honest' films of contemporary relevance was that 'we control the script, the cast, the shooting and the completion of the picture' (quoted in Hill, 1986, p. 40). Despite such radical talk there was, in the early stages of the New Wave, a recognition of certain directors' inexperience. For all his brilliance in the theatre and as a documentary film-maker, first-time features director Richardson was bolstered by the support of production staff with a strong track record in the industry. Indeed such support could be one of the preconditions for funding their projects. Therefore Saltzman's demand for artistic control initially translated into a desire to work with established technicians Richardson considered outstanding. ABPC studio employee Richard Best's account of assembling the crew for *Look Back in Anger* makes this clear:

> *Look Back in Anger* was partly financed by ABPC ... to the extent that they insisted if they were going to put money in it, it was going to be made at Elstree at ABPC studios ... Tony Richardson wanted the crew that Carol Reed had had recently ... The cameraman Ossie Morris and his crew, and he wanted Bert Bates as editor who had cut one or two Carol Reed films. Bert Bates wasn't available ... and the studio wanted me on the film, obviously, because they could make money that way. They paid me my pittance ... and they could charge Woodfall more for me being lent out.

Best retained his credit although the first choice of editor, Bert Bates, was brought in at a late stage to complete the film. Best's account draws attention to the more pragmatic side of the New Wave revolution: Richardson's desire to learn from experienced technicians. After Best and Bates other established editors with similar track records were brought in to ballast subsequent Woodfall productions: Alan Osbiston on *The Entertainer* (1960) and Seth Holt on Karel Reisz's first feature *Saturday Night and Sunday Morning*. *Room at the Top*, directed by industry veteran Jack Clayton, had different origins but was also

supported by an editor whose record was as long and distinguished as its director's. Ralph Kemplen had previously worked with Clayton in the latter's capacity
as associate producer on Romulus and Remus productions including *The Good
Die Young* (Lewis Gilbert, 1954) and *The Story of Esther Costello* (David Miller,
1957). Clayton and Kemplen had also worked with John Huston on his early
1950s productions *Moulin Rouge* and *Beat the Devil*. As film historian Neil Sinyard points out, 'the connection between Clayton's production experience and
the films he went on to direct has more to do with continuity of technical personnel than with, say, continuity of theme' (2000, p. 24).

Frank dialogue was one of *Room at the Top*'s most notable features. For Kemplen 'the most difficult [dialogue scene around a table] I ever cut was in *Room
at the Top* where [Joe Lampton] Larry Harvey told [Mr Brown] Donald Wolfit
he wanted to marry the daughter. It was beautifully played but very long, and
just the two of them talking' (quoted in Musgrave, 1979, p. 16). Editing makes
a potentially static yet decisive sequence containing strong performances cinematically engaging. Kemplen does this by establishing a pattern of playing Mr
Brown's dialogue against Joe's reaction shots. This pattern culminates when Joe
considers Mr Brown's final offer. This is to marry his daughter in a shotgun wedding and take a job with him on condition that Joe stops seeing his lover Alice
Aisgill (Simone Signoret). Kemplen's editing builds upon performance here.
Neil Sinyard argues 'because he is a man in a hurry Lampton's pauses are always
significant and Harvey always times them to electrifying effect' (2000, p. 52).
Confronted with Brown's final offer Joe silently pauses as the camera tilts down
to show his hand reaching for a glass of scotch. This pregnant pause is accentuated by a cut back to Mr Brown waiting intently for an answer. The next shot
resumes Joe's action. He lifts the glass as the camera tilts back to a close-up of
his face and hand. Editing extends a pivotal pause, imperceptibly stretching time
prior to Joe's eventual response: 'How about salary?'

Following the commercial and critical success of Karel Reisz's *Saturday Night
and Sunday Morning* for Woodfall, Tony Richardson, now a more experienced
director with three feature films behind him, was able to exercise a freer hand
with regard to collaborators. Relative newcomers were brought into the fold and
a different type of production ethos began to be implemented. Stylistic innovation was encouraged. Richardson described this in rather romantic terms:

At Woodfall we tried to think in terms of a repertory group of technicians. On most
of my films I tried to have the same people, including prop men and grips. And the
technicians we used, if we were about to set up a production they did try to keep
the date we hoped to start free. We all liked working together and more or less
developed a 'group' feeling. Some people compared our public image with the old

Ealing set-up, but there was a big difference. Ealing was a studio set-up, which Woodfall was not. We were organised like guerrillas, we'd sort of recruit overnight, disappear into the mountains, and disperse when the operation was completed (quoted in Belfrage, n.d., p. 261).

The member of this 'guerrilla' group of technicians who has received most attention is cinematographer Walter Lassally. His and Richardson's creative partnership on *A Taste of Honey* (1961), *The Loneliness of the Long Distance Runner* and *Tom Jones* has been widely and deservedly praised. Less often discussed in the critical literature on these films is the equally important collaboration between Richardson and editor Antony Gibbs. Gibbs was as instrumental as Lassally to the stylistic innovations evident in the films directed by Richardson from *A Taste of Honey* onwards. Gibbs describes this as the 'first movie that I ever sort of fell in love with'. Film historian John Hill in his classic study of the New Wave takes the sequence where Jo (Rita Tushingham) walks along the canal in *A Taste of Honey* as the prime example of how these films combine 'realism' and 'poetry'. He notes how the latter quality has often been interpreted by critics in terms of the director's 'personal expression', with perhaps a nod to the cinematographer's help in realising this (Hill, 1986, p. 132). This contrasts markedly with Richardson's description of the 'group feeling' he encouraged on his later films, and with Gibbs' recollection of his personal investment in the construction of this sequence. He discovered new possibilities in an optical device that, in the early 1960s, was increasingly seen as outmoded (see Chapter 5):

> There were some very lyrical scenes in *A Taste of Honey* when she was walking along the canal and I did these big, big dissolves which was quite something for me at that time because I was against opticals, I wanted to get rid of opticals. But these opticals I did, I can even remember the length of them, they were seven footers, they were seven feet coming into the centre of the dissolve and I held that centre of the dissolve for another two feet and then faded out over three feet. So in other words I just held the centre so that we had the two images 50/50 for longer than one normally gets in a dissolve where one is going in and the other one's coming out. I held the centre like that for a bit and I remember thinking 'This is going to work'.

This lyrical sequence serves the narrative by establishing an enchanting new location. It expresses Jo's delight in the imagined possibilities of a world beyond the confines of her drab existence with her mother and the boredom of the school classroom she has just left. At the same time it has a 'poetic' quality exceeding these functions that emerges from the freedom collaborators were given to experiment.[1] For Gibbs his achievements were very much a consequence of the ethos Richardson promoted, where collaborators supported each other in their efforts to stretch themselves creatively and move beyond received wisdom: 'Knowing nothing of the technicalities of film editing, [Richardson] pushed me farther away from convention than I would have dared to go alone' (quoted in Sharples Jr, 1977, p. 25).

The Loneliness of the Long Distance Runner features an even wider range of bold editing experiments than *A Taste of Honey*. It exhibits another aspect of Gibbs' stylistic preferences during this period:

> I've always liked to play dialogue over long shots. Everybody does it now and I know I wasn't the first to do it but it was one of those things that one did in the 1960s, and it also helped you get out of a scene or lose a scene or put that scene over something else. You could take a nice A to B walking shot across a park or something and put the dialogue over it and I've always loved doing that and found it fun. I don't do it so much now because it's a cliché.

Gibbs uses this device for the long shots in the evocative sequence where borstal boy Colin Smith (Tom Courtenay) walks along a beach at Skegness talking about happier times in his past. Elsewhere in *The Loneliness of the Long Distance Runner* flashbacks emerge unexpectedly, cued through cuts alone rather than through opticals or cuts accompanied by voiceover narration. These abrupt flashbacks culminate during Colin's final race. They form part of an accelerating montage featuring shots of the runners, onlookers, the cup they are running for, plus shots and snippets of dialogue referring to earlier events within the narrative. This accelerating montage provides a cinematically exciting climax to a narrative anti-climax: Colin slowing down and losing the race on purpose in order to spite the borstal governor.

Another of Gibbs' stylistic preferences is 'in a longish dialogue scene ... I like to stop it if I can and start again ... trying another rhythm or something like that' (see Chapter 2). A good example is near to the beginning of *The Loneliness of the Long Distance Runner* where a new housemaster interviews Colin. This three-and-a-half-minute sequence varies its editing rhythms around the actors' delivery of their lines, particularly Colin's alternations between sullen defensiveness, exasperation and sarcasm. Cutaways to a tape recorder Colin is wary of help punctuate the rapid shifts in rhythm in this sequence. Gibbs' adventurous editing style, lyrical and playful in *A Taste of Honey*, and spikier to suit *The Loneliness of the Long Distance Runner*'s harsher characters and environment, was one factor that provoked some contemporary commentators to view the latter film as a departure from earlier examples of British New Wave realism. *The Loneliness of the Long Distance Runner* looked ahead to developments in the style of certain films of the later 1960s, and the verve of Gibbs' editing was central to this transition.

BRITISH FILMS OF THE 1960s

Gibbs established himself as one of 1960s British cinema's most sought after young editors and worked on several of that decade's most memorable films. On *Tom Jones*, his third film with Tony Richardson and the one that broke decisively with earlier New Wave realism, Gibbs enjoyed editing the hunting sequence. He decided:

> I'll start high and move down . . . there's the helicopter stuff, there is the crane stuff, and then there's the moving ground stuff and then there's the static ground stuff, interspersed with a few helicopter shots of jumping over fences but I regard that as a piece of the ground stuff.

Richardson gave Gibbs full credit for his contribution to this section of one of the most successful 1960s British films: 'We shot about three hours of material . . . Although a certain amount . . . was planned a lot was shot off the cuff. Tony Gibbs . . . worked long hours over that sequence. Film, I suppose, is finally made in the cutting room' (quoted in Belfrage, n.d., p. 262).

After *Tom Jones*, Gibbs went on to edit *Girl with Green Eyes* (1964) directed by Desmond Davis, a former member of Richardson's 'guerrilla' group of technicians, *The Knack* (Richard Lester, 1965), and *Performance*. In his willingness to take risks, innovate and experiment, Gibbs belonged to a generation, including Jim Clark, Tom Priestley and John Bloom, who established themselves in the 1960s and promoted new approaches to British film editing. These and other editors contributed significantly to the stylistic audacity film historian Robert Murphy (1992, p. 3) argues is characteristic of some of the more voguish 1960s British films.

Early in the decade Jim Clark contributed some distinctive editing to the Henry James adaptation *The Innocents* (Jack Clayton, 1961). Clark concurs with the high regard many people within the industry held for Clayton as a fastidious, discerning director. He describes their first collaboration as an 'extraordinarily happy, profitable relationship'. What film historian Neil Sinyard describes as psychological and supernatural 'uncertainty and ambiguity' (2000, p. 82) in *The Innocents* is partly rendered, as Clark puts it, through

> a cutting style in which things would appear calm on the surface, but at the same time there would be undercurrents of unease. In order to get this, we would have

quite a number of fairly long takes, with an occasional vaguely disturbing sharp cut (quoted in Hudson, 1966, p. 83).

A number of shots include statues in the background and reflections in water or in windows that 'superimpose' unsettling images within images. These effects are amplified by *The Innocents*' extraordinary dissolves that, in critic Penelope Houston's words, gradually disappear by 'burning out into white instead of fading into the usual black' (1961, p. 115). As Clark explains, this device causes certain images to mysteriously and ominously linger on screen rather than completely give way to what follows them:

> I devised a very special kind of dissolve routine for that film, inspired, I suspect, by George Stevens.[2] I remember it was a form of mixing that involved not having matching overlaps. That's to say they were not like a three-foot mix or a four-foot mix or a six-foot mix where you'd have a centre. We designed the dissolves in that film in a rather special way so that certain things overlapped more than others so that it became more like a montage than a straight mix. I remember we had to devise some special way of doing it at the lab.

These are most prominent in Miss Giddens' (Deborah Kerr's) disturbing dream sequence, approximately halfway through the narrative, which condenses within itself the overall style of the film. It would ultimately be misleading to ascribe creative ownership of *The Innocents*' 'special' dissolves to either Clayton or Clark. Film historian Neil Sinyard, in an auteurist analysis of Clayton's career which acknowledges the collaborative context of production, identifies 'the frequent use of slow dissolves' as one of the director's 'stylistic signatures' (2000, pp. 5–6). This may be a legitimate claim but it is a signature that emerged and gained definition through fortuitous early collaborations with editors of the calibre of Ralph Kemplen and Jim Clark.

With *Darling* Clark began a long-term collaboration with director John Schlesinger. A 'stylistic signature' he attributes to Schlesinger is the use of shots such as that of a parking meter edited into a lovemaking sequence in *Darling* and the similar use of shots of a television and a fruit machine in *Midnight Cowboy*: 'that's all John ... he was always interested in getting those little comments and ideas in'. Where Clark demonstrated his worth on *Darling* was as a creative fixer. For example, Clark's ideas proved essential to maintaining a light satirical touch in a sequence that threatened to introduce dullness into the film:

> There was one rather amusing section ... where Julie Christie is married to the count in Italy, and John shot a tremendous amount of really loosely shot material of

the wedding itself; the wedding and the reception and this and that. It was sitting there looking rather forlorn when we put it all together and it didn't seem to work, it was really rather dull. I had the idea of turning it into a newsreel, which was a nice conceit which John fell for. We stuck that together like the Pathé News and got Bob Danvers-Walker to do the narration for it. So that was a way of saving the material from being rather turgid, turning it into something really rather amusing.

Darling would have been inconceivable in the British cinema of just a decade earlier. Even in the 1960s certain critics derided some of the more modish films, in Robert Murphy's words, as 'an indigenous degeneration in film style' (1992, p. 3). These new films were also not to every editor's taste. For Richard Best, who edited *The Dam Busters*, the film exemplifying how the style and substance of British cinema had deteriorated during the 1960s was the cult favourite *Morgan – A Suitable Case for Treatment* (Karel Reisz, 1966). One succinct example for him was the sequence where Morgan [David Warner] infiltrates his ex-wife's bedroom to plant a bomb underneath her bed:

> He was coming through the window to get to the bed . . . and he came a bit through the window, they took eight frames out or something and he was here, then they took another eight frames out and he was here . . . absolutely ridiculous!

Throughout *Morgan* semi-perceptible jump-cutting of the protagonist's actions is a stylistic strategy that constructs him as a character out of sync with 'normality'. *Morgan*'s editor, Tom Priestley, was the third to work on this film plagued by a troubled post-production history. He was preceded by an experienced commercials but inexperienced features editor who had adopted a mechanistic approach rather than responding to the material. The second to work on the film was a senior, older features editor who 'wasn't in the spirit of the thing'. Priestley's approach proved better suited to *Morgan*'s 'spirit'. His rejection of a strict adherence to continuity (see Chapter 2) extended the growing tendency during this period towards a more 'abbreviated' style of editing.

The search for new modes of cinematic expression and the challenge to preceding stylistic conventions in certain British films of the 1960s energised some relationships between new directors and editors. John Bloom describes the experience of working with Silvio Narizzano on *Georgy Girl* (1966) as 'wonderfully liberating . . . He said "try anything, I'd love you to try any ideas you have, the more outrageous – love outrageous ideas! Do anything you want to do."' Ideas arising from this call for 'outrageousness' included Georgy (Lynn Redgrave) imagining or remembering a jump-cut dance sequence with the children she teaches. Another example is Bloom's editing of the moment when

Georgy and Jos (Alan Bates) realise they are in love: 'suddenly they come face to face and I did those silly little quick cuts [several times between close-ups], something I never would have done but I thought let's try something for Silvio'. The film-makers' delight in their work and relaxed relationship with each other carries through to the finished product where the improvised, exploratory style of the film chimes with its youthful characters' lifestyles.

In certain circumstances the director's encouragement of an atmosphere of genuine collaboration and shared creative discovery could prove liberating, but this was not the only consequence of the decline in studio and rise of independent production in 1960s British film culture. The conception of the director as an independent, autonomous creative artist also gained ground during this period. Several of the new British directors of the 1960s with aspirations to produce work comparable to that of European auteurs tended to be very closely involved with post-production. This was how Jim Clark's relationship with Schlesinger operated, and his perception of other similar collaborations during that period was 'they were always in the cutting room in those days, Lindsay Anderson and Karel Reisz and people of that kind, and Kubrick too I remember was always in the room with Tony Harvey when they were cutting *Dr Strangelove* [1964].' The crucial distinction here is the extent to which the presence of the director in the cutting room involves creative collaboration with an editor as opposed to an attempt simply to dominate the editing by reducing the editor to an unthinking 'pair of hands' obediently implementing the director's will. This situation varied enormously according to the personalities involved and the production context. It was rarely either one extreme or the other.

Lindsay Anderson is a pertinent case in point. *If...* was documentary editor David Gladwell's first features editing credit. One reason for hiring an inexperienced features editor was to facilitate Anderson's desire to exercise strict control in this area. The director made it clear to Gladwell he had 'no intention of being out of the cutting room for one moment until the editing was complete' (Gladwell, 1969, p. 28) and 'all I'd have to do is what he told me'. Anderson similarly 'considered it necessary to assume command' (p. 31) during *If...*'s dubbing. Although Anderson 'admitted to being unable to think visually' (p. 25), and therefore delegated responsibility for the look of the film to cinematographer Miroslav Ondricek, Gladwell had a high regard for his director's 'editor's outlook'. He admired his talent, partly derived from his earlier experience as a film critic, for 'being able to see material and knowing what's good about it and what's not good about it'.

On *If...* Gladwell accepted Anderson's view that 'when a director is making a highly personal film, he does not want an editor to argue every point with him'

David Gladwell at a 16mm pic-sync machine, cutting a documentary in 1963

(Gladwell, 1969, p. 31). Yet Anderson's almost obsessive perfectionism during post-production could border on 'absolute pedanticness', and when it came to the technicalities of editing 'he couldn't handle a Moviola or anything like that'. There were inevitably moments when Gladwell's specific expertise came to the fore and he was able to make significant contributions to editing decisions. These included the order and timing of shots in the short opening sequence where boys return to the boarding school on the first day of term. Gladwell uses 'we' rather than 'he' to refer to the work involved here: 'Many times we would return to the sequence to try something fresh and each time, I think, we improved it' (p. 29).

GOLDCREST

The Goldcrest episode in the early 1980s was the next moment, after the 1960s, when British film production in general attracted international acclaim. This began with the success of *Chariots of Fire*. Publicity surrounding this film led to excessively optimistic talk of a 'British film renaissance'. Several British editors with established reputations played a pivotal role during this period, acknowledged in Academy Awards for John Bloom's work on *Gandhi* and Jim Clark's on *The Killing Fields* (Roland Joffé, 1984). Later, hopes for a renaissance began to evaporate when box-office failures spiked Goldcrest's expansion and led potential investors to lose confidence in British film production.

One of the problems was the struggle to arrive at a release print acceptable to distributors of the troubled musical *Absolute Beginners* (Julien Temple, 1986). Veteran editors Russell Lloyd, Gerry Hambling and Michael Bradsell were brought in for several weeks to see if they could help bring what was perceived as a 'wayward' film into line. According to Jake Eberts, Goldcrest's recently reinstated chief executive, some of the material was 'wonderfully shot, particularly the opening sequence', but 'rudimentary aspects of film-making, such as continuity, had been disregarded'. An overall structure for many 'vignettes' and 'individual scenes' had not yet been found; in conventional terms 'the real problem was the lack of a storyline' (Eberts and Ilott, 1990, p. 575). Lloyd, Hambling and Bradsell undertook the thankless task of working independently on different sections of the film to give some kind of shape to an ambitious project that had initially promised to introduce a new sensibility into mainstream British cinema. Under these circumstances fruitful collaboration proved impossible. Lloyd, for example, hardly met the director and 'didn't approve of some of the other bits that I didn't do and I suppose some of the other editors didn't approve of what I did'.

Absolute Beginners apart, for new directors emerging through Goldcrest the role played by senior editors was similar to that played by their predecessors who contributed to the early stages of the British New Wave. Goldcrest's leading producer David Puttnam operated the time-honoured policy of teaming experienced editors with less experienced directors: 'When you're working with a young director ... it's essential to surround him with as much experience as possible' (quoted in Seidenberg, 1990, p. 37). The pairing of editor Michael Bradsell and director Bill Forsyth on *Local Hero* (1983), Forsyth's first bigbudget project after the modestly scaled *That Sinking Feeling* (1979) and *Gregory's Girl* (1981), was one example of this. Vitally important to Puttnam on two of his major projects at this time was Jim Clark, of whom he has said, 'it's more a question of me getting panic-struck if he's not available ... He's a linch pin' (quoted in Seidenberg, 1990, p. 37). The initial weeks' shooting of *The Killing Fields*, the first feature directed by Roland Joffé, required delicate negotiation. As Clark put it 'I'm not there to upset people' but, as many editors do, he felt his first responsibility was to the film itself. Given that the main production unit was on location in Bangkok while rushes were processed in London, Puttnam charged Clark with a difficult task:

> He basically wanted me to tell him if I thought they could be improved upon ...
> He gave me a lot of trust; it was very gracious of him. Specifically I was quite
> critical of some camera positions in the early days. I thought that Roland was being
> too loose with his angles; he could have gone in closer. There were a number of

things like that which he gradually changed and improved, because he's a very intuitive man and very good with performers. I felt also there was a certain lack of detailed coverage, which I wanted to make a scene work. Like the evacuation scene from the city, shot very largely in long masters with two cameras. What I was looking for were those moments of detail of people who were injured and such. David thought up the idea of the little boy who was lost. The scene needed more highlights, which Roland went out and shot on a separate day. But in general, that film was no problem. It didn't present any difficulties of a creative nature, because I was able to put my finger on the problems at an early stage and get them ironed out. I guess David felt I had this ability to 'read' the rushes, which is important when you're separated by many thousands of miles (quoted in Yule, 1988, p. 238).

Partly due to its capacity, for a brief period, to support projects with larger than average budgets, one of Goldcrest's distinctive contributions to 1980s British film culture was its production of 'liberal' epics in the tradition of *Lawrence of Arabia* (David Lean, 1962). Logistically, this frequently involves editors working at a distance from the main production unit while location shooting takes place. The devolution of considerable autonomy and responsibility is often inherent within such situations. For his cherished project *Gandhi*, director Richard Attenborough was keen to employ John Bloom who had previously collaborated with him on *Magic* (1978). An unusual arrangement was eventually arrived at whereby there was a 'big overlap' between Bloom's work on *The French Lieutenant's Woman* (Karel Reisz, 1981) and *Gandhi*. Bloom began editing *Gandhi* in London and continued working without direct contact with Attenborough for several months while shooting continued in India. Material was flown back and forth each day. Editing a film of this magnitude entailed organising a significant amount of footage over a longer than average post-production schedule.

Structuring devices were necessary to make this lengthy film cohere as a narrative that engaged rather than exhausted its spectator. At certain points in *Gandhi* shots in one location are drained of colour and incorporated into black and white newsreels being watched elsewhere. For Bloom this was 'very useful in being able to jump time, place, history, etcetera'. Shots of trains Gandhi (Ben Kingsley) travels on are also 'used a little bit in that way', for example in the transition from the opening sequence of Gandhi's funeral in 1948 back to his arrival in South Africa in 1893. This dramatic shift between different periods and locations is accomplished through a cut from a long shot, gradually tracking back as mourners slowly advance, to an overhead shot of a train speeding in the opposite direction with a slight camera pan to follow its progress. The reversal of the direction of movement adds to a contrast between the speed of action and between day and night in the two shots. At the same time graphic continuity is maintained through the similarity between the line formed by the funeral procession in the first shot and the rail tracks in the second.

Throughout *Gandhi* Bloom's editing helps compress a fifty-five-year period spanning numerous locations into approximately three hours of screen time in an attempt, as the opening credits state, not 'to give each year its allotted weight' but to 'try and find one's way to the heart of the man'. Gandhi's discovery of and alignment with the 'real' rural India occurs within another train sequence which condenses an unspecified period of time between his return from South Africa and his debut speech for the Congress Party. The first part of this sequence, lasting over two minutes, builds up a gentle, contemplative rhythm. It utilises many dissolves between long shots of the train at different times of day, medium shots and close-ups of Gandhi's intensely receptive face, and point-of-view shots of different parts of the countryside where peasants work the land.

Issues of length and narrative structure are especially pertinent to epic films and editors are often central to these considerations. On *Cry Freedom*, the next liberal epic directed by Attenborough, discussions with editor Lesley Walker

Lesley Walker during the
shooting of *Cry Freedom*, 1987
(Reproduced by kind permission
of Richard Attenborough)

resulted in a major structural change to the narrative. She reveals: 'The funny thing about *Cry Freedom* is it's not as scripted, and that was editorial.' The crucial difference was that 'Biko [Denzel Washington], in the original script and as shot, died in the first four reels and everything from then on was flashback, but it was a great disappointment because ... to go into flashback didn't hold you very much.' The solution was to 'move his death down two reels by using what was flashback into reality'. Keeping Biko alive and active within the narrative longer than was initially intended gives him and the wider context of the anti-apartheid struggle greater prominence. Reducing the length of the flashback lessens the centrality of white liberal journalist Donald Woods' [Kevin Kline's] subjectivity. As critic Judith Williamson noted, although the latter part of the narrative focuses upon Woods' family's escape from South Africa, the finished film evinces 'a considered attempt to counterbalance the drama of the white family' (1993, p. 157). Walker as well as Attenborough deserves credit for this.

Chariots of Fire, another Goldcrest production, has been identified by academics as the first contemporary heritage film.[3] Film historian John Hill, summarising debates about heritage cinema, argues that in these films 'stylistic procedures characteristically exceed narrative or expressive requirements' and 'compositions and camera movements are often motivated more by the desire to "show off" settings than adhere to any strict dramatic logic' (Hill, 1999, pp. 80–1). Holding shots long enough for spectators to appreciate a view is essential to 'showing off' settings. *Chariots of Fire*'s editor, Terry Rawlings, confirms that techniques such as playing several lines of dialogue over a long shot of a landscape, country house or Cambridge college before cutting to a closer shot were 'consciously done ... to set up this visual thing'.

Some later so-called heritage films have been seen as moving away from the showcasing of the visual lustre of opulent interiors, locations and ancient buildings exemplified by *Chariots of Fire*. In these cases editing is equally important, albeit to different ends. Writer-director Philip Goodhew, for example, notes that to complement the dour urban settings in *Jude* (Michael Winterbottom, 1996), 'the stunning landscapes, when they come, are dynamic and evocative, not least because the camera never lingers a fraction longer than is necessary. For this credit is due to the disciplined, finely judged work of editor Trevor Waite' (1997, p. 61). Lesley Walker says of editing *Emma* (1996) that 'being a costume drama and having beautiful houses and drawing-rooms and beautiful clothes ... it was nice to show these to give a breath of fresh air'. However, she also praises writer-director Douglas McGrath's brisk direction for making the film 'not quite as stuffy' as some other examples of the genre. Walker's editing also helps drive the narrative forward, for example, by moving Emma Woodhouse (Gwyneth Paltrow) rapidly through time and space when she impatiently waits for an invitation to and then attends a party.

Film historian John Hill acknowledges that even the first entry in the contemporary heritage film cycle does more than simply showcase beautiful locations. He concludes his discussion of *Chariots of Fire* by arguing that, although the sequence where Abrahams (Ben Cross) confronts the college Masters over dinner 'overtly criticizes the establishment' through dialogue, it also 'appears to relish the visual pomp and splendour with which it is associated' (Hill, 1999, p. 27). For Hill this is demonstrated in the sequence's final shot which tracks back, as Abrahams exits the frame, to dwell on a sumptuous college interior.[4] In Hill's analysis spectacle ultimately overwhelms dialogue even in a sequence that might initially seem to be more concerned with other issues.

Editor Terry Rawlings offers a different assessment. For him 'that's a scene that's played on eyes', in which he worked particularly hard to orchestrate the looks between characters. His editing highlights faces, eyes and looks, underscoring Abrahams' and the Masters' conflicting values of professionalism versus amateurism and the latter's xenophobic attitudes towards Abraham's coach Mussabini (Ian Holm). When he is discussed there is a cut to a reaction shot of the Master of Caius' (Lindsay Anderson's) wide-eyed, disdainfully aggressive stare as the Master of Trinity (John Gielgud) says the word 'Italian'. Abrahams' further revelation that Mussabini is 'half-Arab' is followed by two rapidly edited, disapprovingly silent reaction shots of the Masters. Rawlings' editing underscores what the Masters think but hypocritical social decorum does not allow them to say to Abrahams' face. It also prepares the ground for the Master of Trinity's anti-Semitic remarks at the end of the final shot after Abrahams has left the room. None of this is explored in Hill's analysis. The role of editing in so-called heritage films, particularly its relationship to dialogue and performance, is something academic debate has largely ignored.

BRITISH EDITORS IN HOLLYWOOD

Throughout British film history directors and stars have crossed the Atlantic to work in Hollywood. During the latter part of the post-war period a significant number of leading British editors began to follow suit. In the mid-1970s Bernard Gribble noted that he, Ernest Walter, Peter Tanner, Jim Clark and others had relocated to Hollywood because of the need to go 'where the work is!' (1975, p. 14). Antony Gibbs was another noted British editor who made this transition in the early 1970s. In some cases this was a permanent relocation, in others it has been more fleeting or intermittent. The first significant wave of emigration to Hollywood was partly prompted by the downturn in the British film industry in the late 1960s. Employment on Hollywood-financed productions in Britain often proved to be the best route to establishing contacts and a track record leading to work in Hollywood. In the first wave of emigration there was a tendency for editors to continue in Hollywood creative partnerships initially formed in Britain. Jim Clark renewed his earlier association with John Schlesinger, working on *Midnight Cowboy*, *Marathon Man* (1976) and several of the director's other 1970s Hollywood productions. Tom Priestley, who had edited *Our Mother's House* (1967) for Jack Clayton and *Leo the Last* for John Boorman in Britain subsequently edited *Deliverance* for the latter and *The Great Gatsby* (1974) for the former in Hollywood.

Although the level of investment represented by the MGM-British studios was scaled down during the 1970s some freelance editors with a track record on successful films continued to find work on big-budget American productions in Britain. Anne Coates' credentials as an Academy Award winner for *Lawrence of Arabia* led to work on films such as EMI-MGM's *Murder on the Orient Express* (Sidney Lumet, 1974) and *The Eagle Has Landed* (John Sturges, 1976). Stuart Baird moved from working with Ken Russell to American productions in Britain such as *Superman II* (Richard Lester, 1980) and *Outland* (Peter Hyams, 1981). Nevertheless, both these editors formed part of a second significant wave of emigration to Hollywood after Goldcrest's collapse precipitated another major crisis in the British film industry in the mid-1980s. Like the previous wave, their track records of working on Hollywood–British productions helped facilitate their passage to America. As Coates explained in an interview given in America:

> My films are really American pictures that I've worked on in England, most of them brought over here and shown to the heads of the studios and previewed here. So they are American films really. That was why I'd been over here on so many trips that I knew I'd fit in (quoted in Oldham, 1992, p. 168).

Generalised comparisons between working conditions in Hollywood and working conditions in the British film industry are difficult to make. This is not only because of the interpenetration Coates refers to but also because in each context there exists a variety of different productions set-ups and editors' roles within these. However, the scale of some Hollywood productions has led British editors who have worked in both contexts to note subdivisions of labour that they had not previously encountered within the British film industry. Tom Priestley observed that on big Hollywood productions:

> You have a person called the post-production supervisor who sits in an office and makes the phone calls and juggles the dates and deals with the more practical side of it ... Certainly in Britain, where budgets aren't so huge, the editor had that responsibility. Now to what extent he accepted and exercised that responsibility was obviously up to him and up to the particular set-up. But that was my view, that

everything that happened once the film had passed through the camera was the responsibility of the editor or the editing department.

Antony Gibbs' experience since relocating to Hollywood in the 1970s has been similar. In 1960s Britain 'when you took Tony Gibbs on you took his crew, which wasn't just his assistants but also his sound editors ... Here it's very divorced. They've always, for example, had separate sound houses.' In Britain his creative involvement extended to every area of post-production, including having 'a lot to say about where the music was going to go, and hopefully ... helping the director in the form the music should take'. As someone whose attitudes were shaped by Tony Richardson's ideal of a 'repertory group of technicians', Gibbs finds Hollywood more compartmentalised: 'A vast amount of money is now spent on post-production ... there are just too many people around with their own little area that they just concentrate on.' If this limits the editor's authority and creative autonomy, similar constraints also apply to the director:

> The auteur situation, I don't think it really works today, because there is just so much collaboration and there is so much technicality involved in all of it, and you can't expect any director today to know what every section of every department is doing, whereas twenty years ago you could.

Gibbs nevertheless appreciates working with directors who value editing and positively encourage editors to comment upon the script and contribute during production. He cites Richard Lester, Mark Rydell and Norman Jewison as directors who have involved him in projects from their inception, sometimes, for example, inviting him to sit in on pre-production rehearsals.

Stuart Baird's trajectory in Hollywood has been rather different from that of his other British colleagues. Baird's formative editing experiences in Britain were on Ken Russell's 1970s films, initially as assistant to Michael Bradsell and then as editor in his own right on *Lisztomania* (1975), *Tommy* and *Valentino*. Some of these films unashamedly prioritise spectacle, shock and musical bombast over dialogue and character development. In certain respects working with Russell placed Baird in a better position than many other British editors to make the transition to editing a series of Hollywood action films produced by Joel Silver. Baird's credits as editor here include *Lethal Weapon* (Richard Donner, 1987), *Lethal Weapon 2* (Richard Donner, 1989), *The Last Boy Scout* (Tony Scott, 1991) and *Demolition Man* (Marco Brambilla, 1993).

There has in the past been a tendency on the part of certain critics to look down on contemporary Hollywood action cinema because it privileges visceral and affective responses over intellectual ones. Recently, however, some academics have argued that the whole genre should not be written off simply because it does not conform to more traditional understandings of what good cinema is. José Arroyo (2000), for example, insists that the aesthetic sophistication of action cinema needs to be understood and evaluated on its own terms. Some of these terms could usefully be supplied by practitioners like Baird. One thing he shares with these academic writers is the conviction that this type of cinema is not necessarily inferior to any other:

> To make a really good action picture is just as difficult as making anything else. The dialogue may be a bit puerile ... but the fact is, it is what it is. If you try and break the mould ... you fall between two stools. What you can do is recognise the genre and milk it for the best parts of it, and pace is an aspect of that, and humour is an aspect of that, and tension ...

He underlines the importance of thinking in terms not just of isolated sequences but of everything surrounding them, and each sequence's place within the overall structure of the film. The pacing of an action sequence must relate to the pacing of, for example, a dialogue sequence preceding it. How transitions are effected from one sequence to another is also crucial. On a more local level 'pacing an action beat, so it is just long enough so you are enjoying all it has to offer, but you just cut off ... not exactly where the audience expects it to', can have a powerful impact. Practical aesthetic considerations of the kind Baird discusses could contribute to a more rounded critical appreciation of contemporary Hollywood action cinema.

Baird also emphasises the imperative, from an industry perspective, of completing and releasing contemporary Hollywood films on schedule. The higher the budget the more intense this pressure is likely to be. If a production runs over schedule the time allotted to post-production is likely to be reduced. This further increases the pressure upon editors. In some cases more than one editor can be assigned to a film in order to maximise the possibility of having it ready for its release date: 'On a big American picture ... on a very tight schedule I'd have another editor with me.' This was the case, for example, with *Die Hard 2* (Renny Harlin, 1990), edited by Baird and Robert A. Ferretti. Baird accepts the scheduling imperative within contemporary Hollywood. Indeed his career has flourished as a result of being able to deliver in these terms: 'I made my reputation of being very, very, very fast.' Baird is sanguine about his role within contemporary Hollywood as an editor, film doctor and director, primarily of action films:

> The people who have all the power are the studios. If you make a lot of hit movies, you have a lot more power and you get what you want. But even so, if the studio

wants it to open on a certain date, it's in your interest to open it on that certain date. You do everything you can to open it on that date, because you know you're going to make more money. There are so few weeks in the year and so many pictures open and you want to get an envelope of time to give your picture a chance to hit the marketplace without too much competition. There's all that aspect of it and that's a big aspect. It doesn't affect the English industry because the English industry doesn't operate in those terms ... that's what Hollywood studios pay me and people like me to do. Not just to get the picture done well, but to get it done on time, and with as little aggravation for everybody as possible.

Another practice considered essential to maximising the box-office potential of contemporary Hollywood films is previewing. Studios' interpretations of preview audiences' responses can lead to an insistence upon changes after editor and director have arrived at their preferred cut of a film. Terry Rawlings' experiences, for example, include changes to *The Saint*'s (Philip Noyce, 1997) ending because an initial version where the heroine died was strongly disliked at preview screenings. *Entrapment* lost an apparently stunning car chase near the beginning of the narrative for the same reason. Director Terry Gilliam's contractual agreement on *Twelve Monkeys* allowed him final cut if the film was kept under a certain length, so this became one of editor Mick Audsley's priorities. Poor written responses to preview screenings led to some re-editing of sequences dealing with the romance between James Cole (Bruce Willis) and Kathryn Railly (Madeleine Stowe), a reduction in the amount of screen time given to Cole's prophetic dream sequences, and the use of captions to clarify time lines. However, Gilliam and Audsley held out against making major changes to the film.

Bernard Gribble, although sceptical about the usefulness of previews for predicting box-office success, argues that 'at least if you put the film up with an audience you can easily tell whether something's working or not'. He edited the comedy *Top Secret!* (Jim Abrahams, David Zucker, Jerry Zucker, 1984), and felt it ultimately benefited from post-preview changes. At the same time he notes that preview audiences from different social backgrounds responded quite differently to the film. Tom Priestley suggests the process is most useful with genres demanding an immediate response: 'The two kinds of films that have to be previewed are the films that require maximum audience participation, which are horror films and comedies.' He is less sure with regard to previewing drama: 'Different elements in the audience will react in different ways; they'll be rooting for this character, for that character, a whole lot of other things are going on.' Whether or not such arguments hold sway after a negative preview very much depends upon whether the director is willing and able to defend the version of the film s/he and the editor have arrived at.

British editors working in Hollywood tend to be distinguished by their seniority. In most cases a successful track record editing British films is what makes their transatlantic passage possible. Their credits give them a certain prestige and status but this is sometimes offset against implicit or explicit ageism on the part of potential collaborators and employers. Antony Gibbs suggests that when younger directors interview editors for a job the end result can be that 'they'd rather scramble through the movie themselves with somebody of their own age'. Although his credits include *The Man in the White Suit*, Bernard Gribble admits to omitting much of his earlier work from his CV when he applies for jobs. Anne Coates relishes the challenge of working with younger directors, but is careful to state that 'I don't do a lot of talking about the fact that I've been around a long time and done a lot of movies – only occasionally if they're really annoying me a lot!'

The fact that British editors in Hollywood tend to be senior figures has led a number of them to work regularly or intermittently as film doctors (see Chapter 2). There is a fairly long history of British editors in Hollywood playing this kind of role. One of the earliest examples is when Jim Clark was invited by director John Schlesinger to doctor *Midnight Cowboy*. Clark was brought over to Hollywood to see if he could provide any solutions after Schlesinger and initial editor Hugh A. Robertson had arrived at an impasse:

> There was great stuff in it, wonderful performances, but there were structural problems, particularly with the opening . . . getting Joe Buck [Jon Voight] from his home town to New York. That whole journey, which was crucial to the film, was a mess . . . The only way I could do it was by taking it all to pieces, entirely. I just took the first two reels of the film back to rushes and started afresh . . . I think it took me the best part of three weeks to reassemble it into some new order, some new shape. Then John would come in and look at it, and little by little we found a way of integrating the flashbacks, and using sound and somehow making the sequence have a flow which it hadn't had before. Also I found material which had not been used, which had been shot by a second unit on the road . . . I found little moments which I could inject into this sequence, which helped it a lot.

Clark's ability as a creative fixer was later institutionalised during David Puttnam's tenure as head of Columbia Studios during the late 1980s. Clark was persuaded to accept a one-year contract as a senior production editor: 'It was my job to see all the rushes of current films shooting and report to David if I found anything wrong. Another unenviable task . . . I'd rather make my own mess than clear up someone else's' (quoted in Yule, 1988, p. 439). Clark did not find this role very rewarding, unlike Stuart Baird, whose assignments as a post-production doctor include *Mission: Impossible II* and *Lara Croft: Tomb Raider* (Simon West, 2001). Like Clark on *Midnight Cowboy*, Baird prefers to assess all available footage when he works on a project as a film doctor. His recommendations may include re-writing scenes, altering dialogue, compressing two or more scenes into one, shortening scenes to quicken a film's overall momentum and bring it to the length required by the studio, adjusting the amount of plot information conveyed to the audience at certain points in the narrative, and so on.

Within these broader contexts it is possible to trace certain patterns in the careers of individual editors who have emigrated from Britain to Hollywood. One example, discussed above, is Baird's transition from films directed by Ken Russell to Hollywood action cinema. Anne Coates, a very different example, has purposefully 'chosen very different kinds of movies to do' because 'I don't want to get typecast', but an element of continuity is provided by the type of project she is particularly drawn to: 'mostly non-violent films' and 'mostly character-driven pieces'. Throughout her career Coates has worked on many films, for example *Tunes of Glory* (Ronald Neame, 1960) and *Lawrence of Arabia*, where her sensitivity to the subtleties of relationships has enriched their narratives and the actors' performances within them.

Coates was alert to similar undercurrents in *Erin Brockovich*. In this film secretary Erin (Julia Roberts) and lawyer Ed Masry (Albert Finney) work closely

Anne V. Coates in 2000, editing *Erin Brockovich* on an Avid non-linear system

together over a long period of time and develop a mutual, affectionate respect for each other:

> The characters interested me. Her relationship with the lawyer I liked. Here he is working with one of the sexiest women ... but nothing went on between them, they were just good friends. I mean there must have been a certain little attraction but nothing that ever developed into anything.

Erin's defining characteristic as 'a person pitting themselves and having the guts to go through with what they believed in' is augmented by the film's editing. Coates and Soderbergh worked hard to 'get that drive there' into the progression of the narrative. This is evident in the montage sequence when Erin collects water samples to prove the culpability of the large corporation whose dumping of toxic waste has poisoned a nearby community: 'You can pretty quickly see what she's doing, and it's important to see the various places she goes to, and the time and bother that she takes to do it, but also you don't want to linger.'

Out of Sight (1998), Coates' first collaboration with Soderbergh, provided the opportunity to work on a similarly character-driven piece with a 'more intricate story'. Although hailed as Soderbergh's return to the mainstream, this romantic thriller afforded considerable scope for editing experiments. When bank robber Jack Foley (George Clooney) is sent to jail at the beginning of the narrative the oppressiveness of incarceration is signalled by shots of 'the same fence superimposed three times over itself as you go towards the prison'. 'Very short freezes, a second or something like that', are employed when important characters first appear within the narrative. They are also used as what Coates calls 'heightening points' at key moments of dramatic action. For example, they occur in the stylish seduction and lovemaking sequence between Jack and US Marshal Karen Sisco (Jennifer Lopez). This brings out the subtext of their conversation in a bar by flashing forward to them in a hotel bedroom. As Coates explains, the sequence was largely improvised in the cutting room:

> Where we did the inter-cutting of the cocktail bar with the bedroom, that was not in the script, that was purely a cutting idea. The idea of overlapping one into the other, with maybe some overlaid dialogue just at the beginning, there was some idea to do something there but not what we actually did in the end. Steven and I did that between us and it was really exciting, watching it come together and the ideas working so well ... I cut the two sequences separately as sequences, particularly the dialogue one. Then I cut silent because we had no sound with the bedroom one. I cut that together and got the most erotic stuff that I could out of

Antony Gibbs receiving the ACE
Career Achievement Award in
2002 (Photograph by Pete
Zakhary. © American Cinema
Editors)

it. Then we literally just moulded them together, trying bits here and there that
went together, like the hand on the glass in the bar and then on the knee in the
bedroom … We let the dialogue play over, very often we didn't fit it, in a way. It
was just fantastic how it went together.

Soderbergh's interest in working with Coates, Stuart Baird's doctoring assignments, Antony Gibbs' Career Achievement Award presented by ACE in 2002
attest, in different ways, to industry recognition for the distinctive contributions
certain British editors have made to contemporary Hollywood cinema.

NOTES

All unattributed quotations in this chapter are drawn from the interviews conducted
for this book.

1. Peter Hutchings has recently argued, contra Hill, that many 'landscape shots' in
    British New Wave films are 'explicable within the established conventions of the

establishing shot' (2001, pp. 149–50). Gibbs' description of his work on the film's canal sequence suggests that this example at least is not solely reducible to this function.

2. As with Clark and Clayton, credit for these slow dissolves in *A Place in the Sun* (1951) should be shared between director George Stevens and editor William Hornbeck. Hornbeck says these dissolves were the result of a collaborative experimental process: 'we fooled with it together' (quoted in Thompson and Bordwell, 1983, p. 39).

3. Claire Monk (2002, pp. 192–3) elaborates the important point that the description 'heritage film' is an academic rather than industrial one.

4. There are other possible motivations for this final shot apart from visual display. Rawlings' editing gives the sequence symmetry; a camera movement tracking out at the end reverses the direction of a track in at the beginning. Each of these opening and closing shots are held for approximately fifty seconds, partly to allow the Master of Trinity and Abrahams to deliver quite lengthy, relatively formal speeches outlining their values. Arguably these play better in long shots rather than more intimate close shots.

5

Stylistic Developments

HOLLYWOOD CRAFT STANDARDS AND THE INFLUENCE OF SOVIET MONTAGE

None of the editors interviewed for this book felt there was a distinctive British style of editing between the 1930s and the 50s. Most suggested it was more a matter of individual preferences, modulated according to the material and production context, within a basic set of conventions shared with Hollywood films. The British demand for American editors during the 1930s demonstrates that, whereas German personnel were particularly sought after in areas such as production design, Hollywood editing was seen as setting the international craft standard British films should aspire to.[1] The strongest American editing presence was at Alexander Korda's London Films but former Hollywood editors including Duncan Mansfield, Arthur Tavares, Merrill White, Fred Smith, Otto Ludwig and Jack Kitchin were employed at British and Dominions, Gainsborough, Gaumont-British and Ealing Studios in the late 1920s and 30s. Although most prevalent in the 1930s, this was an established practice. An American editor was brought over as early as 1919 to work on *Twelve-Ten* (Herbert Brenon).

Karel Reisz's book *The Technique of Film Editing* (1953), compiled with help from editors and ex-editors Reginald Beck, Jack Harris, Sidney Cole, Thorold Dickinson, Robert Hamer and David Lean, can be seen as a codification of many years of British editing experience. The book does not distinguish between British and American styles of film editing. It analyses specific sequences from British and American films without differentiating between them. The editing conventions it outlines broadly conform to the system of continuity editing consolidated in Hollywood during the 1910s. *The Technique of Film Editing*'s discussion of basic principles adheres to a classical approach to editing applied to many Hollywood and British productions between the 1920s and 50s. Throughout the book discussions of general topics such as preserving a sense of direction and matching tone from shot to shot are based upon the classical assumption that 'smooth continuity' is essential. The only proviso, itself an equally classical assumption, is that dramatic demands sometimes require that rules for achieving continuity 'are not to be taken as binding or universally valid' (Reisz and Millar, 1968, p. 216). The main distinction, then, is the extent to which the material supplied to American and British editors is different. If, for example, the latter tend to work with different performance styles, or more frequently seek to integrate documentary and location footage into feature films, then specific editing strategies will vary while staying within the broad parameters of the classical approach.

When film historians have ventured cautious generalisations about British editing styles between the 1920s and the 50s they have tended to highlight the impact of Soviet montage cinema, first shown publicly through the (London) Film Society in the late 1920s. Film historian Barry Salt has conducted a 'statistical style analysis' of 1930s films which demonstrates that British cutting rates were somewhere between American and Soviet norms. He suggests that this may be related to the influence of Soviet montage cinema within British film culture (1992, pp. 216–17). Likewise, film historian Richard Dyer claims, 'while British montage may not be exactly what the Russian formalists envisioned, it does certainly go beyond the invisible joins of standard narrative cinema' (1993, pp. 94–5). Yet the influence of Soviet montage cinema and the alternative film culture centred around the Film Society on British editing technique between the late 1920s and the 50s should not be overstated. Even by the end of the 1920s some commentators involved in alternative British film culture were beginning to warn against the employment in British film production of undisciplined editing influenced by Soviet montage cinema.

Adrian Brunel was one of these commentators. In the 1920s he ran a firm specialising in doctoring British films judged by distributors to need further post-production work to improve their pacing and comprehensibility. His business partner Ivor Montagu, a founder of the Film Society, translated the first English edition of Vsevolod Pudovkin's book *Film Technique* (1929). Brunel and Montagu Ltd also re-titled and re-edited foreign films for British distribution. One of the firm's major long-term contracts was the re-titling and re-editing of German, French, Soviet and other foreign art films exhibited by the Film Society. Despite this background Brunel, in his widely read book *Film Production* (1936), recommended inclining more towards Hollywood standards than Soviet montage precedents:

> I do not say we should slavishly imitate the quick tempo of well-cut American pictures; in the majority of cases the American method of quick cutting is the most effective, although I have known it to be applied to subjects that were not designed for such treatment, with rather tragic results. Nor do I say that we should indiscriminately emulate what is called the Russian method. Editors sometimes

amuse themselves with a spot of Russian montage, which is in effect just a spot of bother to a confused audience who are not amused. Such experiments should be kept for the private amusement of technicians, unless there is a legitimate reason and a definite call for the application of such methods in the story (1936, p. 39).

Ian Dalrymple began his career at Brunel and Montagu Ltd and later became an influential editor at Gainsborough and Gaumont-British. He also distanced himself from the term montage. More important to him were considerations such as establishing 'your set clearly so that the audience knows what's happening where', and putting over 'one thing at a time quite clearly and in logical order' (1933, p. 172). These basic principles of continuity editing would have been learned as part of the doctoring work undertaken by Brunel and Montagu Ltd. In Dalrymple's view montage was 'something that happens to Russian films, a few German and French pictures, and the entire output of the Empire Marketing Board. All other films are "cut" ' (1933, p. 170). He asserts his credentials as a no-nonsense cutter of mainstream British feature films. Yet Dalrymple's assertion also reveals a thorough knowledge of where exactly montage can be observed in contemporary film culture.

There are certainly individual cases where the influence of Soviet montage editing was strongly felt. Thorold Dickinson is the most obvious example. His editing of *Sing As We Go* employs some jump-cutting and constructs a humorous montage sequence utilising what one film historian describes as 'optical avant-garde effects reminiscent of Vertov's *The Man with a Movie Camera* [USSR, 1929]' (Higson, 1995, p. 153). Dickinson's editing is clearly marked by the influence of the Film Society screenings of Soviet and abstract films he organised. Referring to Soviet montage, Dickinson said, 'I loved it . . . I used to put elements of that into British films.' Dickinson's description of his work recalls the language used in theoretical writing on editing published in Britain in the late 1920s and 30s, including translated books and essays by Pudovkin and Sergei Eisenstein: 'A montage sequence was like a cadenza in a concerto. I used to enjoy making them' (quoted in Richards, 1984, p. 31). Dickinson's protégé and fellow Film Society member Sidney Cole also reached for an analogy with an established art form when he theorised about his editing:

I can make some attempt, if not at definition, at least at indicating the sort of thing I do in pursuit of rhythm, and the concept I start with. I start from an analogy with ballet. Ballet consists of a series of movements, each complete in themselves, which are linked by the choreographer in varying ways to form different ballets. A series of clear-cut movements. That's what the final succession of edited shots should be (1944, p. 14).

The cultural framework initiated by the Film Society in the 1920s was inherited by some editors who started their career in subsequent decades. Peter Tanner read Pudovkin's *Film Technique*, watched silent films rented from the Wallace Heaton library, and published occasional articles on editing. Jim Clark began his film education and acquired a high regard for editing at an early age. As a child he repeatedly watched a silent version of *Blackmail*, Charlie Chaplin shorts and *Battleship Potemkin* (Sergei Eisenstein, 1925) on his home film projector. Clark became involved with some of the leading institutions of 1940s and early 50s British film culture, such as the Federation of Film Societies and the Edinburgh Film Festival. He read books such as Roger Manvell's *Film* (1944), the period's key text on film appreciation which expounded theories of montage derived from British translations of Pudovkin and Eisenstein. David Gladwell followed a similar path. Although editors remained relatively invisible, editing had a high profile within British film culture between the 1920s and the 50s. Films such as *Battleship Potemkin* were regularly screened at film societies and publications such as Adrian Brunel's *Film Craft* (1933), *Film Production* and Manvell's *Film* emphasised editing's importance.

In some instances certain British editors let enthusiasm for alternative approaches to editing, derived from this strand of British film culture, temporarily get the better of them. Revealingly, these impulses were usually tempered by the need to conform to basic principles of continuity editing. Sidney Cole remembers getting carried away by *Gaslight*'s opening sequence in which a murder is committed. Director Thorold Dickinson 'had a chronological sequence in mind and I had cut it purely on a visual basis of increasing and accelerating tension, so that it had a mounting rhythm in terms of what was happening and was not related to chronology or the topography of the house' (quoted in McFarlane, 1997, p. 136). Dickinson and Cole reworked the sequence together, merging their different conceptions. In the revised version, close-ups of a clock indicate exactly how much time the murderer, whose face is never seen, spends ransacking the house. Shots of his legs going up and down the stairs help to establish the house's topography. Otherwise, the sequence is 'purely visual' insofar as there is no dialogue and the editing rhythm conveys the faceless murderer's mounting frustration at not finding whatever he is looking for. In the upstairs bedroom his hands ransack boxes, drawers and a bed, with these violent actions alternating from left to right after each diagonal wipe. Downstairs the action is concentrated in the left or centre of each shot of a chair and sofa being ripped apart. Dissolves accentuate the impression of time passing yet getting nowhere.

Peter Tanner's initial version of *The Cruel Sea*'s 'survivors' sequence' went through a similar process to Cole's work on *Gaslight*. Captain Ericson (Jack

Hawkins), commanding a Second World War corvette, faces an agonising choice. He must decide whether to depth charge a U-boat suspected to be lurking beneath a group of survivors hoping to be rescued:

> At one time part of it was cut to the rhythm of the ASDIC [undersea submarine sonic detector]. As the pings and pongs got quicker, so did cutting, until it worked up to cuts of only two or three frames each. This was quite effective, but definitely 'arty-crafty' and what used to be termed 'montage'. It just wasn't right, though, in a realistic film such as this and looked contrived. Both the director and I wanted to get a more newsreel approach and so we threw it out and started all over again. This time it was cut entirely for realism and maximum suspense. Notice how, after the depth charges have exploded and the men have been blown up and only the floating debris remains without a trace of the U-boat, the cutting goes back to slow tempo to match the slow almost mockingly peaceful 'ping ping ping' of the ASDIC (Tanner, 1962, p. 298).

Tanner's point of reference for his first version of this sequence was the final part of *Battleship Potemkin* where an accelerating editing rhythm heightens anticipation about whether other ships in the fleet will attack or join the *Potemkin* mutineers. This decelerates when it becomes clear they are not going to attack. Tanner's description of editing *The Cruel Sea* nicely illustrates an awareness of alternative approaches to editing within a context where involving the spectator with the narrative and the psychology of individual characters is paramount. In the finished film 'the story', in Tanner's words, 'told itself in Jack Hawkins' face'; hence the emphasis upon lengthy close-ups of him in the final version of the 'survivors' sequence'. Tanner's original montage might not have achieved the requisite suspense and involvement with character psychology that is integral to a classical approach to editing. At the same time, Tanner's emphasis on 'a newsreel approach' and 'cutting entirely for realism' is quite specific to the type of material he edited at Ealing in the 1940s and 50s (see Chapter 3).

OPTICALS ELIMINATED AND RECLAIMED

One post-war stylistic development many British editors have remarked upon is changes in how the passage of time and flashbacks are signalled. In the original 1953 edition of *The Technique of Film Editing* Karel Reisz asserts:

> The most usual way of joining two consecutive sequences is by means of a dissolve ... Through years of usage, moreover, the dissolve has come to be commonly associated with a passage of time ... Equally, a flash-back, which takes the story back in time, is commonly introduced and terminated in a dissolve.

He goes on to qualify this by pointing out that dramatic considerations, for example the desire to avoid an apparent pause in the narrative, could lead to a cut being used instead. In such cases one possibility would be for 'a phrase of dialogue [to] effectively link the two scenes in such a way that a cut from one to the other would make the transition acceptable' (Reisz and Millar, 1968, p. 268). Prior to the cut, dialogue could help prepare the spectator for the transition. Alternatively dialogue, a sound effect or music could be overlapped across the cut and thus smooth the transition. During the 1950s and 60s these devices became increasingly common, to the point where Thorold Dickinson stated: 'Dissolves are rare enough today to break the illusion and make the modern audience screen-conscious' (notes to Reisz and Millar, 1968, p. 277). Tracing the historical shift from dissolves to cuts for temporal transitions in British films requires close attention to incremental changes in editors' practices.

American editor Ralph Winters argues, at the most general level, that the gradual shift from dissolves to cuts is related to post-war audiences 'looking at a lot of television' where cuts, especially on channels with commercial breaks, more frequently separate segments of broadcast output (quoted in LoBrutto, 1991, p. 42). American editor Evan Lottman concurs: 'The elimination of optical fades and dissolves . . . was probably a television influence' (quoted in Oldham, 1992, p. 233). In Britain, the decisive period for the growth of television audiences and the launch of a commercial channel was between the early 1950s and the early 60s. This was also the period in which an increasing number of British editors, with differing degrees of boldness, began to use cuts rather than dissolves for temporal transitions. Although some editors experimented prior to this, audiences' acclimatisation through television usage probably accounts to a large extent for the eventual widespread acceptance of the new practice.

Debates within the production sector of the British film industry in the immediate post-war period also have a bearing on this issue. Anne Coates recalls a prevalent concern at the beginning of her career in the late 1940s: 'When British films came over [to America], they were considered very slow' (quoted in Oldham, 1992, p. 167). Whether or not British films actually were slower than American films, this perception got taken seriously during the late 1940s. At this time the Rank Organisation, like Gaumont-British in the mid-1930s, was strenuously attempting to make inroads into the American market. Jack Harris, the British industry's most highly regarded editor, was sent by Rank to America for four months in 1945 to investigate distributors' allegations about the slowness of British films.

Within this context of renewed concern about the speed of British films, certain Hollywood films began to be noted within British editing circles for their brisk transitions between sequences. In the 1953 edition of *The Technique of*

Film Editing, for example, Karel Reisz discusses how straight cuts between some sequences in *State of the Union* (Frank Capra, 1948), edited by William Hornbeck, give this film 'tremendous pace' (Reisz and Millar, 1968, p. 245). Cuts marking the passing of time between sequences do not necessarily take up less screen time than dissolves, but they do typically give the impression of moving the narrative along more quickly. *State of the Union* and films like it were not typical of Hollywood production of the late 1940s. Film historian David Bordwell concludes from a broad survey of Hollywood's output that: 'Not until the late 1950s did a few films begin to eliminate such internal punctuation and simply use the straight cut to link scenes and subscenes' (Bordwell, Staiger and Thompson, 1985, p. 44). The shift towards new stylistic norms in British films was similarly uneven and protracted.

Editors working with Michael Powell and Emeric Pressburger's Archers production company played an important role within this shift. Films directed by Powell and Pressburger during their 1940s heyday sometimes indicate flashbacks or the passage of time in ingenious ways. A flashback commences without an edit of any kind near to the beginning of *The Life and Death of Colonel Blimp* (1943). A crane shot starts with an elderly Clive Candy (Roger Livesey) struggling with Lieutenant Wilson (James McKechnie) in a pool in a Turkish bath in 1942. It ends with a young Candy emerging from the pool in 1902. Near to the end of the narrative a graphic explosion is interpolated into a lengthy fade to signal the death in an air raid of Candy's former comrade and servant Montgomery Murdoch (John Laurie). Yet these are exceptions to the general pattern of John Seabourne's editing for Powell and Pressburger. He follows contemporary conventions by employing dissolves for shorter and fades for longer passages of time. Anne Coates, who worked as Seabourne's assistant, credits him with teaching her how to edit 'ruthlessly' (quoted in Oldham, 1992, p. 154), but this attitude manifests itself within sequences rather than in transitions between them. In *I Know Where I'm Going* (1945), for example, Seabourne's editing often propels impatient protagonist Joan Webster (Wendy Hiller) through space. One instance is when Joan first arrives at the house at Port Erraig. Cuts transport her swiftly from the middle of a corridor into a room and then into the centre of another one.

Reginald Mills succeeded Seabourne as Powell and Pressburger's regular editor from *A Matter of Life and Death* (1946) onwards. This was his first major feature and he enthusiastically advocated dispensing with conventional transitional devices:

> It was on *A Matter of Life and Death* that I first decided to try and get away from all the sort of mechanical aids to cutting, try to edit a picture without using fades or

opticals. It's perfectly easily done, and also can be intelligently done if you include
this thinking when the script is being written. In the average script the average
scriptwriter . . . at the end of a scene they would just put in the word, 'dissolve' or
'fade out' . . . It is such an old fashioned device really. I started talking to Mickie
and Emeric about this, and they became interested, and we found the idea worked
(quoted in Belfrage, n.d., pp. 196–7).

Powell's keen interest in technical experiment would have made him receptive
to Mills' idea. Pressburger had worked on German and French films during the
1930s where, according to film historian Barry Salt, transitions without dissolves
were more common than elsewhere (1992, p. 217). Moreover, the Archers were
given considerable creative autonomy under Rank's Independent Producers
scheme during the 1940s. Nonetheless, Mills' preferences were only gradually
implemented. In *Black Narcissus* (1947) some of Sister Clodagh's (Deborah
Kerr's) flashbacks begin or end with a straight cut rather than a dissolve. In *The
Red Shoes* (1948) there are a couple of isolated examples of the passage of time
being indicated in this way. It is only with *The Small Back Room* (1949) that
Mills' use of cuts to bridge the passage of time becomes more systematic. In this
film transitions from sequences in other locations involving Susan (Kathleen
Byron) and Sammy Rice (David Farrar) to later sequences in their flat are
effected by cutting to close-ups of a boiling pot of coffee, a cat on a sofa and a
hand putting a key in a lock. These transitions do not occur at particularly dramatic or emotionally intense moments, except for two in quick succession when
Susan and Sammy reunite at the end of the narrative. In *The Small Back Room*
this new editing convention is routinely used, but it is also an intermediate film
insofar as Mills continues to use dissolves to mark the passage of time between
some sequences.

By the end of the 1940s other British films were showing signs of more flexible approaches to these editing conventions. *The Passionate Friends* (1949), the
first film Geoffrey Foot edited for director David Lean, resembles *Black Narcissus* inasmuch as Mary Justin's (Ann Todd's) flashbacks sometimes begin or
end with a straight cut. *Madeleine* (1950), Foot and Lean's next collaboration,
takes this a step further in its courtroom denouement. This includes a long series
of brief flashbacks to statements made earlier by witnesses. The beginning of
the first in this series is marked by a dissolve, but after this only cuts are used.
Madeleine also contains a prime example of a cut between earlier and later
sequences being used for dramatic emphasis. The final shot in a fraught night-
time encounter between Madeleine Smith (Ann Todd) and her lover Emile
L'Angelier (Ivan Desny) is followed by a daytime shot of one of her servants at
a dispensary attempting to obtain some poison. The narrative never resolves

whether Madeleine murdered her lover or not, but this cut suggests the strong possibility of a direct connection between the disintegration of their relationship and his poisoning.

For Peter Tanner at Ealing, *Kind Hearts and Coronets* marked the beginning of a period of experimentation (see Chapter 3). His next project pushed this further: 'The *Blue Lamp* was amazing ... Geoff Foot may have done one once but ... I said ... we're not going to have any dissolves, or very, very few in it, we're going to jump from one thing to another ... audiences weren't used to it, but it gave terrific pace.' Michael Balcon supported this innovation: 'When we ran the rough cut of *The Blue Lamp*, Balcon sat back at the end of the screening and said nothing. And then he said, "What can I say? There it is. It can go out tomorrow. We don't need music."' *The Blue Lamp* contains even more instances than *The Small Back Room* where cuts mark the passage of time, although dissolves are also used quite frequently.[2] Shifting this balance opens up the possibility for opticals to carry greater expressive weight when they are used. The quietly emotional sequence in *The Blue Lamp* where PC Andy Mitchell (James Hanley) tells Mrs Dixon (Gladys Henson) her husband is dead illustrates this well. In keeping with the narrative's generally brisk pace, a cut rather than dissolve moves the action from PC Mitchell and his superior opening a door in the police station to them arriving by car at Mrs Dixon's house. After she has been told the news and begins to weep the sequence ends with a fade. This rare fade adds to the moment's poignancy.

In a 1962 essay Tanner suggested that cuts between sequences were more appropriate to certain genres than others: 'A dissolve is rather like a paragraph in a book but nowadays often the public will accept a new paragraph without a dissolve, and this is especially true in fast-moving stories, crime dramas, etc.' (1962, p. 296). Fast-moving stories and crime dramas were a relatively minor element in the generic mix at Ealing in the 1950s, so Tanner was presented with few opportunities to extend his break from convention in *The Blue Lamp*. *Cage of Gold* (Basil Dearden, 1950), unusual for Ealing in the prominence it gives to moral transgressions and crimes of passion, maximises their impact through cuts between earlier and later sequences. They occur when Judith (Jean Simmons) announces she is going to marry charming, deceitful Bill Glennon (David Farrar), and when Bill's lover Marie (Madeleine Lebeau) jumps out of a train after shooting him. In *Pool of London* there is a cut between earlier and later sequences as the police investigation into a diamond theft gathers pace. *The Cruel Sea* contains three moments where Tanner cuts abruptly from sequences in which characters begin to express personal feelings to later sequences of them performing public duties. This supports the film's overall emphasis upon the need to stoically curtail strongly felt private emotions in order to effectively perform wartime duties. In general, however, this type of transition was used only sporadically by Tanner and other Ealing editors in the 1950s.

Elsewhere Reginald Mills continued proselytising for cuts rather than dissolves to mark temporal transitions. He recalled: 'Joe Losey was a director who was amenable to the idea. On *Blind Date* [1959] we would plan to shoot the end of a sequence and the beginning of another in such a way they could be cut together smoothly, and without using an optical' (quoted in Belfrage, n.d., pp. 196–7). There are no opticals at all in *The Servant* (see Chapter 4), and there are early signs of a gradual movement away from dissolves and fades even in Mills' and Losey's first collaboration *The Sleeping Tiger* (directed using Victor Hanbury's name, 1954). Transitions to later sequences set in a club or bar where jazz or pop music is being played often provided editors during this period with opportunities to cut straight into a shot of a musician and/or use the music to signal the new time and location. Mills does this once in *The Small Back Room*, twice in *The Sleeping Tiger*, and once in *The Servant*. Peter Tanner uses the same tactic in *Pool of London*. Ann Chegwidden employs a variant on this device in *The Tommy Steele Story* (Gerald Bryant, 1957). She cuts from Tommy's announcement of a forthcoming free concert in Bermondsey to an audience of noisy teenagers just before it begins.

By the late 1950s a small but increasing number of British editors were using cuts for temporal transitions. Editors working for Michael Powell and Emeric Pressburger, such as Arthur Stevens on *Ill Met by Moonlight* (1957) and Noreen Ackland on *Peeping Tom*, continued the tradition begun by Reginald Mills. Yet the dominant practice of exclusively using dissolves and fades persisted in the majority of films. Examples from across the spectrum of British film production include Frank Clarke's work on MGM-British's *Bhowani Junction*, Richard Best's on the otherwise adventurously edited ABPC film *Woman in a Dressing Gown* (J. Lee Thompson, 1957), and Alfred Roome's on Rank's *Nor the Moon by Night* (Ken Annakin, 1958). Established practice was still capable of achieving elegant results; in the latter film the onset of heavy rain builds up to a downpour through two carefully timed dissolves linking shots of the darkening African sky.

Change occurred slowly and unevenly throughout the 1950s. Although he experimented with cuts in *Kind Hearts and Coronets*, *The Blue Lamp* and certain sequences in other early 1950s films, Peter Tanner reverted to exclusively using dissolves and fades for linking earlier and later sequences in mid- to late 1950s Ealing films such as *The Night My Number Came Up* (Leslie Norman, 1955). Although Hammer productions acquired a reputation for the occasional startling use of shock cuts, James Needs and Alfred Cox scrupulously follow classical practice when indicating temporal transitions in the company's earlier horror films such as *The Curse of Frankenstein* (Terence Fisher, 1957) and *The Mummy* (Terence Fisher, 1959).

It fell to the British New Wave to accelerate the tendency that had been halt-ingly gaining ground since at least the late 1940s. Don Fairservice argues that for directors and editors of these films, 'the use of the cut as a preferred transition ... added a degree of no-nonsense rigour ... [helping to] ... fix a trend which soon became a convention' (2001, p. 316). In some of the later New Wave films the bal-ance tilts decisively towards cuts rather than dissolves or fades for temporal transitions and flashbacks. This is particularly the case with those films edited by younger editors. Whereas Richard Best and Bert Bates in *Look Back in Anger* and Ralph Kemplen in *Room at the Top* follow classical practice, Seth Holt frequently employs cuts for temporal transitions in *Saturday Night and Sunday Morning*.

Saturday Night and Sunday Morning's pre-credit sequence featuring Arthur Seaton's (Albert Finney's) famous 'all the rest is propaganda' voiceover uses this device to startling effect. It ends with a cut from a low-angle medium close-up of Arthur cleaning his hands and throwing down a rag to a high-angle long shot of workers leaving the factory some time later. This emphasises Arthur's aggress-ive physicality and establishes a thematic opposition: cuts between sequences are used not only for temporal transitions but also to mark a sharp separation between Arthur's work and leisure time. Brief sequences set in the factory typi-cally begin with a cut, as do those when Arthur visits a pub for the first time in the film, dances at Doreen's (Shirley Anne Field's) house, and visits a fair-ground.[3] Dissolves, fades and even wipes are, however, also used, especially during more reflective moments such as when Arthur and Bert (Norman Ross-ington) go fishing, and when long shots of the town are displayed.

Saturday Night and Sunday Morning proved to be a turning point insofar as subsequent British New Wave films were concerned. Roger Cherrill's ratio of cuts to dissolves for temporal transitions is higher in *A Kind of Loving* (John Schlesinger, 1962) than Holt's in *Saturday Night and Sunday Morning*. Higher still is Antony Gibbs' ratio in *The Loneliness of the Long Distance Runner*, where very few dissolves are used. Within this context their occasional appearance becomes all the more resonant. The most striking example is during a flashback where borstal boy Colin Smith (Tom Courtenay) ruminates about his past while walking along a beach at Skegness. This tendency of later British New Wave films is taken to its furthest extreme in *This Sporting Life* (Lindsay Anderson, 1963), edited by Peter Taylor. There are no dissolves at all in this film, and eye line matches sometimes link the end of one sequence to the beginning of a sub-sequent one later in time.

By the early 1960s younger editors, for example John Bloom in *Girl on Approval* (Charles Frend, 1962) and Anne Coates in *Becket* (Peter Glenville,

1964), were disseminating the emphasis upon cuts rather than dissolves beyond the British New Wave. This became routine as the 1960s and 70s progressed, and some editors and directors explored further possibilities inherent within the new convention. Tony Lawson learned from director Nicolas Roeg 'how to make transitions that are to do with association'. A movement, a colour, or similarities in the composition of disparate shots can provide the link motivating a cut between earlier and later sequences. This makes it possible either to 'lead you where you expect to go but make it surprising', or to 'get away with so many apparently unrelated events, by finding some key thing that's common to them all, and bringing them together, and it seems perfectly natural and yet totally unconnected'. In *Bad Timing*, the first film Lawson edited for Roeg, transitions through association are sometimes achieved through cuts between shots of characters smoking cigarettes. A striking example of an unusual transition in this film occurs at the end of a Moroccan holiday. It involves a cut between a shot of writhing snakes held aloft in a bazaar to a shot of an aeroplane with similarly cursive Arabic writing across its exterior. Both shots are composed against backgrounds of clear blue sky and incorporate a left to right camera pan.

Another comment made by Lawson, who began his career as an assistant during the 1960s and gained his first editing credits in the 1970s, suggests a different perception of optical effects to that held by an earlier generation. Whereas editors would be more inclined in the 1930s, 40s and into the 50s to employ fades and dissolves as relatively neutral devices for indicating a flashback or the passing of time, Lawson describes them 'as a way to slow the film down'. In a historical context where straight cuts between earlier and later sequences are the norm, carefully placed opticals acquire a greater capacity than in the past to contribute to deliberately unhurried pacing and to convey emotion. Jim Clark's work on *The Innocents* and Antony Gibbs' on *A Taste of Honey* are early instances of this (see Chapter 4). Another is the sombre *The Spy Who Came in from the Cold* (Martin Ritt, 1965). Editor Anthony Harvey recounts:

> There were plenty of opportunities for exciting cutting, as in any spy story. But we found it would have been wrong for this particular spy story. We realised during the editing period that, instead of using hard and dramatic cuts, it would be more fitting to use long slow dissolves to match the bleak and austere mood of the story (quoted in Hudson, 1966, p. 83).

Terry Rawlings is the contemporary British editor who has most frequently reclaimed dissolves for atmospheric and expressive purposes, often within rather than between sequences. He uses dissolves primarily to communicate emotional states or accentuate graceful movements rather than simply mark the passing of time. He sees these developing in his work since *Alien* through to more recent films such as *Entrapment* (see Chapter 2). *Yentl*'s languorous narrative was well suited to Rawlings' elegant dissolves. Camera and body movements are choreographed in a sequence where Yentl (Barbra Streisand) sings of her love for Avigdor (Mandy Patinkin) as she undresses, washes and gets into bed. The sensuousness of these movements is enhanced by long dissolves. Rawlings used them to make 'five shots all drift together', and the sequence ends with a fade to black.

MORE DIRECT AND FASTER CUTTING

Whereas for Lawson fades and dissolves are devices for slowing a film down, many older editors perceive a trend towards faster cuts speeding films up from the 1960s onwards. Whether this is regarded positively or negatively, editors with this longer view certainly share a sense that styles have changed since they began their careers in the 1930s. Russell Lloyd laments the pervasiveness of what he sees as more jarring, abrupt editing. Richard Best is disappointed by contemporary films which seem to 'cut, cut, cut, cut all the pauses, make it go like a bomb. That isn't editing ... If you don't respond to the emotional content ... all you're getting is a fast film.' Other veterans eventually accepted some of these changes. Interviewed in the late 1970s, Ralph Kemplen admitted 'even I am a copyist in enjoying the freedoms created by others; not bothering too much about strict continuity any more, not following someone through a door, not dissolving' (quoted in Musgrave, 1979, p. 18). Interviewed in the late 1980s, Geoffrey Foot agreed: 'We're much sharper now ... we go for the job rather than smoothness ... audiences now accept rapid change on the screen.'

Anne Coates found herself on the cusp of various stylistic changes during the formative years of her career in the 1950s and 60s. She and other younger editors identified certain practices as antiquated: 'In the old days, I watched editors who would painstakingly match arms going up ... such a simple thing like somebody crossing a road? You don't need to see the person go through that and cross the road and match it' (quoted in Oldham, 1992, p. 167). Jim Clark, interviewed in the mid-1960s, used the popular example of a character going through a door to illustrate how uninteresting movements could be truncated. He also noted that an older rule of thumb, about cutting to a shot containing camera movement just before the movement begins, now seemed outmoded: 'It was supposed to be ugly on the eye if you cut to a travelling shot from a static shot. But one does it all the time now' (quoted in Hudson, 1966, p. 83). In a similar spirit of directness, future Bond film editor John Glen was 'absolutely fascinated by the new technique' which 'outrageous editor' Peter Hunt employed on the first film in the series:

Dr No [Terence Young, 1962] was clearly the work of people whose philosophy was 'If it's boring, cut it out.' The style of editing was consequently executed in broad strokes and had an almost comic strip feel to it. It didn't seem to matter that an actor had to go from A to B in order to reach C – *Dr No* did without B altogether and eliminated a lot of the pedestrian movement that bogged down so many films of the era. Sean Connery would be seen looking towards a door and it would cut to the corridor outside and him emerge from the doorway. It was an abbreviated style, almost impressionistic. Terence's set-ups and Peter's stylised editing did no less than usher in a new era of film-making with techniques we now take for granted. As a young editor, I watched carefully and was impressed (2001, p. 37).

Many isolated precursors of this approach can be identified, such as Ian Dalrymple's discussion in his 1933 essay 'Commercial Cutting' of how editors can compress actual movements (see Chapter 3), or John Seabourne's 'ruthless' editing of certain sequences in *I Know Where I'm Going*. Nevertheless Coates' and Glen's comments point towards a widespread interest, among younger editors of the 1960s, in experimenting, where possible and appropriate, with new, more direct styles of editing which pay less heed to traditional notions of strict continuity. Statistical indicators, insofar as they are useful, add further weight to Glen's suggestion that Bond films were important to this development. Film historian David Bordwell has calculated that the average shot length of *Goldfinger* (Guy Hamilton, 1964), also edited by Peter Hunt, is significantly shorter than that of most British and American films of the mid- to late 1960s (2002, p. 16).

It is sometimes assumed that television, with its need to engage easily distracted audiences, encouraged a general acceleration of feature film cutting rates. This can lead to assertions, such as Reginald Mills', that since the 1960s there has been 'a steep decline in the art of film editing due firstly to the bad influence of instant television editing' (quoted in Sharples Jr, 1977, p. 25). One problem with sweeping judgments of this kind, whether positive or negative, is that they ignore the changing contexts in which films and television programmes are produced and the diversity of each industry's output.[4] Certainly there has been significant traffic in editors moving from British television into feature film production since the 1960s: John Glen, Tariq Anwar and Jonathan Morris are some of many who could be cited as examples. Yet their experiences have been far from uniform.

A useful approach is to trace specific editors' paths through television into film, rather than relying on generalisations about television and film per se. John Glen, who responded so enthusiastically to Peter Hunt's editing of the early Bond films, links them directly to particular British television series of the 1960s:

'I think it's fair to say that *Dr No* kick-started a wave of spy-themed shows. In the spring of 1964, I joined the team of editors on one of the very best: *Danger Man*' (2001, p. 38). Shot on film, with high production values, and snappily edited, this series (re-titled *Secret Agent*) proved successful in America. Glen edited it for two years and this experience clearly informed his subsequent editing of three Bond films. This is an example of a synergy developed at a particular point in time between specific areas of British film and television production. In this case, fast cutting was part of that synergy. In other cases it has not been a factor. For example, Jonathan Morris' background in television documentary editing fed directly into his work as editor of all the films directed by Ken Loach during the 1990s and early 2000s, but these films do not conform to generalisations about television accelerating feature film cutting rates.

Some British editors have admitted to the influence of the French New Wave in stimulating a trend not only towards more experimental editing in certain British feature films of the 1960s, but also towards a more direct style. John Victor-Smith, editor of *Help!* (1965), and subsequent films directed by Richard Lester, argued: 'when the French New Wave decided that people no longer had to walk in and out of doors, this was an important change' (quoted in Sharples Jr, 1977, p. 25). The biggest influence on David Gladwell, editor of *If . . .* and *O Lucky Man!* (Lindsay Anderson, 1973), was *Hiroshima Mon Amour* (Alain Resnais, 1959) rather than the 'kitchen sink' aspects of the British New Wave. The second enlarged edition of *The Technique of Film Editing*, published in 1968, also testifies to the impact of recent developments in European art cinema. It contains lengthy analyses of sequences from several French New Wave as well as other European art films. British films such as *A Hard Day's Night* (Richard Lester, 1964), edited by John Jympson, and *Help!* have been considered important by film historians for the role they played in mediating French New Wave editing techniques to American film-makers. Although broad patterns of influence along these lines are discernible, further investigation reveals both very specific influences on specific editors and the difficulty of fixing a single point of origin for these developments.

The earliest British film of the 1960s to impact significantly upon American editors was *The Loneliness of the Long Distance Runner*. Dede Allen, editor of *Bonnie and Clyde*, was particularly impressed by Antony Gibbs' editing of this film. She continues to screen it as an example of innovative editing when teaching film students. *The Loneliness of the Long Distance Runner* and *Bonnie and Clyde* are edited, to use Tony Lawson's description of the latter, in an 'incredibly aggressive', 'jarring' and 'extremely effective' manner. Both films conclude with a burst of frenetic, rapid-fire editing. *Bonnie and Clyde* became the key film in what was widely referred to at the time as Hollywood's renaissance. Dede

Allen openly acknowledges the British influence upon her work: 'The "angry young men" films that Tony Gibbs cut . . . had more direct influence on me than anything. I loved the way those pictures were cut. It was incorporated in pictures cut in New York like *Bonnie and Clyde*' (quoted in LoBrutto, 1991, p. 78). Gibbs concurs with Allen's assessment of this influence but modestly places his innovation within a broader European context, albeit one he was relatively unfamiliar with at the time:

> I think Dede is right. I think *Bonnie and Clyde* was the first time that any form of European-style presentation was presented on an American movie and it came to them as a great shock – even though English movies had been coming to America and had been seen.
>
> We were all looking to do new things, particularly with Richard Lester, but I remember on *Long Distance Runner* I'd done some funny work on the close-ups of him running, and I was feeling pretty proud and arrogant about the whole thing, you know, 'this is the way we're going to go, kids'. Then I went and saw *Breathless* [*À bout de souffle*, Jean-Luc Godard, 1959] – and there was this sequence with Belmondo and Seberg in the car and it was jump-cut, jump-cut. I went, 'Oh God', because I'd thought in some silly way that I'd thought of something new and here was someone who'd done it six months earlier, and much better . . . I grew a little older and I realised that there is nothing new under the sun, actually, and that all those things had been done way, way before . . . All these things had been done in silent movies.

Tony Lawson agrees with Gibbs that the issue of where new editing styles emerged from in the 1960s is a tangled one that cannot be reduced to unilateral derivation or imitation. By the late 1960s European, British and American developments had thoroughly cross-fertilised each other. Considering the complex web of influences on his, Michael Ellis' and Murray Jordan's more experimental editing in certain sequences in *Cross of Iron*, Lawson recalls:

> We'd all seen *The Wild Bunch* (Sam Peckinpah, 1969) [edited by Lou Lombardo], and been shocked and amazed, and excited by that. But also it's a question I asked myself . . . when could you pinpoint that type of editing? Actually it goes way, way back . . . *Help!* . . . *Bonnie and Clyde*, Dede's film, it's all there . . . people were ripe for it. Although Sam and *The Wild Bunch* made a very, very strong mark, nevertheless that kind of editing was in the air, was already starting to get used . . . so going back to *Cross of Iron*, it just seemed the natural thing to do, to cut those sequences that way, because that's the way it should be done.

Wider cultural changes 'in the air', a desire among young film-makers in particular to break new ground and be innovative and modern, contributed to the
emergence of new stylistic developments in British film editing from the 1960s
onwards. A more immediate industrial factor, however, is also relevant to the
developments Lawson discusses. There was a gradual shift, throughout the 1950s
and 60s, from long-term employment by a single studio or production company
to editors, directors and other technicians working on a freelance basis on independent productions. This impacted upon stylistic developments. In a studio
context such as Gainsborough in the 1940s, editors like Alfred Roome or R. E.
Dearing might have relatively limited contact with a director during post-production, and therefore be inclined to edit broadly in accordance with established
conventions. Freelancing and independent production could on occasion permit
more latitude for experimentation. Jim Clark, for example, noted a significant
contrast between his closer, more open-ended collaborations with directors
including Jack Clayton, John Schlesinger and Roland Joffé, and his earlier work
on three films directed by Stanley Donen. Clark recalls that with Donen, an old-
style Hollywood professional, general guidelines for editing were clear and the
director simply expected them to be followed in his absence: 'it would have been
amazing to see him in the cutting room three times in three pictures. There was-
n't that much experimentation' (quoted in Wyeth and Grantham, 1984, p. 64).

The 1960s saw significant stylistic developments in certain areas of British film
editing. These included consolidating the use of cuts rather than dissolves for
temporal transitions between sequences, the abbreviation of actors' movements
within certain sequences, less adherence to strict continuity and, in some cases,
a tendency towards faster cutting. A more recent consideration has been the
possible impact upon film style of the advent, in the 1990s, of non-linear editing systems (see Chapter 6). In an attempt to systematically explore these
stylistic developments, film historian David Bordwell (2002) has surveyed a wide
range, primarily of Hollywood films, from 1961 to 2000.[5] One conclusion he
arrives at is that a general tendency towards faster cutting that began in the
1960s has definitely accelerated in certain types of films in more recent decades.
His examples include Gerry Hambling's work on *Pink Floyd The Wall* (Alan
Parker, 1982), and Stuart Baird's even faster editing of *The Last Boy Scout*. This
approach tends to be more prevalent in action-orientated films or those influenced by music video. Films identified as British tend not to fall into the action
genre, whereas music video has had an impact upon films as diverse as *The Last
of England* (Derek Jarman, 1987), edited by Peter Cartwright, and *Lock, Stock
and Two Smoking Barrels* (Guy Ritchie, 1998), edited by Niven Howie.

One point needs to be reiterated within the debate about a general trend
towards faster cutting. A primary concern for most British editors continues to

be, within broadly accepted parameters, to fashion a style and pace of editing appropriate to the material they are working with. If there is some credence in John Hill's (1999) and other film historians' argument that a significant sector of British film production has drawn closer to the traditions of art cinema since the 1960s, then Barry Salt's observation about one of the consequences this has for editing styles needs to be considered. Salt argues that from this time onwards long takes 'largely came to be associated with high artistic ambition in feature films from any country' (1992, p. 266).

Salt's generalisation is open to debate, partly because some French New Wave films also incorporate rapidly edited sequences. Nevertheless it highlights a relevant point. Salt cites as an example Reginald Mills' work on *The Servant*, where shots held for over a minute are not uncommon. Another British film containing numerous, comparatively static shots held for almost as long is *My Way Home* (Bill Douglas, 1978), edited by Mick Audsley. To a more limited extent, Jon Gregory and Lesley Walker also eschew fast cutting in the films they have edited for director Mike Leigh since the 1980s. A relatively unhurried editing pace is also characteristic of many examples of the so-called heritage films that have been particularly identified with British cinema during recent decades. In this respect Terry Rawlings' measured pacing of *Chariots of Fire* and Andrew Marcus' of *Howard's End* (James Ivory, 1992) fit into a tradition that can be traced back at least as far as *Comin' Thro' the Rye* (Cecil Hepworth, 1924) (Higson, 1995, p. 78).

Trainspotting, one of the most influential and widely discussed British films of the 1990s, does conform to the faster cutting trend noted by Bordwell. Masahiro Hirakubo's editing also introduces a limited amount of ambiguity into the construction of space and the chronological order of certain events. Yet an important part of Bordwell's argument is that, although editing conventions have changed in certain respects since the 1960s, a traditional armature persists in the majority of contemporary feature films. This is the case in *Trainspotting*. For all its playfulness it adheres to several tried and tested conventions. Shot/reverse shot, eye line matching and matches on action stitch together a basic coherence to its narrative and most of the spaces its characters pass through (Stollery, 2001, pp. 45–8). The illumination of emotion and character psychology through editing also continues to be important. Praising Hirakubo's contribution to their later collaboration *The Beach* (2000), director Danny Boyle states: 'Masahiro . . . becomes intimate with the psychology of the major characters and knows them like he has written the novel [the film is based upon] himself' (quoted in Unattributed, 2002b). This is not that far removed from veteran editor Richard Best's emphasis upon the importance of responding to a film's emotional content. British editing styles have changed over time, but many underlying objectives remain the same.

NOTES

All unattributed quotations in this chapter are drawn from the interviews conducted for this book, apart from the quotation from Geoffrey Foot, which is drawn from his interview for the BECTU History Project.

1. The Austrian Oswald Hafenrichter is often cited as one of the most important foreign editors to have worked in Britain. John Glen cites him as 'the greatest influence on my editing' (2001, p. 27). Bernard Gribble argues there is a discernible difference between the films directed by Carol Reed which Hafenrichter edited and those he did not. Nevertheless Hafenrichter arrived in Britain in the 1940s, later than most of the American editors, and is an individual exception to the general trend.

2. Like Mills remembering *A Matter of Life and Death*, it is probably the later wide acceptance of his experiments that leads Tanner to overstate their frequency in *The Blue Lamp*.

3. The only factory sequence that doesn't begin with a cut is the final one in the film. This is after Arthur has been beaten up and is beginning to settle down with Doreen. By this point in the film he is perhaps moving away from his rebellious attitude of disdaining work and living only for pleasure.

4. Comparative studies of cutting rates in American television and film during the 1960s (Salt, 1992, p. 266; Bordwell, 2002) suggest there is no conclusive evidence that television editing was primarily responsible for accelerating film editing.

5. One limitation of this statistical approach is that, although it can index general trends, it cannot grasp the specific ways in which pacing is developed within individual films and sequences. The calculation of an average shot length would not register, for example, how a film might combine shots held on screen for a very long time with a rapid series of one or two frame cuts.

6

The Future of Editing and Technological Change

Press the wrong button nowadays, and something magical might happen.
Peter Honess (2002), editor, *LA Confidential* (Curtis Hanson, 1997)

THE CHANGING BACKGROUND

Nothing in the history of cinema, except for the coming of sound, parallels the impact made by digital technology on feature film editing. The explosion of new media technologies that have transformed film and television post-production in the past decade or so stands in stark contrast to the slow evolution of mechanical systems that developed from the 1920s until the end of the century. Don Fairservice has noted that from the very beginnings of cinema until about 1916 there was no specialised film editing equipment. The only means of viewing the processed film was either by running it through a projector, or by viewing it over a light box. Editors were able to cut film in the hand, requiring little more than scissors and glue to assemble the film, which was weighed on finely balanced scales to calculate its duration (Fairservice, 2001, p. 331). While it was possible for editors to compare shots by eye, the development of continuity editing and the need for matched action cuts required a mechanised form of film transportation to assess timing and rhythm. The arrival of the electrically powered Moviola editing machine in the 1920s (and the advent of the sound version in 1930) was one of the most significant developments in film editing and these machines became a staple for editors on both sides of the Atlantic. American editor Walter Murch referred affectionately to 'the humble Moviola – that frog-green fixture of every editing room over the last seventy years' (1995, p. 75). This was an upright editing machine usually equipped to run one reel of vertically mounted picture and a separate reel of perforated magnetic soundtrack. Due perhaps as much to its apparent antiquity as to the racket of its pedal operation, the Moviola was referred to by some editors as 'the Gatling Gun'. Its accuracy, reliability and adaptability made it a great favourite with many editors. Bert Bates wrote a letter in March 1970, describing the editing of *The Battle of Britain* (Guy Hamilton, 1969) and celebrating the versatility of a machine which could be used on location as well as in the studios:

We were operating from a couple of caravans which were towed around the various airfields, and our power came from a portable generator. One day my Moviola came to a grinding halt and T. G. was sent to discover why, and came back with the news that we had 'run out of petrol'. Surely a new first! (1970, p. 17).

The design of the Moviola was not suited to all kinds of editing. In Germany and Italy flatbed, table-styled editing machines were developed which rivalled, complemented and sometimes replaced the venerable American upright. The advantage of the flatbeds was a capacity for much longer takes, since the film and sound were spooled horizontally from revolving plates, making it especially suitable for documentary editing. Most commonly used of these flatbed machines were the German-designed Steenbecks and KEMs, introduced into feature film editing in the late 1960s. Flatbeds allowed both director and editor to sit side by side during cutting, and review complete rolls of film while running multiple soundtracks. John Bloom (who continued using a Moviola until 1995) considers this to have produced a significant change, by bringing editor and director together during cutting, unlike the solitary working encouraged by editor and Moviola:

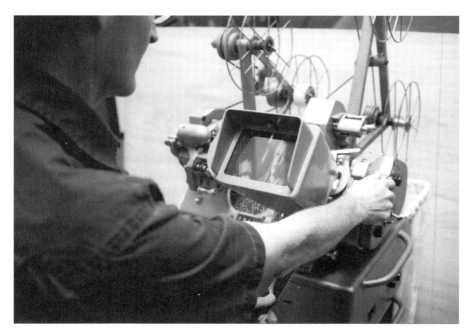

Hollywood upright Moviola, little changed since its introduction in 1930 (Courtesy of Salon Ltd, London)

The flatbed was the first innovation which was important because of the ability to sit with the director without the clackety-clack of the Moviola, or having always to go into the theatre to see reels. That was a big advance, actually.

The standard practice had been for the editor to work alone (with assistants) and to show the edited reels to the director in the viewing theatre. The director would then give the editor notes of recommended changes, and these alterations would be made back in the cutting room, and re-evaluated during cutting and subsequent projection. It was rare for the director to oversee the immediate editing process in the cutting room, and so the relationship between editor and director was often rather detached. Some editors have argued that this additional 'space' allowed them more autonomy in the cutting process, but this would also depend on the working preferences of individual directors and editors. It is certainly true that the small viewing screen of the Moviola, with its standing operation, discouraged joint working, and the arrival of the Steenbeck and KEM flatbed editing tables, with their larger screens, encouraged the director to spend more time with the editor. Film engineer and Steenbeck agent Mel Worsfold considers that by 1970 the Steenbeck was the preferred tool of many editors, but also acknowledges that the Moviola was (and still remains for some),

> an editor's machine. That's the reason a lot of editors still use a Moviola, because they can keep the director's head out of the way. They can stop the director getting too involved in the cut. The Steenbeck came along and it was perceived as the director's toy because now the director could sit there and see exactly what the editor could.

Jim Clark, looking back to his time cutting *The Innocents*, compared working on Moviolas with present practices encouraged by both Steenbecks and modern computerised editing systems: 'Like all directors of that period, [Clayton] rarely appeared in the cutting room. We didn't have at that time what we have now, which is a sort of constant presence in the cutting room of the director.' When working on *The Saint* television drama series in the 1960s as an assistant, Jonathan Morris also remembers the cramped conditions produced by editing on an early version of an upright which 'had a little lens you look through, and only one person at a time could look through as he was pressing the pedals'. For Antony Gibbs, cutting film on the Moviola meant that the work of director and editor took place in the film viewing theatre. Directors only visited the cutting rooms socially:

> I'd say 'I've got a bottle of champagne', and they'd come in and have a drink and maybe I'd show them something on the Moviola, but it was something I'd say [in

passing], 'Well, while you're here' ... They never came into the cutting rooms at all. Tony [Richardson] never came into the cutting rooms. I mean, it just wasn't their sphere, you know. Their sphere was to see it up on the screen and say, 'I don't like this', 'there's a better take of that', and you took your notes.

For a director, the difference between viewing a reel in the theatre and over-seeing the edit in the cutting room could be significant. Rather than offering an opinion in the theatre, working in the cutting room would normally imply a closer involvement in the editing process. Antony Gibbs acknowledges that there are occasionally directors who 'have to be there, who have to say to the editor, "I want you to cut there" '. But he feels, as do many editors, that it is far from ideal and he has largely avoided working in that prescriptive context. To have a director stand over an editor cutting on a Moviola would be both diffi-cult and trying, but where directors and editors have wanted to work in parallel, this has been facilitated by technology, as Gibbs points out: 'I think it's certainly since the Avid, and it may have happened to other editors with the Steenbeck. It's become a habit over here [in Hollywood] and probably in England.' For the director, the move to the cutting room that developed with the arrival of flatbed editing machines during the 1970s introduced a style of working that would become more widespread with the advent of digital non-linear editing (NLE) systems. Technology is only one of the factors here, however. While a number of directors insist on remaining in the cutting room, there are still those who would not wish to 'cramp' the style of an editor, and others who might be pre-occupied with setting up new projects. Editors differ in their views. Although Anne Coates is aware that the introduction of flatbeds like the KEM brought directors into the cutting rooms, she still prefers to edit alone, regardless of technology:

> A Moviola is almost impossible to share with anybody, which was what I loved about it, in that you could cut quietly by yourself. So that when I moved to electronic cutting I couldn't really have anybody sitting beside me because I'm so used to cutting on my own.

Steenbecks became a standard fixture in British television editing during the 1970s but the hold of the Moviola in features post-production was a source of frustration to some editors. Norman Wanstall's letter of resignation to the Guild of British Film Editors offered numerous reasons for leaving the industry, including having to work on what he considered to be a diet of third-rate *Carry On* films; he also mentioned the poor working conditions and having to use Moviolas, which 'still hadn't been re-designed to incorporate the advantages of the Steenbeck' (1978, p. 26). Other editors, however, were still unconvinced of the advantages of the flatbed and Ralph Kemplen felt that although it was a good adjunct to the Moviola, he still 'couldn't actually cut on one' (quoted in Musgrave, 1979, p. 14). Writing to Russell Lloyd in 1977, Reginald Beck complained that:

> Here in Munich, having agreed to work on a Steenbeck, I am struggling to master an impractical machine, with film snapping in all directions. It is hard to convince the locals of the need for simplicity in the tools they work with (1977, p. 8).

The widespread use of Steenbecks in Germany is unsurprising given the machine's Hamburg origins, but the conservatism of many editors in their choice of editing equipment reflects the critical importance of system reliability as well as the slow evolution of mechanical film editing. The few technical innovations there have been required only limited revisions to working practices. Walter Murch has pointed out that although film is a very expensive medium, there is comparatively little professional film equipment in the world, and thus little commercial incentive to improve it (1995, p. 77). The vast majority of research and development has occurred in the production, transmission and reception of global TV, and it is these professional and domestic markets that

Tape joiner or splicer resting on a 35mm Steenbeck flat-bed editing machine (Courtesy of Mel Worsfold Ltd, London)

have forced the pace in feature film post-production. The convergence of film and television technologies has increased the profit potential for equipment manufacturers and software designers, and this has essentially driven the film industry's digital revolution.

The first example of a video image inset into the main television picture was accomplished in 1976 by Quantel, who later pioneered the first digital non-linear editing system called 'Harry' in 1985, followed by systems from Avid and Lightworks, among others (Unattributed, 2002c). Avid, whose name has become synonymous with non-linear editing, sold its early units into the cor-porate and commercials sectors in Los Angeles in the early 1990s before introducing its computer film editing system, the Avid Film Composer, on which Steve Cohen edited *Lost in Yonkers* in 1993 (Hartman, 2000). During the fol-lowing two years, hundreds of feature films for theatrical release were edited digitally, but despite the enormous inroads made by NLE it was not until 1996 that the first digitally edited feature film, *Braveheart*, cut by Steven Rosenblum on Lightworks, received an Academy Award for editing. Film editing, which for a century had relied on manual labour, was now increasingly performed in the digital domain. Discussions about Moviolas versus Steenbecks and various attempts to synthesise film and video technologies were to be overshadowed by

Tariq Anwar in 2003, editing *Sylvia* on a Lightworks non-linear system

the arrival of computer-based editing systems, resulting in significant changes to the editor's working environment. These developments have profoundly affected post-production, and in 1994 a survey based on research undertaken by Chris Thompson for Skillset, the UK's leading media training body, signalled, 'the recognition by broadcast television professionals of a current revolution in the practice of picture and sound editing' (Stafford, 1995, p. 1).

If the impact of new technology was of concern to broadcast television professionals who had already been forced to adapt to numerous changes in film and videotape formats and equipment, the effect on feature film editing practices was even more far-reaching. For many, the rapid transition from what was essentially nineteenth-century technology to that of the twenty-first represented a 'fear of the unknown', according to Jonathan Morris, and some editors considered it to be less a change than a leap into the abyss. Today, non-linear editing (or 'electronics' as described by some film editors) has become the standard for editing feature films, commercials, TV dramas and mini-series, television shows and corporate video. But, as noted in a *Screen Digest* report assessing the impact of digital technology on the British film industry, the changeover from analogue (film) to NLE was remarkable in that 'any economic advantages of the benefits (speed and ease) were not immediately apparent' (2000, p. 24). It was in part the need to be at the cutting edge of technological development that drove post-production companies to make the first massive investments in non-linear systems. The considerable advantages offered by NLE – namely the speed and flexibility of editing on computer discs – were initially accompanied by a sacrifice in image quality and spiralling costs in data storage. Although some of the problems inherent in NLE have been addressed by the computer industry, dissenting voices remain, unconvinced of the improvement to either the overall quality of feature film editing, or to the editor's working environment.

FILM EDITING ON SYNCHRONISERS, MOVIOLAS AND FLATBEDS

Digital technology has generally been welcomed by the industry at large, and many television editors were keen to make the earlier move away from film cutting rooms to cleaner videotape editing suites. In television much of the cutting had been performed on Steenbecks and the British-designed Acmade picture synchronisers, introduced in 1965. The synchroniser (or pic-sync as it is commonly referred to) is a simple but quite ingenious bench-mounted device which consists of a picture viewer and four sound heads across which picture and soundtracks can be manually wound, or driven by an electric motor. Although apparently technically unsophisticated, the pic-sync was preferred as a cutting tool to the Steenbeck by many editors. The infinitely variable speed allowed by manual control offered probably the most tactile relationship between editor, machine and material: the editor could physically sense the rhythm of the cut sequence as it was wound through the small picture viewer. Picture and soundtracks could be locked together, maintaining correct synchronisation (unlike the drift between picture and soundtracks that sometimes occurs on flatbeds), and the physical placement of sound in relation to picture facilitated minute adjustment and experimentation. Editors often preferred to make changes 'on the bench', where precision cutting could be guaranteed. The advantages offered by the Steenbeck and the KEM were more pronounced at the viewing stage, where large rolls could be shuttled quickly forwards and backwards, and an overall sense of timing could be better gauged. Synchronisers, film splicers (joiners), rewinds, Moviolas and, latterly, flatbed editing tables such as the Prevost, KEM and Steenbeck, comprised the standard cutting room equipment that served editors for the best part of a century.

A few distinguished editors still remain sceptical of the advances in non-linear editing systems, and even reject the previous generation of flatbed film editing machines. Gerry Hambling, considered by many of his peers to be Britain's most accomplished editor, still chooses to cut on the Moviola. According to Lesley Walker, American editor Michael Kahn (who has worked for much of his career with director Steven Spielberg) also preferred to work on the Moviola, as did the veteran British editor, Peter Tanner, who considered NLE systems to be 'too mechanical'. One of Britain's best-regarded editors, Tom Priestley, explained his preference for working on the traditional American upright:

> I'm an old Moviola man, but for a very technical reason, which is quite simply this: a Moviola goes backwards and forwards at twenty-four frames per second. I mean alright, there is a picture-only fast forward thing you can do if you're just viewing, but it means that going backwards, going forwards, you're learning the interior rhythm of the shot, and I think that the fault, the disadvantage of a flatbed – never mind tape or anything that you can whizz very fast – is that you are confusing yourself. You are actually giving yourself messages that are unnecessary and unhelpful. If you are learning a shot, you just want to see it, and what happens within it, at the correct speed, so that going back, you're learning it as much as going forwards. And then you are seeing it at the correct speed.

Priestley suggests that editing with a Moviola clarifies cutting procedure by enabling the editor to see the film in terms of its discrete cutting points rather than as a series of endlessly overlapping possibilities, which can be the effect of rolling fast backwards and forwards on flatbeds or computers. The Steenbeck film editing table, like the KEM, though having the advantage of being able to run large rolls of film at variable speeds, has to be slowed down before hitting an exact frame. The immediate hand–eye co-ordination between editor and film is perhaps more easily achieved on a Moviola, through the use of a highly effective braking system. Antony Gibbs was also nostalgic about the accuracy of cutting on the Moviola:

> The most precise editing tool that's ever been invented is the Moviola. It's the only machine that will stop on a frame. It will stop on *that* frame. The Steenbecks and the flatbeds, they go whirr, and so does the Avid. I can do it with the Avid, but I've really got to kick it on the actual frame. I cut a picture in Poland, and all they had there was a Steenbeck. I was obliged to cut on it and hated it, just hated it. The moment they finished shooting and then came back to Twickenham to finish the movie, I just put it on the Moviola and trimmed it up by frames.

Frame-accuracy in editing is of vital importance. Miscutting by a few frames can be significant in action sequences, and for editing dialogue, precision is essential. A scene that was consistently two or so frames 'out' for its total duration would quickly look sloppy to the practised eye, and the necessity for maintaining exact synchronicity between picture and sound is self-evident.

A feeling for editing rhythm may be more easily achieved by standing at a pic-sync or a Moviola, rather than by sitting at a flatbed, or at a computer where cutting remotely through a keyboard and mouse makes the relationship between film and editor far less physical. The introduction of a variable speed lever (similar to that used by the Steenbeck) to control the running speed of the digitised film was a tacit acknowledgment by the Lightworks company that the keyboard-intensive operation of non-linear editing systems was not popular with many film editors. But even the flatbed editing table, though able to accommodate larger rolls of film than the Moviola, was compromised as an editing tool, according to Tom Priestley. Steenbeck had patented a revolving polygon, which back-projected the film image onto a large ground glass screen, the quality of which caused Priestley some problems:

> Flatbeds, wonderful for viewing material. If you've got a reel you want to look at, terrific. The other thing about it is that with a Moviola there's light, film, lens – so you are genuinely seeing the light coming through the film. Now the flatbed is a series of mirrors, so that the image is not as sharp. I can see more on a Moviola with a [screen of] three inches square. I can see more detail than I can see on a Steenbeck screen which is perhaps four times as big, because there is a kind of cloudiness about it.

The direct transmission of light through photographic emulsion – best achieved with a light-box – allows the most critical reading of film tonalities. Many editors (including Rawlings and Audsley) look at the actor's eyes to cue their editing, difficult to do when the film image is degraded. The relatively small, though sometimes crucial, differences in image quality between flatbeds and Moviolas were insignificant when compared to the problems posed for editors by the pixellated images from the first generation of computerised editing systems, produced in the late 1980s and early 90s. According to Avid engineers, due to their poor image resolution the early machines were only considered acceptable for television editing, where the use of close-ups predominated: 'The Avid was much better for TV rather than film. You couldn't even see a person's mouth move if the shot was too wide' (Hartman, 2000). The quality of picture was to improve dramatically, but many editors had started to run conformed 35mm film edits copied from the computer-generated electronic versions as a visual check, before finally having the negative cut. Mel Worsfold noted how the initial enthusiasm of many editors (and producers) to get to grips with the newly emerging computer editing systems was to be qualified by the experience of working with them:

> A big picture, a Bond-type picture, would have had three Steenbeck tables, three complete cutting room kits, on the picture for six to nine months. Today they'll have £1.5 million of networked computers and massive storage banks, and they will still have two Steenbecks. Now, that really tells you what is happening in film cutting rooms. If they didn't need those two Steenbecks, they wouldn't have them. And it's not simply to see the results of their cut. It's clearly to do fine cutting, because they've also got synchronisers, they've got joiners. They're working with it. And it's because of this requirement to dovetail in film, to see it optically, to be able to fine cut it. It's still a necessary requirement to produce a good result. And actually on one of the Bond pictures, they did not do that, and they suffered.

Film's continuation as a medium of image acquisition and distribution, although challenged by the digital revolution, still requires the assistance of machinery that has evolved over the last hundred years. What has changed is the value allocated to it: the hire of a film cutting room for one week is now equivalent to the cost of a few hours' editing on a high-end non-linear system.

CROSSING OVER TO NON-LINEAR

After cutting on film for many years, Mick Audsley was an enthusiastic convert to non-linear editing. He had hoped to cut *Twelve Monkeys* digitally, but the cost at that time (1995) was prohibitive:

It would have been perfect for that film, but that wasn't possible. That was just the nature of the financial aspect of editing the film. Crossing over – initially I found it very difficult to read a movie off a television screen, because I'd spent ten or fifteen years looking at Moviolas and Steenbecks. What's going on in people's eyes, and all that, reads so perfectly. So that [loss of] quality is the disadvantage [of TV monitors] – still.

The image degradation resulting from transferring 35mm film to videotape, and then into the computer, required Audsley to make notes from the original film rushes. The final check was to screen the cut material, conformed back to 35mm film, in a viewing theatre: 'I would never judge a film off tape. I've got to sit in the movies and watch this big great thing going through, rolling by, to be sure of how it's going to read.'

Terry Rawlings at first moved reluctantly from the Moviola to a Lightworks non-linear editing system, using the same medical metaphor as a generation of television editors who made the change from film to videotape:

Having the operation, the lobotomy? I didn't want to do it at all, though I'm glad I did. But I decided to take some time off, and I haven't a clue how the machine works at the moment. I was talking to Jim Clark who said, 'I take two or three months off, I go back and I think, what do I press to start now?' And the crazy thing is we never forget how to use the Moviola, cut film, work synchronisers.

Lesley Walker's initial response to working with the new systems was not entirely favourable, and she remarked on the notorious difficulty of judging the correct timings for cutting points, one of the most important aspects of an editor's work, as well as relating parts of the edit to the whole:

I have to say I think the timings change [on non-linear] ... I was one of the last people to go over to it ... I don't bother with half the buttons, I mean who needs them? I wondered what was worrying me when I first started, and it's that I can always tell how long something is by just looking at it. You can't do that on Avid. I'd be cutting something on film and I'd look back on the bench, and look at the next cut. I wouldn't even have to put it up and say, 'Oh, that's fine'. I mean [I could judge it] within a few frames. I'm afraid I still like film.

Editors of Walker's standing were able to continue working on film, despite the advent of NLE. Reports that initial problems with non-linear systems had caused a reversion to cutting on film were confirmed by Walker: 'Spielberg's editor [Michael Kahn], he reverted to film. There's several that did. If I said to Richard [Attenborough], "I want to cut on film", he'd be quite happy.'

Anne Coates has cut numerous films on Avid, but was careful at first to integrate the Moviola into the new electronic environment, for reasons of familiarity and reliability:

> I think Avids are only a tool and it was really when I started to realise that they were just a tool like a Moviola that I stopped fighting them. I had quite a difficult time going from the Moviola and the KEM onto them. Because I was really cutting on the Moviola still. You know, my first cut.

For Tony Lawson, the initial uncertainty of working with non-linear systems was short-lived, and he found that working electronically on Lightworks retained some of the advantages of film editing on a Moviola, in contrast to the problems he had encountered when working on Steenbecks. The common requirement to choose takes and join them together on a long roll can make editing unwieldy on the Steenbeck, as well as forcing the editor to make what might be premature decisions in selecting material:

> If I was working on a Moviola the film would be broken down into slates and takes. If I'm working on electronics it's the same, in a sense. They're broken down into individual sections. You've got to select, working on a Steenbeck. I did work on one film on a Steenbeck, and that was *Barry Lyndon* with Stanley [Kubrick] and even he found it impossible. We ended up with something like five Steenbecks in the room, with one Steenbeck having all the material for one character in a scene, and the next Steenbeck having all the material for another character, and so on, so we could constantly refer to all the material. But if you've got one Steenbeck, it's desperately limiting ... I work in individual takes as opposed to a roll, but I'm always looking at the material. I like working on a Lightworks, and that does allow you to see individual takes, even if it's just a little frame to remind you they're all there.

The advantages offered by disc-based computer editing include the ability to quickly modify a cut, experiment with different versions, along with the substantially increased speed of accessing and extending shots without having to ask an assistant editor to search for a few frames of a shot extension. These benefits also relate to sound editing, and the freedom to make a preliminary sound mix without having to go into a dubbing studio adds to the convenience of working digitally. For Lawson, the introduction of NLE systems like Lightworks has been of immense benefit: 'It has tremendous potential for what I think editing is about. To be able to re-shape a film, and look at it immediately is just extraordinarily helpful.'

Jim Clark retains little nostalgia for cutting on film. His first film on Avid was *Nell* (Michael Apted, 1994), which needed networked computers:

> We needed four machines all joined up. So I had to learn the Avid. I took to it very quickly. There's no way I would ever go back to film. I don't think I could cut on film any more. And furthermore, I quite believe that if I'd had these machines in the days of *The Killing Fields*, I would have had a better result.

SOME ADVANTAGES OF NON-LINEAR – AND SOME DRAWBACKS

For an outsider the scene inside a traditional film cutting room, often not more than twelve feet square, might suggest a tiny museum devoted to relics of industrial archaeology. Film students are often sceptical when told that the mechanical devices in front of them are responsible for post-producing most of the films that have been made to date, and that the picture quality of footage emanating from a 35mm cutting room is superior to that produced by state of the art digital video cameras and computers. They also question the laborious nature of the work that takes place there, the arduous rewinding of thousands of feet of film, and they look in disbelief at the antiquated rubber-numbering machines, introduced in 1932 to stamp synchronising code along the edges of both film and soundtrack (see Chapter 3).

Mick Audsley began by editing British Film Institute productions without having to serve the obligatory number of years as an assistant film editor. He is ambivalent about cutting film the old way:

> I'm happy to see the thing go. It was great while it lasted. I enjoy handling film, but the crick in your neck or keeping things in sync, the fact that your mind would race ahead and it would take you a long time to catch up to realise what you had imagined. Now you can free think it straight there, and you're not worrying about the physicality of it. It's great. I love it.

Electronics have liberated him from the physical drudgery of working with the sheer weight of 35mm film rolls.[1] This has increased the creative energy and editing opportunities available to him:

> The fact that you can skip through the tapes very quickly rather than winding them [35mm film rolls] all down is fantastic. I mean it literally is twice as fast. To assemble a scene in a day would now literally take me half a day … Before I would be on my knees by the end of the day because just physically handling it would be so time-consuming.

For some editors, however, the sheer operational convenience and speed of computer-based editing undermines a cardinal virtue of working film the old way: the opportunity for 'thinking time'. The time taken to rewind film, to lace it up on a Steenbeck, to find extensions or file film off-cuts in a trim bin, allows the editor a space to ponder and deliberate. These laborious mechanical processes often discouraged premature editing decisions, unlike the electronic process of laying shots down first and changing them afterwards. Tom Priestley considered that editing on film offered a more reflective mode of working:

> So, it's time to think. The moment we were doing the physical part was also thinking time. So you're then putting the other versions in your head, and you're thinking – 'actually, instead of starting with her, start with him'.

The breaks from cutting at the bench or Moviola, and moving around the cutting room are for Lesley Walker an essential part of the considered approach she takes to her work, in contrast to the mandatory breaks required while working at a computer:

> Because [electronic editing] is so immediate you sort of rush at it like some lunatic, instead of slowly going through it. It takes your thinking time away and I find that annoying ... I like to look at it and sit and think about it. The Avid and me are not the greatest pals, really, in that way. I do move around, I do take more breaks but it actually breaks my concentration, whereas I would never take a break while I was cutting on film, because my breaks would be wandering over to the trim bin, to put a trim up.

In his role as a film post-production doctor, Stuart Baird recognises the advantages of speed offered by electronic systems, but notes that a radical appproach to re-cutting can make use of more traditional methods. Making a colour or black and white film duplicate of the cutting copy, which he likened to making a Xerox, allows him to 'attack' the original edit. For him what is important is not the technology, but the approach. Like Priestley, Baird likes to appraise material as often as he can at a natural film-running speed:

> It's quicker to do certain things but speed is not the essence. As I've said to younger editors working on the Avid stuff, just because you can do certain things, it doesn't mean to say that you have to do them. Think about it. Think – it's much more important than doing. The best impression you're going to get of the film is in the theatre.

Maintaining a critical distance from the edit, rather than being seduced by the speed and digital possibilities offered by an Avid, is crucial to Baird's understanding of the relationship between film editor and audience. How the film looks on a computer screen may be far removed from the effect it will have in a cinema auditorium. The interdependence of scenes and the way the film narrative builds should be assessed on the big screen at twenty-four frames per second, rather than as a series of discretely constructed sequences viewed on a computer. The instantaneous access to any footage stored within computer hard drive systems without having to wind through a large film roll may hasten editing, but according to Baird this also has the disadvantage of removing shots from their context, unlike viewing rushes on a flatbed: 'The Avid doesn't work like that. It means you don't keep analysing the material. As an editor your job, really, is to keep looking at the material. There may be gems in there.'

The rapidity of scanning rushes electronically makes the viewing process more convenient than before. But this increased speed and immediacy may actually reduce an editor's detailed knowledge of the material, previously gained by constantly shuttling through the film rushes. For Mick Audsley, however, time saved from labour-intensive cutting room tasks can be used more creatively, allowing him the opportunity to experiment with different versions of a cut which can then be saved electronically. This becomes a part of his private preparation:

> Sometimes the alternative versions are things which, if you like, I would never share with anybody else. It's just me, like a sketch or using a certain kind of pencil to make a drawing ... It's a wonderful freedom rather than chopping loads of frames up, and knowing I'm going to have to look at all that Sellotape for months on end.

The computer's capacity to store different versions of a cut electronically and to produce immediate optical effects, like a wipe or a dissolve, gives Lightworks and Avid a significant advantage over film editing, which entails waiting for optical effects to be processed in the laboratory. Terry Rawlings found that Lightworks facilitated his characteristic use of long dissolves:

> The thing I like about it is you can experiment, and you can try things and you can see them before your very eyes. It's like the sequence in *Entrapment*, going under the wires. If I was going through and doing that on film, it may never have happened that way because it would have meant too much expense to check to see if things work. I'd have to do temporary dissolves to see if it looked right. And then you'd say, 'No, it doesn't look right that long, it should be longer, or it should be shorter.'

Most of the editors interviewed, whatever their general feelings about working with electronic systems, agreed that re-editing following the first cut was made much easier by working digitally. Jim Clark felt that the flexibility of electronic editing helped to resolve differences of opinion between director and editor, particularly because the system can store both a director's and editor's preferred version of a cut sequence. These can then be compared, and from them a third 'amalgamated and adjusted' version can be created (see Chapter 2). This is one of the reasons why Clark is 'totally converted to digital. It's the most forgiving machine a film editor could ever wish for.' This facility to synthesise the creativity of editor and director affirms what is best about post-production. But, as Terry Rawlings points out, digital editing has an amenability to endless modification and change which can introduce problems previously discouraged by the comparative intractability of film:

> It's got built-in indecision. And it doesn't come from the editor. It comes from the director, or the producer – 'Let's try a bit of this.' And it gets to the point where you don't know whether you're coming or going because you have so many choices. You've got to be strict with yourself. I'd keep three things. I would chuck the rest, or file it into the boys' [assistant editors] room, so it would still be with me. If you have too many things to look at, you get so confused.

The perception of non-linear editing's increased speed in particular has influenced the amount of re-cutting expected of an editor. This has not, however, as Mick Audsley points out, succeeded in reducing feature editing schedules:

> We don't make the film any quicker now. In fact I'd say we make them slightly slower. And that's because it's seen as being a medium which is more malleable, is more plastic, and everybody gets involved. They will request many more things because the time it takes me to do it is half or less. They are investing less in my time when they ask for these changes.

THE IMPACT OF NON-LINEAR TECHNOLOGY ON EDITING STYLE

Design engineer Mel Worsfold has supplied Steenbeck flatbed editing machines to the British and overseas film industries since his involvement started with the Hamburg-based company in 1967. He has talked to many of the world's leading editors, and has been a keen observer of the impact made by technology on editors' working methods, and how the interaction between editor and machine has affected cutting style. Using an analogy from computer-aided design, Worsfold maintains that it is easier to see the interrelation between the various components of a design on a large drawing board than on a twenty-two-inch computer monitor. Similarly, he considers that the overview an editor needs is better maintained when working on film, a process that starts while viewing rushes:

> Editors can see all of those cuts in their minds beforehand. Then they will make what a lot of students today will think is a quick assembly. But by God it's within a few frames of being right the first time. And then they'll put the Steenbeck into play, and they will stand back from it. They are taking the long view, the audience view, because they know that if you get too close, too intricate, then you're going to miss the overall effect. You can't do that with a computer system, because you are locked into this video game, this business of being locked into a feedback loop ... It says, 'that's your result, try again'.

Worsfold argues that computer editing changes the relationship of the editor to the film being cut, which becomes a series of 'differentiated events' lacking overall integration, and believes that the editor becomes drawn into a kind of stimulus-response cycle similar to that of computer-gaming. The danger of getting too 'intricate', in Worsfold's phrase, and losing an overview is echoed by Tom Priestley, who considers that computer editing can encourage unnecessary elaboration. Priestley believes that what historically distinguished the best of European from American cinema was the former's tendency to work through the audience imagination, whereas the Hollywood approach has always been more of an assault than an invitation. 'It's all there', in Priestley's words. But he has noticed a general increase in ostentatious cutting in both Europe and America, stimulated by the widespread take-up of non-linear editing systems:

> I can spot a film that's been cut with the new technology. It tends to be over-quickly cut and uses too much material. There's an impatience about it in terms of 'we have to keep making it interesting' – sort of adding little bits, because we can do it. It's easy, you just press a button and it happens. It's like nudging the audience all the time – 'Look, now are you looking? Now we're doing this', rather than just letting the audience relax and sort of go with the experience of seeing the film.

The move from cutting on film to non-linear was welcomed by Jim Clark, but despite his enthusiasm for working with the Avid, he is aware that the new technology may be a contributory factor in changing both the nature and pace of picture editing:

I'm still slightly leery of things which are too fast, which are not telling the story in a coherent way. I think the craft of film editing is being debased very largely by people who are misusing these machines. I don't think it's in my nature, personally, to overcut films and make them scrappy and fast and flashy. It isn't me, I can't do it, although on the last James Bond film, *The World Is Not Enough* (Michael Apted, 1999), I tried to make the action scenes as gutsy and as punchy as I could. There's a lot of fast cutting in that film, but I don't think I overcut it. I'd like to think I didn't go too far with it.

Clark's refusal to overcut, despite the ease with which it can be done electronically, underlines his preference for an approach which favours narrative coherence.

American editor Walter Murch considers that the goal of editing is to make as few cuts as possible because 'cutting – that sudden disruption of reality – can be an effective tool in itself' (1995, p. 77). The style of cutting epitomised by *Natural Born Killers* – the first film said to have been edited with the full functionality of the Avid (*Screen Digest*, 2000, p. 24) – appears to contradict Murch's principle, and indeed a number of editors interviewed revealed a particular dislike of the relentless style of cutting which characterises that film. This change in editing style has been identified by both practitioners and film academics as rapid, self-conscious and often obtrusive. The trend is commonly considered to have emerged from the 'post-classical' period of American film-making following the demise of the studio system in the 1960s, and is widely held to consist of a 'fragmentation of style and a reduction in narrative coherence' (Bordwell, 2002, p. 16). Although scholars disagree about the extent to which film aesthetics have changed in the past forty years, there is little doubt that the rate and visibility of cutting has increased. This is more easily accomplished on non-linear editing systems which, in addition to making straight cuts easier, also allow instantaneous access to digital effects: mixes, dissolves, wipes, freeze-frames, filters and a myriad of others – all previously impossible to use on film without lengthy laboratory processes.

The rapid adjustments enabled by non-linear editing have led to a phenomenon called 'frame fucking', where shots are shaved a frame at a time, leading to a highly accelerated pace of cutting (Bordwell, 2002, p. 23). This can produce disastrous results when played on the big screen, as American film academic David Bordwell recounts: 'After cutting the car chase from the *The Rock* (1996) on computer, [director] Michael Bay saw it projected, decided that it went by too fast, and had to "de-cut" it' (p. 23). British-born editor Peter Honess has similarly observed that a lot of films are 'far too choppy' when cut using a computer monitor, and he is therefore cautious when judging the timing and rhythm of shots destined for cinema projection (Honess, 2002).

The importance of screening the cut has become rather more important in non-linear editing because of problems inherent in working from a video image transferred from film. Cutting decisions made on Lightworks or an Avid can prove misleading, as post-production engineer Mel Worsfold explains.

> It's a basic fact that whether the image is stored on a computer, or on videotape, at the moment it is being presented through a video-type channel, [there is] a built-in persistence to hold the image ... because it is being scanned in a totally different way. And therefore you've almost got an automatic built-in dissolve. It's a natural one- to one-and-a-half-frame dissolve, which you don't have optically [on film]. The persistence softens the cut.

When this cut is transferred from the computer back to film, what was originally a 'soft' (dissolved) video-edit becomes a hard-edged optical film cut, intensified by the magnification of film projection. John Bloom contrasted the impression gained from the routine projection of film edited sequences at Shepperton Studios, with the surprises produced by projecting a digitally edited film on a big screen for the first time:

> At Shepperton there were lots of smaller rooms you could use if you were wanting to run a little bit. So one's first impression would be on the bigger screen, which was actually quite useful, because the difference between what you see on a small screen or on a television set, and actually running it on a big screen is so huge. I remember the first time running a two-hour cut on the Lightworks [monitor], and I'd fooled myself. We thought it was working pretty well, and it wasn't until a bit later when we ran it in the theatre, it was a totally different experience ... Your sense of pacing just seems so different when you get it on the big screen.

Some editors still maintain that assessing pace or rhythm is best done using traditional film technology. Gerry Hambling has stated his dislike for the style of much modern editing, which he considers is comprised primarily of 'quick flashes', and admits that he gets 'livid with television where you can tell the Avid influence' (quoted in Young, 1999). Although recognising the speed advantages offered by non-linear, Hambling notes that the more premeditated approach to the overall arc of cutting may in the long run save time in the post-production schedule. There seems little chance in the near future that Hambling, described by Tony Lawson as 'high on the list of practitioners who will be remembered', will abandon his preferred mode of cutting on a pair of Moviolas.

Stylistic changes in film-making are the result of a multiplicity of factors and extend well beyond the domain of editing, into the fields of camera support, lens design, film emulsion technology, trends in television production, and stylistic influences from commercials and music videos. Tony Lawson considers MTV and television video editing to have been a significant influence in accelerating the pace of feature film editing, and noted that the trend for faster cutting preceded the introduction of non-linear editing in the early 1990s. In the 1960s a more primitive order of technology may also have influenced the aesthetics of editing. Lawson points out that the appearance of a new design of film splicer – used for cutting and joining film – may have contributed to changes in editing style: 'In terms of editing techniques, and going back to *Performance* and *Bonnie and Clyde*, it was round about that time that the splicer changed, and I wonder whether that had some bearing on style and experimental editing.'

The Italian CIR transparent tape splicer, introduced in 1964, had the advantage of allowing tape joins to be quickly made and unmade, unlike previous models of splicer which overlapped the adjacent frames of the edit with a permanent cement join. With cement joins, re-cutting would entail either losing frames or re-printing film, which discouraged making changes to the original cut. The tape or butt splicer, by contrast, encouraged experimentation. Barry Salt's analysis of film style and technology shows almost a doubling in the percentage of six-second duration shots, and a halving of the rate of ten-second shots in American productions between 1964 and 1969, compared with 1958 to 1963 (Salt, 1992, p. 266). The tape splicer's ease of operation may have been a contributory factor here in increasing the rate of cutting. Certainly the American editor of *Jaws* (Steven Spielberg, 1975) Verna Fields, interviewed in 1977, considered the introduction of the butt splicer to have been the most important development in film editing since the 1960s, freeing the editor 'to try different possibilities for cuts' (quoted in Sharples Jr, 1977, p. 25).

Statistical evidence is hard to come by, but it would appear that the advent of digital technology may have short-circuited the training of feature film editors. There is likely to be an increasing number who have television, commercials and pop promo editing backgrounds, blurring traditional demarcations between various sections of the industry. Antony Gibbs, one of the great innovators in British cinema, sees problems for this new generation of editors, arising from the fast career-tracking encouraged by the widespread use of electronics:

> The standard of film editing and presentation of films nowadays has fallen dramatically. I've walked out of some movies because they've been so badly edited. I just cannot take the irresponsibility of somebody who has no control over a scene in terms of timing or presence of an actor, and one sees that more and more today. I see it now, whereas I wouldn't see it ten years ago.

Generalised concerns about the impact of computerisation were expressed by American editor Mary Sweeney, David Lynch's collaborator on *Mulholland Drive* (2001):

> I worry that people trained as editors on Avid and other digital systems will not work material as hard as it can be worked. There seems to be a tendency to make quick decisions and quick changes. The process seems to be less thoughtful and have shorter attention spans. [It] feels more restless to me, more agitated (2002, p. 2).

It is too early to know with certainty what stylistic changes have arisen in the change from film to electronic editing. British documentarist and features editor David Gladwell has noted a significant increase in the past seven years in the number of cuts and transitions, which he attributes to digital technology, but is convinced that nothing new has happened in editing that had not already been pioneered by Eisenstein and the experimentalism of the European cinema of the 1960s. Anne Coates has noticed an increase in the speed and visibility of editing, although she cautiously notes that a flamboyant cutting style facilitated by non-linear systems can also be effective:

> It seems to have made a lot of flashy cutting. I'm not against flashy cutting, it can be great. But I don't see the point of a lot of cuts where you don't see what's happening at all. I think that's going over the top with this, and it's very easy to do it on these machines.

Like Jim Clark, Anne Coates ultimately believes that the requirements of storytelling and narrative clarity precede editorial self-indulgence, although she has displayed a readiness to use freeze-frames, jump-cuts and time-shifting when appropriate in *Erin Brockovich* and *Out of Sight*, both edited electronically.

A revealing stylistic comparison between film and electronic styles of editing, spanning fifty years, can be made by examining Ralph Kemplen's elegant, understated but impeccably timed editing of *Moulin Rouge*, the opening sequence of which he rates as one of his best (quoted in Sharples Jr, 1977, p. 13), and Jill Bilcock's later version for director Baz Luhrmann, where the velocity of cutting can be both breathtaking and disorientating in equal measure. One inherent defect of non-linear systems observed by some editors – the reflexive, agitated style of cutting it appears to encourage – can be turned to advantage. The success of *Trainspotting*, one of the highest-grossing UK films in the history of British cinema, is partly due to the energy of its editing by Masahiro Hirakubo, whose display of editing virtuosity also respects the self-effacing subtleties of classical film cutting. He is more than prepared to slow the pace where the narrative demands, and his discriminating approach may reflect his long experience at the BBC, cutting a diverse range of programmes from current affairs to drama. Stuart Baird has compared the 'wonderful, fresh and interesting' style of *Trainspotting* to the peaks of British 1960s film innovation, but adds that it was the only film of that calibre in a decade of British film-making: 'Maybe all that energy has now gone into MTV or commercials or rock videos.'

Despite Jim Clark's earlier admission that *The Killing Fields* would have benefited from being edited on an Avid, he does suggest that in the end the creativity and the craft of the editor should transcend technology, especially in relation to non-linear editing:

> Of course, there are always disadvantages, like it's too easy, or anyone can do it. That is one of the disadvantages, but I still believe that no matter what system you're using, whether you are on an Acmiola with a bull's eye magnifying glass or whether you are on the most sophisticated Avid, that the mind, the mentality of the film editor still has to be properly used.

THE NEW EDITING ENVIRONMENT

The Moviola required an assistant to be constantly on hand to rewind shots for the editor, and to pass over the shorter film lengths which needed to be fed separately into the machine. Film editing also required assistants for synchronising and coding rushes, laboratory liaison, and for generally running the cutting rooms. The editorial department post-producing on film typically consisted of an editor, a first and second assistant, a third assistant/trainee, along with a sound editor, assistants and additional specialist music and dialogue editors on larger productions. The value of this working arrangement was that assistants could observe the film editing process at first hand and, if they were fortunate, cut sequences under editorial supervision. There have been many successful pairings of editors with assistants who, in their turn, have become highly regarded in the industry: Antony Gibbs assisted Ralph Kemplen, Jim Clark worked for Jack Harris, Anne Coates assisted Reginald Mills and John Seabourne, Lesley Walker trained with John Bloom. During a fifteen-year apprenticeship, Peter Honess was mentored by Antony Gibbs and Thelma Connell: 'Thelma was quite an extraordinary woman,' recalls Honess, 'I was absorbed by how she edited. She cut very, very fast. That was also true of Tony [Gibbs]. He'd cut the film in his head at dailies' (quoted in *Unattributed*, 2002a). The combined talents of Connell, who edited *Alfie* (Lewis Gilbert, 1966), and Gibbs – whose ability to mentally construct sequences at rushes viewings must have impressed directors he worked with – provided Honess with an editorial lineage and quality of training difficult to equal. What concerns Honess now is that the film editing skills passed on so generously to him are less easily transmitted in the digital editing environment, where the role of the assistant editor is much less concerned with the immediate cutting process than before:

> I do quite a lot of talking at seminars and universities, and everybody asks how the assistants learn to edit. It's gotten harder now, because when I cut on an Avid, what can an assistant be doing in the room? They don't have time to sit and watch, and sadly, you don't need them there to help, like you used to (Honess, 2002).

By working in the same room as the editor, even the process of filing trims was turned to good advantage by an ambitious film assistant, who could learn how a scene had been constructed from various takes:

> You knew, because you had to put the bloody stuff away. And you learned by osmosis. Every time you put a piece of film away, you realised what he was using, and every time you pulled a trim out, you were part of the process that was going through the editor's head. Unfortunately, we're not able to do that now. It's a major responsibility for all of us editors – how do we pass the craft on? It's all done so quickly now and you're not going to be sitting at an Avid explaining every cut (Honess, 2002).

The skills base of feature film editing has been fundamentally changed by the introduction of new technology. One of the cost advantages to a production, apart from the increased speed of cutting, is the increasing redundancy of the traditional roles of the assistant. In the digital environment editor and assistant rarely share the same work space, and sometimes not even the same working hours. On a low-budget production the assistant editor may be brought in at night to digitise rushes into the computer, which will save the cost of having to hire an additional NLE system. Unsurprisingly, younger assistants entering the industry have shown less interest in film and laboratory processes, though this is still very much required, as noted by Lesley Walker:

> You still need the other basic film technology, and a lot of them that are coming in do not have that, and some don't want to actually. I mean, they buy the computer, being of a computer age. Fascinating, I'm not denying it, but they are not that interested in the physical side of film-making . . . My first [assistant editor] actually is very film-minded, and he teaches the younger assistants about film, like rushes, etc. But very few second assistants at the moment know how to sync up rushes on film.

For many high-ranking features editors with traditional film editing backgrounds, the technical reliance on assistant editors in the digital domain has
actually increased. Whereas previously the editor could have performed the
assistant's basic chores, the new editing environment requires a different set of
skills. Although many assistants may not have had film training, their increased
levels of computer literacy nevertheless make them indispensable to their editors, as Mick Audsley acknowledges: 'I'm much more reliant on them now
because of the digital technology. I just haven't come from that background.'
Those assistant film editors who have not converted to working on electronics,
through choice or circumstance, face a bleak employment future, however. One
film director, well aware of the changed working circumstances of the new
digital environment, still prefers to cut on film, which suits editor Jonathan
Morris:

> When I work with Ken [Loach], we work on film. But it's rare. I mean people
> walk past our door, and say, 'Oh film, look at that'. It's exotic now. And I have two
> assistants. My brother works with me, and I have another assistant, and they only
> work, virtually, when I am working on film with Ken. So they work for about eight
> months out of every eighteen. Ken likes people around. I think there is a slight
> worry of the unknown, and I don't think he finds the Avid environment very
> friendly … And I won't talk him out of it, because I enjoy working on film from
> time to time, and also I'd put my brother out of work, and my other assistant out
> of work for ever.

An inevitable and unfortunate consequence of the tide of new technology driving film post-production is the loss to the British film (and television) industry
of a number of highly gifted film and sound editors who did not want, or were
not easily able to make, the transition brought about by the digital revolution.
As previously noted, it is probably the editorial department that has been most
affected by these changes, and any diminution of the skills base gives cause for
concern, especially in relation to bigger-budget productions where experience is
at a premium. The collapse of domestic feature production by 40 per cent
between 2001 and 2002 underlines the importance of inward investment to the
British film industry, historically prone to economic instability and the lure of
Hollywood, which continues to attract its best technicians (Minns, 2002, p. 1).
There is a compelling requirement to create a new generation of British editors
who have absorbed traditional editing skills but who are also digitally compet-
ent. Steven Spielberg has often complimented the high standards of British film
crews, and the continuing availability of technicians of the calibre of BBC-
trained Frances Parker, who edited an award-winning episode of Spielberg's

production *Band of Brothers*,[2] is contingent on nurturing and retaining the UK's world-class skills base.

NON-LINEAR EDITING AND THE WIDER CONTEXT

The move to digital editing has allowed a wider access to post-production, displacing the once exclusive film technology. When editing on film, producers or actors would visit the cutting room, where the film could be discussed with the editor. Increasingly requests are now made for multiple copies of the edit, from people further removed from the cutting process but still wanting to influence its outcome, as Mick Audsley points out:

> Before, they used to come in, sit down, lace the film up. Now tapes fly around the world, and I'm nervous of what that is. And the way in which responses come back based on those sorts of perceptions is worrying to me.

John Bloom's experience of editing on both the East and West coast of America signals a change in working conditions, and he echoes Audsley's concerns about the increased pressures placed on directors and editors:

> You're up against the technology, which allows everybody to have their little say. And that doesn't merely mean people sitting around an Avid. It means continuously having to send out videos. And believe me, it doesn't just go to the studio. It goes to the producer, then the producer's wife, and then the producer's student son. Everybody is able to put in their twopenny-halfpenny's worth. That's one of the worst things with it.

In contrast to computer-based systems, the physical editing of film was considerably more specialised, which for Bloom retained certain advantages:

> You know, there was always a mystique [on film]. Let's face it, every editor, if they haven't wanted to do something – particularly for producers, who are usually the natural born enemy most of the time – always managed to find some excuse. You know, 'Well, I can do this, but it's going to take a week, and it's not going to work', and you can talk them out of it. You can't do that on these machines. Everybody knows how quick it is. You can't *not* try something for somebody. You have to do it.

Lesley Walker agrees that the convenience of electronics has increased the access of producers (and directors) to the immediate cutting process:

> On re-cutting, the Avid is a great advantage if you want to start swapping stuff around all over the place. It takes, you know, three seconds. It's not putting a reel

of film up, taking something out, pulling it about. And it's far easier for the producer, and it's easier for the director. It's a producer's tool more than it is anybody else's tool, because before, when it was film, they didn't get so involved with it because it was on a Moviola – and a Steenbeck if you were lucky – and it's not the same thing.

The reluctance of an editor to respond to every idiosyncratic suggestion from beyond the cutting room found a natural alibi in the intractability of film – the time taken to find picture and sound extensions, make adjustments to the soundtrack and rearrange the order of edited sequences. This also protected the editor from accusations of preciousness. But more importantly, it helped protect the cut agreed by editor and director from front-office pressures, as Bloom explains:

> Unless a director is very strong, and can keep producers away, it's becoming more and more a producers' [and] studio medium ultimately, which it is on the big Hollywood film. Horrible. It's changed so much. Nowadays, everything is governed by previews, and preview results.

For Antony Gibbs, now resident in California, there has been a decline in the overall status of the feature film editor compared to his previous experience in the UK, as a result of the increased complexity of digital technology, and the larger budgets and crews available to Hollywood productions:

> The finishing of a film has now become terribly complicated with the advent of the Avid and the computer. Somehow, that has made the presence of the editor decline quite a lot in the last few years. Here [in Hollywood] the picture editor's domain has become that much smaller than I was used to in England. As far as I was concerned, I was responsible for everything that happened once the picture came off the floor.

John Bloom, too, regrets the way in which editing has become an increasingly homogenised process. The uniqueness of each film he once cut, with directors like Karel Reisz, has been sacrificed to the preview-driven electronic production line:

> Really the editor nowadays is fighting a rearguard battle in simply trying to preserve things. Trying somehow to preserve the integrity of the film and not simply turn it into what is so often seen as a piece of commerce. The pleasure syndrome is very much gone. Too many pressures.

THE FUTURE OF EDITING

The transition from film to digital editing will almost certainly be followed by the eventual demise of film as both an acquisition and distribution medium, for reasons of cost and convenience, if not yet of quality. The significant advantage of image resolution that film still possesses over high-definition digital video (calculated to be 4,000 rather than 1,000 lines)[3] ensures the continuation of some film editing technology for the foreseeable future (*Screen Digest*, 2000, p. 17). Film still needs to be dovetailed back into cinema post-production for final negative cutting, as well as being projected at various stages to check both the quality and progress of editing, regardless of whether it is being cut electronically or on film.

Despite the prestige of film and the large community of specialist film technicians, rapid improvements in the quality of high-definition video technology and the inherent cost savings have produced a shift away from shooting on film[4] for American TV series for example, a trend that seems certain to affect cinema production (Mitchell, 2002, p. 6). Distinctions between amateur and professional equipment have been blurred by the widespread uptake of the DV format, which has come to replace 16mm film as the preferred low-budget alternative to 35mm film. In 1999 10 per cent of the submissions for the Los Angeles Film Festival were on DV; by 2001 this had risen to 60 per cent (*Screen Digest*, 2000, p. 7). The market share of very expensive digital editing systems such as Avid and Lightworks is now being challenged by much cheaper systems from Media 100, Apple Macintosh's Final Cut Pro and Pinnacle, which can be bought for a few thousand pounds. The availability to secondary-school students of entry-level computer editing packages like iMovie, combined with the decline of traditional film editing apprenticeships and the reduction of broadcast training, means that film schools and media courses will become more significant in the future training of editors, along with a myriad of post-production houses and small editing boutiques. The preservation of editing guild standards is something that concerns Antony Gibbs:

> The only problem now, of course, is that anybody can do it, and they all think they can. And now that the new iMac [computer] has a film editing disc that goes with it, in about ten years' time you're going to have eighteen-year-old kids saying 'I've been cutting for the past ten years, and here's my work and I can do it.' So, I'm worried about the future of film editing.

For many practitioners, much of the exhilaration of film production comes from the exacting skills level demanded, as well as from the contribution they make to a collaborative process. It has been argued in this book that one of the most important and most frequently overlooked of these collaborators is the editor. But as technology moves away from the exclusive province of film, many of the distinctive craft skills relating to film editing are becoming either devalued or redundant. Critiques that have proposed film-making as an individualised, authorial activity may to some extent be realised before long. Directors who might never have touched a Moviola are now editing their own films and operating their own cameras – both made possible by the introduction of digital technology. Tariq Anwar, when taking over post-production on *American Beauty*, noted an enthusiasm for computer editing shown by Sam Mendes, new to film directing: 'Of all aspects of making a film, Sam openly admits the most surprising and most rewarding is editing.' Director Steven Soderbergh used a semi-professional DV camera to personally shoot *Full Frontal* (2002), which was edited by Sarah Flack on one of the less expensive editing systems, Final Cut Pro.

Combining writing, editing, directing and camera is clearly an enticing prospect for young film-makers. Students on media courses are often encouraged to illustrate theoretical models in their practice, and many of the presumptions of film theory (including the primacy of the director) are reflected in student productions. At the University of Westminster, Joost Hunningher has reflected on the problem this poses in preparing students for a media career, and how it can detract from the valuable experience of student collaboration:

> In our culture there is a romantic perception that commercial and experimental films 'authored' by one writer/director are artistically superior to those made by collaboration. Many film courses encourage this perception by promoting the model of 'the total film-maker' or student 'auteur' in their teaching programmes (2000, p. 172).

The problem presented by the auteur model, particularly for the teaching of editing as a distinctive practice, is compounded by the technological changes affecting the professional training of future generations of editors and assistants. Lesley Walker has noticed a declining interest in learning the art and craft of editing at film school:

> Most of the people doing their little films there weren't interested in editing. All of them wanted to be directors, or writer-directors. Editing wasn't anything they were interested in until you showed them – maybe it's part of the teaching, I don't know – until you showed them what you could do as an editor.

Director Stephen Frears, who has always acknowledged the importance of collaboration in film production, reported on his experience of working with students at the National Film and Television School:

I was asked to talk to students about collaboration, but I could not think why it had to be talked about. It seemed so obvious. However, I have noticed that students find it very, very difficult. I suppose this is because of thirty-five years of the 'auteur' theory (quoted in Ross, 2000, p. 37).

One of the film editor's most important collaborators has always been the assistant. Much of the work previously done by the assistant film editor is now done by computer, while the new responsibilities demanded by electronic editing (digitising rushes, making copies) mean that the editor may now only see the assistant at the end of the working day. Terry Rawlings points out: 'I think it's becoming much more isolated, you're very much on your own now, whereas before you did have your assistants in with you.' Walter Murch values the feedback he has often received from his 'first audience', his assistants, and questioned some aspects of a brave new world where the editor works alone at the computer: 'If this is ever achieved technically, it will be interesting to see the films that result, and to discover whether the collaboration that is the essence of film-making is not in some way compromised by this technical "advance"' (1995, p. 103).

Whatever advantages the new digital systems may offer over cutting on film, narrative skills will continue to be central to the editor's role. For Jim Clark nostalgia for the 'lost craft' of film is misplaced:

If the craft existed because a bit of celluloid was joined to another piece of celluloid, by a bit of plastic, then we have lost it. But I don't believe that's what it was. I think whichever method you use to join one image to another is still a valid method. It's a craft where material exposed to light is crafted into a story of some kind which has a beginning, middle and end. I'm not too happy about it when it doesn't.

The process of finishing a feature film has undoubtedly become more complex, with increasing pressure on editors to acquire new digital skills. However, Tony Lawson is emphatic that one component remains vital to the future of editing:

It has to be storytelling. If you're not telling the story in an involving way, then there is no future. I mean what MTV editing taught us, or should have taught us, is that you can build an enormous edifice to fast cutting, and it will mean absolutely Jack Shit. So you've got to have a point. Whatever you're doing has to have a point. And in that sense, the future is the past. The future is storytelling.

Film editing is beginning to be better understood beyond the cutting room. Michael Ondaatje, who wrote both the novel and screenplay of *The English*

Patient, realised during the film's production that the editing role was of far greater significance than he had previously thought. For Ondaatje (2002b), this role is equivalent in importance to that of the writer and director:

> As Walter [Murch] says, the editor is the only one who sees all of the jigsaw puzzle, and the whole film has to go through this one garden gate, which is where the editor is. Letting some things in, leaving some things out. It just seems to me that those three roles [editor, writer, director] are equal.

Ralph Kemplen, an 'editor's editor' of the old school, described at the end of a distinguished career how he saw the role:

> I think editing is an art form: it's creative within the limitations of the material one's given. I also feel strongly that, next to the writer (whom I'd almost put before the director), the editor is the most important person on the film (quoted in Musgrave, 1979, p. 14).

The opinions of a prize-winning author may carry more weight among academics than the views of Ralph Kemplen, an editor with half a century's experience of cutting feature films, but their conclusions are remarkably similar. Ondaatje (2002b) goes on to say that 'We don't know what the editor does, and we don't really know how to talk about what the editor really does.' Listening to editors – to their own definitions of their role in the film-making process – is an essential step towards understanding and articulating their contribution to the art of film.

NOTES

All unattributed quotations from editors are drawn from the interviews conducted for this book.

1. The rationalisation of the film editing environment by computerisation is illustrated by the storage facility at the British Pathe film archive. The digitised archive now occupies five square feet in their Camden office, in contrast to 10,000 square feet of vaults at Pinewood Studios (British Pathe, 2002).
2. Frances Parker received the ACE 2002 award for the best-edited episode from a television mini-series, for *Band of Brothers* ('Day of Days').
3. Despite the much vaunted superiority of 35mm film over high-definition video for image acquisition (a quality differential of 4,000 to 1,000 lines), an International Telecommunications Union study in 2001 concluded that perfectly exposed and processed 35mm film, when optimally projected in cinemas, produces a resolution of just 600–750 lines (Brennan, 2003, p. 46).

4. Figures derived by Sony from research carried out by BBC Production
   Development suggest that the cost of a sixteen-week shoot for a six- to eight-part
   drama series would be 50 per cent cheaper using a High Definition Sony CineAlta
   camera and HDCAM post-production process, than using 35mm film and Digital
   Betacam for editing. Although these figures should be interpreted with some
   caution, they point to the increasing economic advantages of dispensing with film
   (Unattributed, 2003).

Appendix: Selected Filmographies

The careers of British editors can be related, in general terms, to the distinction between artists and craftspersons, and to issues of class, education and gender. These provide a broad context for the diverse backgrounds, achievements and attitudes of the selected British film editors profiled in this appendix's filmographies.

ART, CRAFT, CLASS AND EDUCATION

Cultural historian Raymond Williams has pointed out that, after the emergence of Romanticism in the late eighteenth century, the previously interchangeable terms 'artist' and 'craftsman' began to acquire different connotations. The 'artist' became characterised 'by an emphasis on sensibility' and genuine creativity, whereas the 'artisan' and the 'craftsman' began to be defined primarily by an 'emphasis on skill' (1958, p. 60). In the early 1930s Adrian Brunel imported these now widely accepted distinctions into his discussion of editing. He suggested that craft and technique relate to the word cutting, and creativity and artistry to editing. For him both were valid as a description of what editors do:

> Use whichever you feel like. If you feel that this is the job of work of a technician who knows and is proud of his craft, then Cutting is a good, workmanlike word. But if you feel that it is something more than just this, if you consider that it is a creative task requiring a more dignified word than Cutting, then you can adopt Editing (1933, p. 94).

Elements of this distinction recurred in many of the interviews given for this book. Some editors took pride in describing themselves as unpretentious technicians, possessing craft skills they had developed over many years. Yet many of the same interviewees also argued that editing involves the sensibility and aesthetic judgment associated since the eighteenth century with the words 'art' and 'artist'. Editors therefore undermine absolute distinctions between the artist and the craftsperson. They simultaneously exercise creativity and technical skills, to the point where it is often impossible to tell when one ends and the other begins. This is one of the central issues raised by Dai Vaughan's biography of British documentary film editor Stewart McAllister (see Chapter 1). Vaughan argues that, because it does not fit neatly into either category, McAllister's career requires new ways of thinking about creative labour within the film industry (1983, pp. 189–94).

Historically, although they have predominantly been white and male, British editors have come from quite diverse class and educational backgrounds.[1] One of the reasons for this diversity is because editing has never been defined as the exclusive domain of either artists or craftspersons. Consequently, some editors have undermined stereotyped expectations, based upon their class and educational backgrounds, of what their capacities are. For example, Teddy Darvas, working as his assistant, registered surprise at the sensibility editor Sid Stone brought to bear on *The Heart of the Matter* (Brian Desmond Hurst, 1954). The initial impression Darvas received of Stone, as a 'cockney' with 'everything outside', led him to assume 'there was no sensitive editor in there'. These preconceptions were shattered when, on a film which was 'a Graham Greene mood thing, his timing, his first cut, it was absolutely brilliant'. Another example is Alfred Roome, an early school leaver who saw himself as quite different from the 'very studious, very academic' Oxbridge graduate editors Thorold Dickinson and Ian Dalrymple. Nevertheless, the lengthy interview Roome gave to the BECTU History Project contains a wealth of fascinating insight, and reveals an editor for whom being 'free to put your own ideas into things' was of crucial importance.

There is a risk that editors like Stone and Roome could be overlooked or undervalued in a historical account of British editing. One of the ways artists' biographies have traditionally been written is to cite ideas and books that have directly influenced them. This approach can be applied, to a limited extent, to editors who have gone through higher education or pursued an interest in intellectual film culture. It does not work especially well for editors whose education has primarily been a practical one. This approach must therefore be combined with careful attention to other processes that are more important for understanding many editors' careers. Assisting and interacting with other editors, and learning through experience, are vital elements of most editors' development. On the naval film *Forever England* (Walter Forde, 1935), for example, Alfred Roome witnessed a type of editing other British editors of his generation might first have encountered reading Vsevolod Pudovkin's book *Film Technique* (1929) or watching *Battleship Potemkin*:

> There was a sequence of a chase by the cruiser after the German one ... And there were the scenes everybody loved doing of the engine room and the stake hold and the pistons going, and all the rest of it, and I remember Otto [Ludwig] cut this so meticulously ... he never showed the outside of the ship, and you could feel it

gathering speed, and by the end of it, you were going flat out. And it was done by
just shortening everything a little – it was so meticulously done … From the time I
met [Otto], my cutting became much better.

Tony Lawson suggests that many editors intuitively reflect on their past practice,
as well as the work of editors they respect, and thereby develop personal rather
than academic theories to guide their future practice. This ongoing process of
reflection provides 'a way into the craft, a way for [editors] to understand what
they're doing', and helps stimulate further creativity. Whatever their background, most of the editors profiled in the filmographies clearly engage in the
reflective process Lawson describes.

WOMEN IN BRITISH EDITING

Film historian Sue Harper has argued that throughout British film history
'women encountered less outright prejudice in editing than in other technical
fields' (2000, p. 231). Anne Coates recalls that, although harbouring ambitions
to direct, she began her career in editing because in the 1940s this was 'what
women could do at that time'. Women have never been adequately represented
in this field, but historically they have had more of a presence in editing than in
cinematography or direction. There is no single reason for this, but several possibilities have been suggested. Coates feels that some women of her generation
make good editors because they are accustomed, in their personal lives, to providing support for others, dealing with the egotism of 'cantankerous
personalities' such as children and husbands, and 'disagreeing in a certain way'
which avoids outright confrontation. Another significant factor is the historical
equation between male and female and public and private spheres. Editors typically operate within a more private space than directors and cinematographers.
The director's authority and cinematographer's mastery of technology are often
publicly displayed. Editors frequently exercise both these functions more dis-
creetly.

The Second World War was a significant period for women training as assistant editors. This arose more from necessity than magnanimity. As Harper points
out, 'conscription was decimating the industry of male workers, and producers
had to make do with what they could get' (2000, p. 234). Thus Freddie Wilson
recalls 'cutting room crews were at a premium during the latter days of the war,
generally they were 100% female' (1979, p. 11). Alfred Roome also noticed that
the number of female assistants increased in the later 1940s and early 50s. By
the 1950s enough women had graduated to becoming editors for director
Muriel Box to operate a policy of employing suitably experienced candidates
whenever she could. Jean Barker edited several films for her, including *The*

Noreen Ackland (r) with assistant editor Alma Godfrey in 1960

Happy Family (1952), *The Beachcomber* (1954) and *Simon and Laura* (1955), and Anne Coates edited *The Truth about Women* (1958). Noreen Ackland enjoyed the friendly and mutually supportive atmosphere Box and Barker generated when she worked with them as a dubbing assistant on films including *Subway in the Sky* (1959) and *Too Young to Love* (1960). Ackland does not describe herself as a feminist but has affirmed sympathy with the argument that women should be afforded the same opportunities as men. She knew of several directors who did not agree with women being employed in the cutting room. When she got her break as editor of *Peeping Tom*, Ackland followed Barker's and Box's policy. She chose Alma Godfrey, 'someone I could trust', as her assistant: 'I could talk to her and she would give me confidence: "Go on Nor. Do it!" she would say.'

On the negative side, Lesley Walker suggests that even into the 1960s 'a lot of [male] editors at that time wouldn't have a woman assistant'. One objection she remembered coming from less progressive members of the 'old school' was 'this thing about not carrying film [due to its weight] and not being able to do the work; it's absolute rubbish actually. You built up a good right arm, got a good workout!' However, for Walker 'that was a different time', and the situation for women editors has improved: 'There are more now of the next generation than there were with me.' Women campaigning within the Association of Cinemato-

graph and Television Technicians (ACTT) for effective implementation of the
Equal Pay Act (1970) and Employment Protection Act (1975) focused attention on this issue, as did the union's publication of a major report on patterns
of discrimination, and its establishment in the early 1980s of the post of Equal-
ity Officer (ACTT, 1983, pp. 73–7). The example set by illustrious predecessors
such as Coates and Walker has also undoubtedly had a positive effect. Very few
male editors would now openly voice the objections Walker occasionally encountered when she began her career. Even fewer women would now define
themselves in the restricted terms accepted by certain assistants Ackland knew
during the 1940s: 'Some girls, if they were working [in the cutting rooms],
didn't expect to do the heavy work as well, they were still dainty ladies.'

Discussions of women in editing sometimes veer into speculation about gen-
dered styles. Film historian Sue Harper ventures a bold generalisation along
these lines:

> In general female editors tend to cut on *mood* rather than action. This makes their
> films run more slowly, but with greater attention to emotional nuance. The films of
> Anne Coates and many other female editors are like this, and they are good at
> respecting expertly timed performances by actors and actresses, rather than
> truncating them. They are qualitatively different from the styles of male editors,
> who are more businesslike (2000, p. 232).

This sort of overarching hypothesis needs to be treated with caution. Harper
implicitly qualifies her generalisation when she praises Coates' particular style as
'buccaneering: wild, adventurous and unpredictable' (p. 231). This aspect of
Coates' style relates to her enthusiasm for direct editing: eliminating fades and
dissolves and truncating action when it is possible and appropriate to do so. It
is a preference she shared with a number of male editors during the 1960s. Many
other factors apart from gender, including broader stylistic developments, production contexts, the specific material being edited, and relationships with
collaborators, need to be considered when assessing any individual editor's work.

FILMOGRAPHIES

Due to limitations of space only features credits have been included here; television work, documentaries and short films have been omitted. For the same
reason directing, producing and other non-editing credits are not listed, and former editors who spent a significant part of their working life as directors have
not been included. Limitations of space also dictate that only a representative
selection of British editors can be profiled. The filmographies included here have
been selected to illustrate a range of different types of career. Inclusion or exclu-

sion does not imply a judgment about the quality of a particular editor's work. Limitations of space also prevent Oswald Hafenrichter and William Hornbeck, the two most significant foreign editors in British film history, from being profiled.[2] Some films are listed twice when more than one editor included in these filmographies has been credited for working on them, or when a supervising editor as well as editor credit has been given. Co-editors are not listed in the filmographics, but every effort has been made to cite them in the main body of the text. All filmographies have been checked where possible.

NOREEN ACKLAND
Called up for war work in 1942, Ackland was placed by Thorold Dickinson in the cutting rooms of the Army Kinematograph Unit. There she began a long stint as assistant to Reginald Mills, following him when he began editing for Michael Powell and Emeric Pressburger during their late 1940s heyday. In the 1950s, when the Archers were less prolific, she continued to work as one of their assistant editors, but also filled in as a dubbing assistant on Rank films including *You Know What Sailors Are* (Ken Annakin, 1954), *Simba* (Brian Desmond Hurst, 1955) and several films directed by Muriel Box. When Mills suffered a heart attack Ackland made a significant contribution to editing *Passionate Summer* (Rudolph Cartier, 1958). Her break came two years later when Michael Powell invited her to edit *Peeping Tom*. After a second film for Powell she edited a Norman Wisdom comedy and three films produced by Virginia and Andrew Stone. Thereafter Ackland abandoned features editing for jobs that allowed her to devote more time to family commitments. She worked intermittently in television, children's films, newsreels, and occasionally as a dubbing assistant on features such as *Nicholas and Alexandra* (Franklin J. Schaffner, 1971).

Filmography
The Secret of My Success (Andrew Stone, 1965)
Never Put It in Writing (Andrew Stone, 1964)
The Password Is Courage (Andrew Stone, 1962)
The Girl on the Boat (Henry Kaplan, 1962)
The Queen's Guard (Michael Powell, 1961)
Peeping Tom (Michael Powell, 1960)

TARIQ ANWAR
Employed at the beginning of his career as a runner and junior assistant director for a small production company, Anwar was drawn to the cutting room which struck him 'as being an altogether more civilised place' than the studio floor. During the late 1960s and early 70s he freelanced as a second assistant editor on films

as diverse as *Cromwell* (Ken Hughes, 1970) and *Au Pair Girls* (Val Guest, 1972). Anwar then moved on to permanent employment at the BBC, being promoted to editor after five years as an assistant. Despite the institution's hierarchical and bureaucratic nature, one advantage at that time was: 'The BBC was a great place to learn and make mistakes and not worry about being sacked.' Like many editors, Anwar felt he was often more 'liberated from the constraints of conventional cutting' on documentaries. One major difference between editing television drama, compared to feature films, was that 'there were again few people, as in documentaries, to defer to: the director, producer and head of department. The cut that left the cutting room was pretty much the one transmitted.'

After such a long time in television Anwar's transition to editing features was not easy: 'Having come out of eighteen years of television, notwithstanding major awards and nominations, I was not acceptable as a movie editor ... I was not studio approved.' For example, Anwar worked with the director Robert Young several times in television, 'yet when he went on to direct features his requests for me were rejected'. The break came when 'Nick [Hytner], with encouragement from producers Stephen Evans and David Parfitt, gave me the chance to cut *The Madness of King George* and the success of that film made me suddenly acceptable.' Since then Anwar has been very active, editing all of the features subsequently directed by Hytner as well as other notable films including *The Wings of the Dove* (Iain Softley, 1997) and *American Beauty*. One of his contributions to the latter film was to work with Sam Mendes on compressing its original ending. This was 'a beautifully orchestrated sequence in terms of design, execution and content ... built solely of tracking shots', but rather too long to retain in its entirety.

Filmography
Sylvia (Christine Jeffs, 2003)
Leo (Mehdi Norowzian, 2002)
Focus (Neal Slavin, 2001)
Green Fingers (Joel Hershman, 2000)
Center Stage (Nicholas Hytner, 2000)
American Beauty (Sam Mendes, 1999)
Tea with Mussolini (Franco Zeffirelli, 1999)
Bodyworks (Gareth Rhys Jones, 1999)
Cousin Bette (Des McAnuff, 1998)
The Object of My Affection (Nicholas Hytner, 1998)
The Wings of the Dove (Iain Softley, 1997)
The Crucible (Nicholas Hytner, 1996)
The Grotesque (Nicholas Hytner, 1995)

The Madness of King George (Nicholas Hytner, 1994)
Under Suspicion (Simon Moore, 1992)

MICK AUDSLEY

Whereas previous generations of editors typically began as assistants, Audsley progressed through a different kind of apprenticeship. After studying at Hornsey College of Art and the Royal College of Art he worked as a sound and then picture editor on various projects for the BFI Production Board. There Audsley encountered Bill Douglas, whom he describes as 'one of the few real poets of cinema'. He learned an enormous amount about the practical aesthetics of editing from working with Douglas on *My Way Home*. On these smaller productions Audsley did every manual task relating to the editing himself. Working on his first 'proper' feature *An Unsuitable Job for a Woman* (Christopher Petit, 1981) involved a process of adjusting to having assistants and being part of a more formal hierarchy. Since then he has established an enduring collaboration with Stephen Frears as well as working with other leading directors.

Before embarking upon a project Audsley reads the script and asks himself the questions: 'Do I want to live with this and take it home with me for a year of my life? Is it the sort of film I care about?' Another consideration is the quality of his working relationship with the director; trust, empathy and supportive frankness are vital factors here. Audsley has great respect for Frears' craft skills, and Frears is a director who has repeatedly acknowledged the invaluable contributions made by his collaborators. Limited budgets dictated that *My Beautiful Laundrette* (1986) and *The Snapper* (1993), both directed by Frears, were shot quickly and 'we didn't spend a lot of time cutting these [television-funded] films'. The craft skills of all involved helped make the most of these limited resources. Audsley particularly enjoyed orchestrating the complex series of looks between several characters after the opening of the laundrette in the earlier film.

Above and beyond the feelings individual sequences can communicate to an audience, Audsley's primary focus is the overall dramatic structure of the film. The narration of pertinent story details was a particular concern during the editing of *Twelve Monkeys*. He was

> continually anxious that it is in the nature of this movie that the 'set-up' of
> information is complex and rather slow, in order for the conflict and resolution, i.e.
> the second half, to work and pay off. Will the movie engage its audience quickly
> enough? (quoted in Petrie, 1996b, p. 142).

More generally, Audsley refers to the crucial process of modulating the emotional 'temperature' of different strands of a film's narrative:

I ask myself 'In this scene, what has changed by the end of it? What's gone up and what's gone down? . . . What's the temperature change?' If I can't explain that or understand it in myself or read it I know there's something not firing right. So I'm asking myself those questions all the time about the dramatic structure.

Filmography
Mona Lisa Smile (Mike Newell, 2003)
Dirty Pretty Things (Stephen Frears, 2002)
Captain Corelli's Mandolin (John Madden, 2001)
High Fidelity (Stephen Frears, 2000)
The Avengers (Jeremiah Chechik, 1998)
The Serpent's Kiss (Philippe Rousselot, 1997)
The Van (Stephen Frears, 1996)
Twelve Monkeys (Terry Gilliam, 1995)
Interview with the Vampire: The Vampire Chronicles (Neil Jordan, 1994)
The Snapper (Stephen Frears, 1993)
Accidental Hero (Stephen Frears, 1992)
The Grifters (Stephen Frears, 1990)
We're No Angels (Neil Jordan, 1989)
Dangerous Liaisons (Stephen Frears, 1988)
Soursweet (Mike Newell, 1988)
Comrades (Bill Douglas, 1987)
Prick Up Your Ears (Stephen Frears, 1987)
Sammy and Rosie Get Laid (Stephen Frears, 1987)
My Beautiful Laundrette (Stephen Frears, 1986)
Walter and June (Stephen Frears, 1986)
Dance with a Stranger (Mike Newell, 1985)
The Hit (Stephen Frears, 1984)
The Terence Davies Trilogy (Terence Davies, 1984)
An Unsuitable Job for a Woman (Christopher Petit, 1981)
My Way Home (Bill Douglas, 1978)

Other editing credits:
Shakespeare in Love (John Madden, 1998) (special thanks to)

STUART BAIRD
While studying for a degree at University College London in the late 1960s Baird attended film screenings and discussions organised at the Slade School of Fine Art by Thorold Dickinson, then Director of Film Studies. His break came when he was appointed assistant to the director on *If . . .* This enabled him to observe

all stages of the production process. He was then employed as assistant editor to Michael Bradsell on films directed by Ken Russell from *Women in Love*) onwards. Baird developed a good working relationship with the mercurial director. Thanks to this, and Bradsell's openness, he found himself at an early stage in his career assisting the director, acting as music editor and editing certain sequences. Baird attributes his decisive approach to editing, his preference for aiming directly for a fine cut, to his unconventional apprenticeship: 'I never worked for those old-time editors who assembled the materials, showed it to the director ... and then tried to tighten it.'

After his first full editing credit for *Tommy*, Baird moved rapidly into working on Hollywood-financed productions and employment in Hollywood itself. *The Omen* (1976) marked the beginning of a long association with director Richard Donner, most of whose action films of the 1980s and 90s he edited. Baird also branched out into second unit directing, producing and establishing a reputation as an effective film doctor. He has edited numerous films produced by Joel Silver. Silver produced Baird's first film as director, *Executive Decision* (1996), an airborne action thriller. Baird continues to work as a film doctor as well as directing. Recent assignments include some doctoring work on *Lara Croft: Tomb Raider* and directing *Star Trek: Nemesis* (2002).

Filmography
Executive Decision (Stuart Baird, 1996)
Maverick (Richard Donner, 1994)
Demolition Man (Marco Brambilla, 1993)
Radio Flyer (Richard Donner, 1992)
The Last Boy Scout (Tony Scott, 1991)
Die Hard 2 (Renny Harlin, 1990)
Lethal Weapon 2 (Richard Donner, 1989)
Gorillas in the Mist (Michael Apted, 1988)
Lethal Weapon (Richard Donner, 1987)
Ladyhawke (Richard Donner, 1985)
Revolution (Hugh Hudson, 1985)
The Honorary Consul (John Mackenzie, 1983)
Five Days One Summer (Fred Zinnemann, 1982)
Outland (Peter Hyams, 1981)
Superman II (Richard Lester, 1980)
Superman (Richard Donner, 1978)
Valentino (Ken Russell, 1977)
The Omen (Richard Donner, 1976)
Alice Cooper: Welcome to My Nightmare (David Winters, 1976)

Lisztomania (Ken Russell, 1975)
Tommy (Ken Russell, 1975)

Other editing credits:
Lara Croft: Tomb Raider (Simon West, 2001) (uncredited)
Mission: Impossible II (John Woo, 2000) (special thanks)
Die Hard 2 (Renny Harlin, 1990) (supervising editor)
Tango & Cash (Andrei Konchalovsky, 1989) (supervising editor)
Scrooged (Richard Donner, 1988) (post-production consultant)

REGINALD BECK

After emigrating with his family from Russia to England in 1915, Beck entered Gainsborough's Islington Studios in 1927, initially as a camera assistant, on films including *The Vortex* (Adrian Brunel, 1928) and several directed by T. Hayes Hunter. Beck was briefly associated with the specialist film doctoring firm Brunel and Montagu Ltd. His first major assignment there was to edit a section of the travel film *Dassan* (Cherry and Ada Kearton, 1930), which featured 'penguins courting, penguins playing, hunting, slipping on ice, and from this mass of stuff I had to devise a story' (quoted in Belfrage, n.d., p. 81). Beck assisted John Seabourne before establishing himself as an editor in the 1930s. Independently minded, he prided himself on always freelancing rather than being tied to a particular studio. In this early phase of his career Beck worked primarily on quota quickies, including some at the more expensive end of the spectrum produced at Fox's Wembley Studios in the mid-1930s.

This Man Is News (David MacDonald, 1938) and *The Stars Look Down* helped move Beck's career beyond quota production. Of Carol Reed he said: 'He would cover a scene in a variety of angles all the way through so you never knew what he envisaged. Even during editing, Reed would want to try out different ways of cutting scenes' (quoted in Eyles, 1985, p. 39). Employed to edit *In Which We Serve*, Beck left in protest after David Lean re-cut one of his sequences without consulting him. Beck's major achievement during the Second World War was his work on *Henry V* (1944), which included helping inexperienced director Laurence Olivier write the detailed shooting script. Subsequent assignments included an associate producer credit for *Hamlet* (Laurence Olivier, 1948) and one film as co-director, *The Long Dark Hall* (1951). Beck also supported another first time (solo) director, Emeric Pressburger, on *Twice Upon a Time* (1953).

Beck concluded his career editing sixteen films for director Joseph Losey. In *The Go-Between* (Joseph Losey, 1971) sharply cut, initially cryptic alternations between time-past and time-present are deftly integrated into the narrative.

Impressed by his work on this film, German director Rainer Werner Fassbinder
sought Beck out to edit the American version of *Despair* (1978). As film historian Thomas Elsaesser points out, *Despair* was Fassbinder's first attempt at a
European art film: 'For a Fassbinder film, the narration makes quite unusual
demands on an audience, with imagined scenes and flash-forwards abruptly
interspersed in the narrative flow' (1996, p. 76). Beck already had considerable
experience of this type of editing through his work with Losey. Losey considered
him such a vital collaborator that he coaxed the octogenarian Beck out of retire-
ment to edit *Steaming* (1985), the last film both men worked on.

Filmography
Steaming (Joseph Losey, 1985)
Don Giovanni (Joseph Losey, 1979)
Despair (Rainer Werner Fassbinder, 1978)
Les Routes du sud (Joseph Losey, 1978)
Un amour de sable (Christian Lara, 1977)
The Romantic Englishwoman (Joseph Losey, 1975)
Galileo (Joseph Losey, 1974)
A Doll's House (Joseph Losey, 1973)
The Assassination of Trotsky (Joseph Losey, 1972)
Something to Hide (Alastair Reid, 1972)
The Go-Between (Joseph Losey, 1971)
Figures in a Landscape (Joseph Losey, 1970)
Secret Ceremony (Joseph Losey, 1968)
Boom (Joseph Losey, 1968)
Accident (Joseph Losey, 1967)
Robbery (Peter Yates, 1967)
Modesty Blaise (Joseph Losey, 1966)
Eva (Joseph Losey, 1963)
The Leather Boys (Sidney J. Furie, 1963)
Over the Odds (Michael Forlong, 1961)
The Trunk (Donovan Winter, 1960)
Desert Mice (Michael Relph, 1959)
Serious Charge (Terence Young, 1959)
The Gypsy and the Gentleman (Joseph Losey, 1958)
Harry Black and the Tiger (Hugo Fregonese, 1958)
Island in the Sun (Robert Rossen, 1957)
King's Rhapsody (Herbert Wilcox, 1955)
Lilacs in the Spring (Herbert Wilcox, 1955)
The Beggar's Opera (Peter Brook, 1953)

Trouble in the Glen (Herbert Wilcox, 1953)
Twice Upon a Time (Emeric Pressburger, 1953)
The Lost Hours (David MacDonald, 1952)
The Wonder Kid (Karl Hartl, 1951)
The Angel with the Trumpet (Anthony Bushell, 1950)
Henry V (Laurence Olivier, 1944)
Freedom Radio (Anthony Asquith, 1941)
Quiet Wedding (Anthony Asquith, 1940)
The Stars Look Down (Carol Reed, 1939)
This Man in Paris (David MacDonald, 1939)
This Man Is News (David MacDonald, 1938)
Who Goes Next? (Maurice Elvey, 1938)
Father O' Nine (Roy Kellino, 1938)
Catch as Catch Can (Roy Kellino, 1937)
Strange Experiment (Albert Parker, 1937)
The Return of Raffles (Mansfield Markham, 1932)
Born Lucky (Michael Powell, 1932)

RICHARD BEST

Eager to work in the film industry, Best urged his mother to write to her former neighbour, J. Arthur Rank, when he read about his financing *Turn of the Tide* (Norman Walker, 1935). This led to the film's producer John Corfield placing Best at the British and Dominions cutting rooms at Elstree. Over the next few years he assisted editors including David Lean on *As You Like It* (Paul Czinner, 1936) and Reginald Beck on *This Man in Paris*. During the Second World War David MacDonald assigned him to the Army Film Unit (AFU). On *Desert Victory* (1943), Best recalled that director Roy Boulting 'gave me a pattern to go on', and possibly some notes, but 'it was left to me to choose the order and more or less the timing, which was obviously left loose at that stage and we gradually tightened things up as we went along' (quoted in Burton, O'Sullivan and Wells, 2000, pp. 262–3). After the war Best edited three films for the Boulting brothers. As independent producers they did not have 'executives looking at the rushes as far as I can remember. That provided a welcome freedom' (p. 265). This helped inculcate Best's attitude that his first loyalty was to the director rather than producer. Throughout the 1950s and 60s he worked at ABPC's Elstree Studios. After a period of freelance work Best found continuity of employment again, editing documentaries at British Transport Films between the late 1970s and early 80s.

At ABPC Best became part of what J. Lee Thompson described as his 'very comfortable and talented team' (quoted in Chibnall, 2000, p. 37). Best's favourite film is *Ice Cold in Alex*. One of the sequences he relished editing is when an ambulance is painstakingly winched up a hill. Trusted by Thompson, Best began editing while the crew were still on location in Libya. In terms of guidance for this sequence 'there was nothing in the script', and no notes. Best decided 'the whole point of that sequence was effort . . . not only effort, but will they get there? Tension, really.' To underline the amount of time involved, the uncertainty of the outcome, and the strain experienced by the characters, he used many 'dissolves to increase the effort'. As he puts it, 'dissolves are very important; they do a lot emotionally'. In Best's second favourite film, *The Dam Busters*, emotional involvement with the narrative was achieved by different means. For a British film of this period a significant number of cuts rather than dissolves between earlier and later sequences are used. Often they help to emphasise the urgency of an operation working to strict deadlines. At a more local level interest is sustained by dispensing with redundant action. For example, when three bombers taxi across a runway and take off on their mission, Best repeatedly cuts before the third has exited the frame. To cut later 'would be boring; the third one you know what's going to happen . . . that's timing'.

Early in his career Best worked out some practical concepts to guide his editing. Having trouble editing close-ups of a romantic dialogue between the hero and heroine of *The Dancing Years* (Harold French, 1949), he added frames from before and after they delivered their lines in order to extend the performers' timing. Lengthening their pauses gave a previously flat exchange of dialogue unspoken depths of feeling and meaning. This sparked the realisation that, within individual sequences, 're-timing' was 'one of the big things of editing . . . you can speed up, and you can slow down'. 'Pacing', for Best, relates to a longer view of every sequence's place within the narrative; this 'comes later, when you have the whole film together and it's dragging in a certain part, then you come to the pacing of the whole film'.

Filmography
Dominique (Michael Anderson, 1978)
Take Me High (David Askey, 1973)
The Best Pair of Legs in the Business (Christopher Hodson, 1972)
Psychomania (Don Sharp, 1971)
Please Sir! (Mark Stuart, 1971)
Satan's Skin (Piers Haggard, 1971)
The Most Dangerous Man in the World (J. Lee Thompson, 1969)
Otley (Dick Clement, 1969)
The Double Man (Franklin J. Schaffner, 1967)
The Bargee (Duncan Wood, 1964)
The Cracksman (Peter Graham Scott, 1963)

Go to Blazes (Michael Truman, 1962)
The Pot Carriers (Peter Graham Scott, 1962)
We Joined the Navy (Wendy Toye, 1962)
The Rebel (Robert Day, 1961)
Bottoms Up (Mario Zampi, 1960)
Sands of the Desert (John Paddy Carstairs, 1960)
School for Scoundrels (Robert Hamer, 1960)
Ice Cold in Alex (J. Lee Thompson, 1958)
Look Back in Anger (Tony Richardson, 1958)
No Trees in the Street (J. Lee Thompson, 1958)
Interpol (John Gilling, 1957)
The Moonraker (David MacDonald, 1957)
The Silken Affair (Roy Kellino, 1957)
Woman in a Dressing Gown (J. Lee Thompson, 1957)
Yield to the Night (J. Lee Thompson, 1956)
Now and Forever (Mario Zampi, 1955)
The Dam Busters (Michael Anderson, 1955)
Valley of Song (Gilbert Gunn, 1953)
The Weak and the Wicked (J. Lee Thompson, 1953)
The Good Beginning (Gilbert Gunn, 1953)
The Yellow Balloon (J. Lee Thompson, 1953)
24 Hours in a Woman's Life (Victor Saville, 1952)
The Elstree Story (Gilbert Gunn, 1952)
The Magic Box (John Boulting, 1951)
The Woman with No Name (Ladislas Vajda, 1950)
The Dancing Years (Harold French, 1949)
Britannia Mews (Jean Negulesco, 1949)
The Guinea Pig (Roy Boulting, 1948)
Mine Own Executioner (Anthony Kimmins, 1947)
Fame Is the Spur (Roy Boulting, 1946)

JOHN BLOOM

As the brother of British and later Hollywood star Claire Bloom, John was
exposed through his family to theatre from an early age. He began his film career
in the 1950s as a script reader in the story department at Pinewood. Having
gained his union card, Bloom found his niche in the cutting rooms, starting as
second assistant to editor John Trumper on *Heart of a Child* (Clive Donner,
1958). His break as an editor came with the 'B' picture *The Impersonator* (Alfred
Shaughnessy, 1960), produced by Anthony Perry. During the 1960s Bloom
worked frequently with director Guy Hamilton and also edited the acclaimed

The Lion in Winter. The director who most actively encouraged Bloom to experiment during this period was Silvio Narizzano on *Georgy Girl*. This resulted in
the playful editing of certain sequences and Bloom's proposal that 'the opening
of the film just has to have a song on it'. The initial choice was the title song
from the musical 'Funny Girl', but the prohibitive cost of obtaining the rights
led to the production team settling for the now fondly remembered Seekers'
song 'Georgy Girl' instead.

Bloom's favourite among the films he has edited is *Who'll Stop the Rain* aka *Dog
Soldiers* (Karel Reisz, 1978), but *Gandhi* won him an Academy Award and international recognition. Attenborough wrote in his book on the making of this epic:

> Immense technical skill is required as far as the editor is concerned; however
> overriding all else is his sense of taste and judgment ... [Bloom's] application to
> the job and his creativity in my opinion are without parallel and much credit for the
> film that audiences will see is due to him (1982, p. 226).

Gandhi seemed to herald a renaissance of British film production, but this was
short-lived and since the mid-1980s Bloom has worked primarily in Hollywood
and New York. Working on projects as diverse as *Air America* (Roger Spottiswoode, 1990) and *Nobody's Fool* (Robert Benton, 1994), he has proved
adaptable to different kinds of film-making and changing styles in editing and
narrative construction. For example, in Bloom's view *Shaft* (John Singleton,
2000) is 'full of narrative non sequiturs', but rather than bemoan this he concludes from observing test screening audiences that 'if they're having a good
time they don't care'.

Filmography
Shaft (John Singleton, 2000)
The Deep End of the Ocean (Ulu Grosbard, 1999)
Last Dance (Bruce Beresford, 1996)
The First Wives Club (Hugh Wilson, 1996)
Nobody's Fool (Robert Benton, 1994)
A Foreign Field (Charles Sturridge, 1993)
Damage (Louis Malle, 1992)
Prague (Ian Sellar, 1992)
Air America (Roger Spottiswoode, 1990)
Jacknife (David Jones, 1989)
Bright Lights, Big City (James Bridges, 1988)
Black Widow (Bob Rafelson, 1987)
A Chorus Line (Richard Attenborough, 1985)

Betrayal (David Hugh Jones, 1983)
Gandhi (Richard Attenborough, 1982)
The French Lieutenant's Woman (Karel Reisz, 1981)
Dracula (John Badham, 1979)
Magic (Richard Attenborough, 1978)
Orca (Michael Anderson, 1977)
The Message (Moustapha Akkad, 1976)
The Ritz (Richard Lester, 1976)
The Abdication (Anthony Harvey, 1974)
Henry VIII and His Six Wives (Waris Hussein, 1973)
Travels with My Aunt (George Cukor, 1972)
To Catch a Spy (Dick Clement, 1971)
The Last Valley (James Clavell, 1970)
In Search of Gregory (Peter Wood, 1969)
The Lion in Winter (Anthony Harvey, 1968)
The Last Safari (Henry Hathaway, 1967)
The Party's Over (Guy Hamilton, 1966)
Funeral in Berlin (Guy Hamilton, 1966)
Georgy Girl (Silvio Narizzano, 1966)
Runaway Railway (Jan Darnley-Smith, 1965)
Man in the Middle (Guy Hamilton, 1964)
Girl on Approval (Charles Frend, 1962)
The Impersonator (Alfred Shaughnessy, 1960)

Other editing credits:
Who'll Stop the Rain aka *Dog Soldiers* (Karel Reisz, 1978) (supervising editor)

JIM CLARK

Even as a boy, Clark's ambition was always to work in film production. At the age of ten his father bought him a Pathe Ace 9.5mm film projector,

> the great toy of my life, which changed it . . . It one day occurred to me that in some way the scenes changed from one angle to another, and I became interested in the reason why. Then I became interested in the manipulation of images to tell a story.

He ordered films from the Wallace Heaton film library, read everything he could about cinema, and established a school film society. Clark then worked in his father's printing business for three years but continued to pursue his passion by remaining involved with the Federation of Film Societies and regularly attending festivals and National Film Theatre screenings. At these events Clark got to know both established film-makers and aspiring ones such as Lindsay Anderson and Karel Reisz.

A brief stint as a runner in a documentary production company was followed by an unexpected invitation to join Ealing Studios as a cutting room assistant. Clark assisted sound editors Gordon Stone and Mary Habberfield and editor Jack Harris. His first break proved to be a false start. Basil Wright asked Clark to edit a children's film he was producing. Unable to find work in mainstream features after this detour, Clark returned to assisting Jack Harris, who eventually recommended him to edit *Surprise Package* (Stanley Donen, 1960). In the 1960s Clark edited two films for Jack Clayton and then commenced a long-standing creative partnership with John Schlesinger on *Darling*. Schlesinger described Clark as someone 'who has saved my bacon many times' (quoted in McFarlane, 1997, p. 512). Between the mid-1960s and mid-70s Clark directed four eclectic low-budget features, but returned to full-time editing because he found this role more satisfying. He did however enjoy directing some documentaries for Granada Television during this period.

Clark believes an editor's role should be a creatively supportive one. He also feels an editor should, when asked to, advise on performances during production. Clark has come to be seen, for example by producer David Puttnam in the 1980s, as someone able to solve problems and give tactful assistance to new features directors: 'people do come to me for advice on scripts, and looking at cuts, and seeing films and advising and commenting'. Since the late 1960s Clark has often worked in Hollywood. He considers one of his projects there, *The Day of the Locust* (John Schlesinger, 1975), an excellently directed, 'incredibly underrated film'. Clark is particularly proud of his work on its apocalyptic finale, set at a Hollywood premiere. Cuts on violent action accentuate the force of a panicked crowd rioting, fires spreading and wreckage falling. A series of dissolves, which begin and end with shots of blinding bright light, intensify the delirium experienced by wounded art director Tod (William Atherton) as chaos engulfs him.

Filmography

City by the Sea (Michael Caton-Jones, 2002)
Kiss Kiss (Bang Bang) (Stewart Sugg, 2000)
The Trench (William Boyd, 1999)
Onegin (Martha Fiennes, 1999)
The World Is Not Enough (Michael Apted, 1999)
The Jackal (Michael Caton-Jones, 1997)
Marvin's Room (Jerry Zaks, 1996)
Copycat (Jon Amiel, 1995)

Radio Inside (Jeffrey Bell, 1994)
Nell (Michael Apted, 1994)
A Good Man in Africa (Bruce Beresford, 1994)
This Boy's Life (Michael Caton-Jones, 1993)
Meeting Venus (István Szabó, 1991)
Memphis Belle (Michael Caton-Jones, 1990)
Spies Inc. (Anthony Thomas, 1988)
Young Toscanini (Franco Zeffirelli, 1988)
The Mission (Roland Joffé, 1986)
The Frog Prince (Brian Gilbert, 1984)
The Killing Fields (Roland Joffé, 1984)
Privates on Parade (Michael Blakemore, 1982)
Honky Tonk Freeway (John Schlesinger, 1981)
Agatha (Michael Apted, 1979)
Yanks (John Schlesinger, 1979)
The Last Remake of Beau Geste (Marty Feldman, 1977)
Marathon Man (John Schlesinger, 1976)
The Day of the Locust (John Schlesinger, 1975)
The Adventure of Sherlock Holmes' Smarter Brother (Gene Wilder, 1975)
Zee and Co. (Brian G. Hutton, 1972)
Darling (John Schlesinger, 1965)
The Pumpkin Eater (Jack Clayton, 1964)
Charade (Stanley Donen, 1963)
Term of Trial (Peter Glenville, 1962)
The Innocents (Jack Clayton, 1961)
The Grass Is Greener (Stanley Donen, 1960)
Surprise Package (Stanley Donen, 1960)
One Wish Too Many (John Durst, 1956)

Other editing credits:
Twilight (Robert Benton, 1998) (special thanks)
Palookaville (Alan Taylor, 1995) (thanks)
War of the Buttons (John Roberts, 1994) (consulting editor)
Midnight Cowboy (John Schlesinger, 1969) (creative consultant)

FRANK CLARKE

School friend Ralph Kemplen secured Frank Clarke his first job as an assistant on Gaumont-British's *First a Girl* (Victor Saville, 1935), edited by Al Barnes. Clarke followed Kemplen to Twickenham Studios, then briefly freelanced before being called up at the outbreak of the Second World War. He worked for several years at the AFU, editing training films and working on the famous documentaries *Desert Victory* and *The True Glory* (Carol Reed, Garson Kanin 1945). Clarke's relationship to the directors and producers of these compilation films was one where 'you did a lot of the searching and getting the backbone of the thing together, then they came in on it'. This experience convinced him of the greater scope for creativity editors could sometimes exercise on documentaries.

After editing films directed by Gilbert Gunn and Herbert Wilcox in the immediate post-war period Clarke was invited by former AFU producer Hugh Stewart to join MGM-British as a supervising editor. There, over the course of nearly twenty years, he worked with major Hollywood directors including John Ford and George Cukor, as well as British directors such as Anthony Asquith. Directors Clarke rated highly as efficient craftsmen included Asquith and Guy Green. His experience of working with acclaimed Italian director Michelangelo Antonioni on his first English-language film *Blow-Up* was less happy. Clarke was used to the more traditional British working method of being left alone to assemble his own first cut of a film before discussing changes with the director. Antonioni was present throughout the entire editing process and, in Clarke's view, 'interfering all the time' and 'controlling too much as far as I was concerned'. These difficulties were compounded by the fact that *Blow-Up* was quite different from the more conventional MGM-British productions Clarke had previously worked on. He refused a credit on the film. Later, after the MGM-British Borehamwood Studio closed down at the end of the 1960s, Clarke rounded out his career by teaching at the London Film School.

Filmography
No Blade of Grass (Cornel Wilde, 1970)
Staal Burger (Daan Terief, 1969)
Lock Up Your Daughters (Peter Coe, 1969)
Pretty Polly (Guy Green, 1967)
The Yellow Rolls-Royce (Anthony Asquith, 1965)
Come Fly with Me (Henry Levin, 1963)
The Golden Head (Richard Thorpe, 1963)
The V.I.P.s (Anthony Asquith, 1963)
I Thank a Fool (Robert Stevens, 1962)
Light in the Piazza (Guy Green, 1962)
A Matter of Who (Don Chaffey, 1961)
The Green Helmet (Michael Forlong, 1961)
The Day They Robbed the Bank of England (John Guillermin, 1960)
Libel (Anthony Asquith, 1959)

I Accuse! (José Ferrer, 1958)
Tom Thumb (George Pal, 1958)
Action of the Tiger (Terence Young, 1957)
The Barretts of Wimpole Street (Sidney Franklin, 1957)
Bhowani Junction (George Cukor, 1956)
Bedevilled (Mitchell Leisen, 1955)
Beau Brummell (Curtis Bernhardt, 1954)
Knights of the Round Table (Richard Thorpe, 1953)
Mogambo (John Ford, 1953)
Time Bomb (Ted Tetzlaff, 1953)
Never Let Me Go (Delmer Daves, 1953)
Ivanhoe (Richard Thorpe, 1952)
Calling Bulldog Drummond (Victor Saville, 1951)
The Miniver Story (H. C. Potter, 1950)
Conspirator (Victor Saville, 1949)
Elizabeth of Ladymead (Herbert Wilcox, 1948)
Spring in Park Lane (Herbert Wilcox, 1948)
Return to Action (Gilbert Gunn, 1946)
Domestic Service (Gilbert Gunn, 1946)
Routine Job (Gilbert Gunn, 1946)
Take Cover (Leslie Hiscott, 1938)
Sportsmen All (John Betts, 1938)
Clothes and the Woman (Albert de Courville, 1937)

Other editing credits:
Blow-Up (Michelangelo Antonioni, 1966) (uncredited)

ANNE COATES
Best known for editing *Lawrence of Arabia*, and her involvement in its subsequent restoration, Coates has become one of the most visible British film
editors. She began her career at a company making religious shorts. From there
she progressed to features, working as an assistant to Reginald Mills on *The Red
Shoes*. Coates' mentor was John Seabourne, who she assisted on various films
including *The Rocking Horse Winner* (Anthony Pelissier, 1949). He gave her
sequences to edit and influenced her preference for brisk editing that avoids
unnecessary transitional actions by 'hit[ting] right to the centre of scenes'
(quoted in Oldham, 1992, p. 168). This is not however an invariable formula.
Tunes of Glory, for example, involves several instances where shots are held for
over a minute as two or more actors perform lengthy pieces of dialogue. In one
sequence Lieutenant Colonel Basil Barrow (John Mills) reveals his feelings to

Captain Jimmy Cairns (Gordon Jackson) as they sit in a jeep. Neither looks directly at the other and their dialogue is played in a single medium shot lasting over two minutes.

Lawrence of Arabia firmly established Coates' reputation, and since then she has 'tried to keep a balance between the bigger films and the smaller films. At one time I was only being offered the really big epic films and I never wanted to get into that situation.' Of her collaborations with Jack Gold during the late 1960s and 70s Coates says: 'I'm somebody that has quite a lot of ideas to offer . . . He likes my ideas, and allows me to make a creative contribution to the films' (quoted in Wyeth and Grantham, 1984, p. 66). Her favourite is *The Bofors Gun* (1968), the first feature Gold directed, and she co-produced *The Medusa Touch* (1978), their last project together. Relocating to Hollywood in the mid-1980s, Coates worked on diverse films with a range of directors and established a fruitful collaboration with Steven Soderbergh in the late 1990s. Throughout her career she has also edited many powerful performances, including Peter O'Toole and Omar Sharif in *Lawrence of Arabia*, John Hurt in *The Elephant Man* (David Lynch, 1980), Robert Downey Jr in *Chaplin* (Richard Attenborough, 1992), and Julia Roberts and Albert Finney in *Erin Brockovich*. Coates sees herself as 'an emotional editor' who looks at performances for 'genuineness, somebody who's really acting from the heart, they've thought it from the inside'.

Filmography
Unfaithful (Adrian Lyne, 2002)
Sweet November (Pat O'Connor, 2001)
Erin Brockovich (Steven Soderbergh, 2000)
Passion of Mind (Alan Berliner, 2000)
Out of Sight (Steven Soderbergh, 1998)
Out to Sea (Martha Coolidge, 1997)
Striptease (Andrew Bergman, 1996)
Congo (Frank Marshall, 1995)
Pontiac Moon (Peter Medak, 1994)
In the Line of Fire (Wolfgang Petersen, 1993)
Chaplin (Richard Attenborough, 1992)
What about Bob? (Frank Oz, 1991)
I Love You to Death (Lawrence Kasdan, 1990)
Farewell to the King (John Milius, 1989)
Listen to Me (Douglas Day Stewart, 1989)
Masters of the Universe (Gary Goddard, 1987)
Lady Jane (Trevor Nunn, 1986)
Raw Deal (John Irvin, 1986)

Greystoke: The Legend of Tarzan, Lord of the Apes (Hugh Hudson, 1984)
The Pirates of Penzance (Wilford Leach, 1983)
Ragtime (Milos Forman, 1981)
The Elephant Man (David Lynch, 1980)
The Bushido Blade (Tom Kotani, 1979)
The Legacy (Richard Marquand, 1979)
The Medusa Touch (Jack Gold, 1978)
The Eagle Has Landed (John Sturges, 1976)
Aces High (Jack Gold, 1976)
Man Friday (Jack Gold, 1975)
Murder on the Orient Express (Sidney Lumet, 1974)
11 Harrowhouse (Aram Avakian, 1974)
A Bequest to the Nation (James Cellan Jones, 1973)
Follow Me (Carol Reed, 1972)
Friends (Lewis Gilbert, 1971)
The Adventurers (Lewis Gilbert, 1970)
The Bofors Gun (Jack Gold, 1968)
Great Catherine (Gordon Flemyng, 1968)
Hotel Paradiso (Peter Glenville, 1966)
Those Magnificent Men in Their Flying Machines (Ken Annakin, 1965)
Young Cassidy (Jack Cardiff, 1965)
Becket (Peter Glenville, 1964)
Lawrence of Arabia (David Lean, 1962)
Don't Bother to Knock (Cyril Frankel, 1961)
Tunes of Glory (Ronald Neame, 1960)
The Horse's Mouth (Ronald Neame, 1958)
The Truth about Women (Muriel Box, 1958)
To Paris with Love (Robert Hamer, 1955)
Lost (Guy Green, 1955)
Forbidden Cargo (Harold French, 1954)
Grand National Night (Bob McNaught, 1954)
The Pickwick Papers (Noel Langley, 1952)

Other editing credits:
Lawrence of Arabia (David Lean, 1962) (editorial consultant for 1989 reconstruction and restoration)

IAN DALRYMPLE

Best known as the head of the Crown Film Unit during the Second World War, Dalrymple's early career acquainted him with both alternative film culture and commercial film-making. This inclined him to support during wartime both the experimentally edited *Listen to Britain* (co-directed by Humphrey Jennings and editor Stewart McAllister, 1941) and the development of the narrative documentary. At Cambridge University Dalrymple met Ivor Montagu and edited the literary journal *Granta*. His practical film education began at the specialist film doctoring firm Brunel and Montagu Ltd where, in Adrian Brunel's view, working on foreign art films imported by the Film Society provided 'excellent training for junior members of the firm' (n.d.[b]). Brunel and Montagu Ltd's connections with Michael Balcon's Gainsborough studios led, in the late 1920s, to Dalrymple's employment there, and then at Gaumont-British, primarily as an editor but also as a writer and producer.

Promoted to supervising editor, Dalrymple was responsible for the final edition of all Gaumont-British releases from *Rome Express* (Walter Forde, 1932) onwards. In the same year he helped establish a training scheme that introduced trainee editors such as Hugh Stewart to the industry. As an editor of films with lavish production designs by Alfred Junge and Alex Vetchinsky, Dalrymple was aware of the need to balance different imperatives:

> Make what you can of the 'production angle'. Don't let the company spend a mass of money on a set and play the whole action in close-up ... At the same time, don't waste screen. Come in as close as you can for significant dialogue, reactions, etc. (1933, p. 172).

He worked closely with leading director Victor Saville on several films including *The Good Companions* (1933) and *Evergreen*. After leaving Gaumont-British in the mid-1930s Dalrymple worked mainly as a writer, producer and occasional director rather than editor.

Filmography
Her Last Affaire (Michael Powell, 1936)
The Iron Duke (Victor Saville, 1935)
Little Friend (Berthold Viertel, 1934)
Evergreen (Victor Saville, 1934)
The Ghoul (T. Hayes Hunter, 1933)
There Goes the Bride (Albert de Courville, 1932)
Love on Wheels (Victor Saville, 1932)
Jack's the Boy (Walter Forde, 1932)
The Faithful Heart (Victor Saville, 1932)
Lord Babs (Walter Forde, 1932)
Sunshine Susie (Victor Saville, 1931)

Michael and Mary (Victor Saville, 1931)
The Ghost Train (Walter Forde, 1931)
The Man They Couldn't Arrest (T. Hayes Hunter, 1931)
The Hound of the Baskervilles (V. Gareth Gundrey, 1931)
The Ringer (Walter Forde, 1931)
Third Time Lucky (Walter Forde, 1931)
Taxi for Two (Alexander Esway, Denison Clift, 1929)
The Crooked Billet (Adrian Brunel silent, 1929, sound, 1930)

Other editing credits:
Turn of the Tide (Norman Walker, 1935) (uncredited)
Friday the Thirteenth (Victor Saville, 1933) (production personnel)
The Good Companions (Victor Saville, 1933) (production personnel)
The Lucky Number (Anthony Asquith, 1933) (production personnel)

ANTONY GIBBS

After eighteen months working on the studio floor and four years assisting Ralph
Kemplen and Alan Osbiston, Gibbs worked briefly in television before establishing himself as a features editor. In the early years of his career Osbiston's
recommendations enabled him 'to pick up movies that Alan couldn't do'. Osbiston edited *The Entertainer* prior to Gibbs' first collaboration with Richardson on
the stylistically innovative *A Taste of Honey*. This marked the beginning of a
remarkably productive period for Gibbs. He worked with Tony Richardson on
five more films during the 1960s. In different ways each one afforded opportunities for experimental editing within the parameters of mainstream narrative
film-making. This decade also saw Gibbs editing notable films for other young
directors, such as *The Knack* and *Performance*. With a string of impressive credits to his name, Gibbs played a crucial historical role in contributing to new
stylistic trends in 1960s British cinema.

Since the 1970s Gibbs has been based in Hollywood, collaborating most frequently with directors Norman Jewison, and more recently Mark Rydell and
John Frankenheimer on both film and television projects. On their films
together Jewison gave Gibbs considerable latitude rather than getting closely
involved with the editing. Gibbs has worked across a variety of genres, from the
musical *Fiddler on the Roof* (Norman Jewison, 1971) to the science-fiction film
Dune (David Lynch, 1984). Gibbs sees himself as 'an actor's editor', and was
particularly pleased by Meg Tilly's recognition of how he helped make her performance in the title role of *Agnes of God* (Norman Jewison, 1985) even more
powerful. Gibbs' sometimes unconventional approach to editing is partly dictated by a commitment to selecting takes featuring the strongest moments of

performance, regardless of whether they occur in close-up, medium or long shot. He suggests that because he uses

> bits that maybe other directors and editors . . . [would consider] . . . the wrong size of shot . . . you will never be able to look at any of my movies and say, yes, well he's cut this in the classical manner, and it's graceful, and we're moving to the right size of shot, because I don't do that, I'm looking for the acting all the time.

Filmography
Reindeer Games (John Frankenheimer, 2000)
Ronin (John Frankenheimer, 1998)
Don Juan DeMarco (Jeremy Leven, 1995)
The Man without a Face (Mel Gibson, 1993)
The Taking of Beverly Hills (Sidney J. Furie, 1992)
In Country (Norman Jewison, 1989)
Stealing Home (Steven Kampmann, William Porter, 1988)
Russkies (Rick Rosenthal, 1987)
Tai-Pan (Daryl Duke, 1986)
Agnes of God (Norman Jewison, 1985)
Dune (David Lynch, 1984)
Bad Boys (Rick Rosenthal, 1983)
Ragtime (Milos Forman, 1981)
The Man from a Far Country (Krzysztof Zanussi, 1981)
The Dogs of War (John Irvin, 1980)
The Wildcats of St Trinian's (Frank Launder, 1980)
Yesterday's Hero (Neil Leifer, 1979)
Butch and Sundance: The Early Days (Richard Lester, 1979)
F.I.S.T. (Norman Jewison, 1978)
A Bridge Too Far (Richard Attenborough, 1977)
The Sailor Who Fell from Grace with the Sea (Lewis John Carlino, 1976)
Rollerball (Norman Jewison, 1975)
Juggernaut (Richard Lester, 1974)
The Black Windmill (Don Siegel, 1974)
Jesus Christ Superstar (Norman Jewison, 1973)
The Ragman's Daughter (Harold Becker, 1972)
Fiddler on the Roof (Norman Jewison, 1971)
Walkabout (Nicolas Roeg, 1971)
All the Right Noises (Gerry O'Hara, 1969)
Performance (Donald Cammell, Nicolas Roeg, 1968)
Petulia (Richard Lester, 1968)

The Birthday Party (William Friedkin, 1968)
Mademoiselle (Tony Richardson, 1966)
The Loved One (Tony Richardson, 1965)
The Knack (Richard Lester, 1965)
The Luck of Ginger Coffey (Irvin Kershner, 1964)
Tom Jones (Tony Richardson, 1963)
The Loneliness of the Long Distance Runner (Tony Richardson, 1962)
Tiara Tahiti (Ted Kotcheff, 1962)
A Taste of Honey (Tony Richardson, 1961)
Offbeat (Cliff Owen, 1961)
Snake Woman (Sidney J. Furie, 1961)
During One Night (Sidney J. Furie, 1961)
Dr Blood's Coffin (Sidney J. Furie, 1961)
Oscar Wilde (Gregory Ratoff, 1960)
The Unstoppable Man (Terry Bishop, 1960)

Other editing credits:
The Sailor from Gibraltar (Tony Richardson, 1967) (supervising editor)
Girl with Green Eyes (Desmond Davis, 1964) (supervising editor)

DAVID GLADWELL

The film that kick-started Gladwell's career was his short *Miss Thompson Goes Shopping* (1957). Positive responses to this film from luminaries such as Lindsay Anderson and Basil Wright helped Gladwell make the transition from amateur film-making and an art school training to a job as an assistant editor at British Transport Films. Much of his professional career has been in documentary editing, and also some directing, including one feature *Memoirs of a Survivor* (1981). Gladwell also directed short films supported by the Experimental Film Fund, later the BFI Production Board. Given the films' limited budgets this would sometimes involve using cutting rooms and equipment he was being paid to use professionally during the day. The most notable features Gladwell has edited are *If . . .* and *O Lucky Man!*, both directed by Lindsay Anderson who he knew from his Free Cinema period. Whereas the first film was economically shot, the latter had much more coverage because Anderson, suffering from creative fatigue, was at times unsure about the film's direction.

Filmography
Lost Angels (Hugh Hudson, 1989)
O Lucky Man! (Lindsay Anderson, 1973)

Bombay Talkie (James Ivory, 1970)

If . . . (Lindsay Anderson, 1968)

BERNARD GRIBBLE

A chance encounter with John (Monck) Goldman led to Gribble securing a job at the Crown Film Unit's picture library during the Second World War. Impressed by *San Demetrio London* (Charles Frend, 1943), Gribble chased Sid Cole for a job at Ealing and eventually entered the cutting rooms as third assistant to editor Michael Truman on *Johnny Frenchman* (Charles Frend, 1945). An early break came when Truman was indisposed, allowing Gribble to put together the entire first cut of *It Always Rains on Sunday* (Robert Hamer, 1947). Truman gave Gribble the Hanover fair sequence to edit on *Saraband for Dead Lovers* (Basil Dearden, 1948), and then recommended him to edit *Another Shore* (Charles Crichton, 1948). As a relatively junior editor Gribble was loaned out by Michael Balcon to work on the lower-budget Group 3 production *Laxdale Hall* (John Eldridge, 1952). Working outside the confines of Ealing gave Gribble the confidence to become a freelancer from 1953 onwards. He credits Wolf Rilla as the first director to encourage him to exercise more creativity by preparing his own first version of a film before altering it in consultation with directors and producers.

A significant proportion of Gribble's work in features editing has been in comedy, from *The Man in the White Suit* and *The Green Man* (Robert Day, 1956) through to broader efforts such as *Steptoe and Son* (Cliff Owen, 1972) and *Top Secret!*. Gribble has also worked in diverse production contexts. During the late 1950s and early 60s he primarily edited 'B' films and several episodes in a series of Edgar Wallace mysteries. In the 1960s and 70s he edited eight films directed by the prolific Michael Winner, who had similarly spent the late 1950s and early 60s working on British 'B' films. Gribble worked on several films Winner directed in Hollywood. He also edited *White Dog* (Sam Fuller, 1982), working closely with producer Jon Davison to condense a large amount of footage into a manageable length. Most of Gribble's subsequent work has been for American television.

Filmography

Aces: Iron Eagle III (John Glen, 1992)

Caddyshack II (Allan Arkush, 1988)

Top Secret! (Jim Abrahams, David Zucker, Jerry Zucker, 1984)

White Dog (Sam Fuller, 1982)

Motel Hell (Kevin Connor, 1980)

The Sentinel (Michael Winner, 1977)

Silver Bears (Ivan Passer, 1977)

Won Ton Ton, The Dog Who Saved Hollywood (Michael Winner, 1976)

Ace Up My Sleeve (Ivan Passer, 1975)

Bedtime with Rosie (Wolf Rilla, 1975)

Death Wish (Michael Winner, 1974)

The Banana Boat (Sidney Hayers, 1974)

Steptoe and Son Ride Again (Peter Sykes, 1973)

The Lovers (Herbert Wise, 1973)

Tales That Witness Madness (Freddie Francis, 1973)

Steptoe and Son (Cliff Owen, 1972)

Mr Forbush and the Penguins (Arne Sucksdorff, Albert T. Viola, 1971)

The Games (Michael Winner, 1970)

Can Hieronymus Merkin Ever Forget Mercy Humppe and Find True Happiness? (Anthony Newley, 1969)

Hostile Witness (Ray Milland, 1968)

I'll Never Forget What's 'is Name (Michael Winner, 1967)

The Jokers (Michael Winner, 1966)

You Must Be Joking! (Michael Winner, 1965)

Cairo (Wolf Rilla, 1963)

West 11 (Michael Winner, 1963)

The Share Out (Gerald Glaister, 1962)

The Frightened City (John Lemont, 1961)

Mary Had a Little (Edward Buzzell, 1961)

What a Whopper! (Gilbert Gunn, 1961)

Your Money or Your Wife (Anthony Simmons, 1960)

And Women Shall Weep (John Lemont, 1960)

Piccadilly Third Stop (Wolf Rilla, 1960)

Witness in the Dark (Wolf Rilla, 1959)

The Headless Ghost (Peter Graham Scott, 1959)

The Shakedown (John Lemont, 1959)

Alive and Kicking (Cyril Frankel, 1959)

The Scamp (Wolf Rilla, 1957)

The Extra Day (William Fairchild, 1956)

The Green Man (Robert Day, 1956)

John and Julie (William Fairchild, 1955)

Make Me an Offer (Cyril Frankel, 1955)

The End of the Road (Wolf Rilla, 1954)

Meet Mr Lucifer (Anthony Pelissier, 1953)

Laxdale Hall (John Eldridge, 1952)

The Man in the White Suit (Alexander Mackendrick, 1951)

Bitter Springs (Ralph Smart, 1950)
The Magnet (Charles Frend, 1950)
Train of Events (Sidney Cole, Charles Crichton, Basil Dearden, 1949)
Another Shore (Charles Crichton, 1948)

GERRY HAMBLING

The opinion voiced by Tony Lawson that Hambling is 'probably the best English editor' currently working is one shared by a number of his peers. Hambling started as an assistant to Hugh Stewart and Ralph Kemplen, who gave him his first break. He went on to build a solid reputation as an editor specialising in comedies, particularly a string of films starring Norman Wisdom in the 1960s. During this period Hambling also worked as a sound editor, for example on *Freud* (John Huston, 1962), edited by Kemplen, and *The Servant*. When production in Britain declined during the 1970s Hambling found work editing commercials and television programmes. He returned to features editing with *Bugsy Malone* and has subsequently edited every film Alan Parker has directed.

Hambling's reason for continuing to work with a Moviola after the advent of non-linear editing is: 'Speed isn't everything' (see Chapter 6). Working on a Moviola is less instantaneous than an electronic system, but for Hambling as for some other editors this means: 'You spend time thinking about the next cut, or some aspect of the film' (quoted in Young, 1999). Hambling rarely talks publicly about his work but its quality is recognised by many of his colleagues. Don Fairservice devotes a lengthy section of his book on film editing to analysing Hambling's contribution to a sequence where FBI agent Rupert Anderson (Gene Hackman) confronts a racist barman in *Mississippi Burning* (Alan Parker, 1988). Fairservice notes how he optimises the impact of physical action, builds tension and handles dialogue with particular subtlety (Fairservice, 2001, pp. 295–8). Hambling's mentor Kemplen was a noted dialogue editor, so Hambling can be seen as carrying on this tradition. More praise comes from Tony Lawson, who cites 'the interviews during *The Commitments* [Alan Parker, 1991] where they try to find another band member, with everyone knocking on the door', as a sequence primarily, and expertly, constructed through editing.

Filmography
The Life of David Gale (Alan Parker, 2003)
Mrs Caldicot's Cabbage War (Ian Sharp, 2000)
Angela's Ashes (Alan Parker, 1999)
Talk of Angels (Nick Hamm, 1998)
The Boxer (Jim Sheridan, 1997)
Evita (Alan Parker, 1996)

White Squall (Ridley Scott, 1996)
The Road to Wellville (Alan Parker, 1994)
In the Name of the Father (Jim Sheridan, 1993)
City of Joy (Roland Joffé, 1992)
The Commitments (Alan Parker, 1991)
Come See the Paradise (Alan Parker, 1990)
Lenny Live and Unleashed (Andy Harries, 1989)
Mississippi Burning (Alan Parker, 1988)
Angel Heart (Alan Parker, 1987)
Leonard Part 6 (Paul Weiland, 1987)
Absolute Beginners (Julien Temple, 1986)
Invitation to the Wedding (Joseph Brooks, 1985)
Birdy (Alan Parker, 1984)
Another Country (Marek Kanievska, 1984)
Pink Floyd the Wall (Alan Parker, 1982)
Shoot the Moon (Alan Parker, 1982)
Heartaches (Donald Shebib, 1981)
Fame (Alan Parker, 1980)
Midnight Express (Alan Parker, 1978)
Bugsy Malone (Alan Parker, 1976)
The Adding Machine (Jerome Epstein, 1969)
The Magnificent Two (Cliff Owen, 1967)
Press for Time (Robert Asher, 1966)
The Early Bird (Robert Asher, 1965)
The Intelligence Men (Robert Asher, 1965)
A Stitch in Time (Robert Asher, 1963)
She'll Have to Go (Robert Asher, 1962)
The Kitchen (James Hill, 1961)
The Bulldog Breed (Robert Asher, 1960)
The Poacher's Daughter (George Pollock, 1960)
Left Right and Centre (Sidney Gilliat, 1959)
The Whole Truth (Dan Cohen, John Guillermin, 1958)
Dry Rot (Maurice Elvey, 1956)

JACK HARRIS

With the partial exception of David Lean, Harris was regarded by many of his peers as the doyen of British film editors between the 1930s and 50s. His career stretched back to 1921, when he joined the original Shepherd's Bush Gaumont Studios. By the end of the decade he was working as assistant director to Maurice Elvey and Victor Saville. It was not until the coming of sound that Harris settled into editing at Twickenham Studios. There he became the prime example of an editor able to work wonders with quota quickies. He kept up with the furious speed of production despite being, in Richard Best's words, a meticulously 'slow thinker' who would scrutinise material intensely before making his cuts. David Lean, shortly after he became a director, moved quickly to secure Harris' services beginning with *This Happy Breed* (1944). After a brief stint in the late 1940s as a supervising editor at Pinewood the final two decades of Harris' career included a number of films at Ealing Studios, including *Where No Vultures Fly* (Harry Watt, 1951), *The Ladykillers* (Alexander Mackendrick, 1955), and various Hollywood-financed British productions.

Two of many examples which could be cited of Harris adding distinction to his 1930s films are: several carefully timed series of close-ups of women at a tea party inadvertently drunk on vodka in the Ivor Novello vehicle *I Lived with You* (Maurice Elvey, 1933); dynamic inter-cutting and matching on action which enlivens the otherwise quite static opening section of the Tod Slaughter 'melodrama of the old school' *The Face at the Window* (George King, 1939). The care and thought Harris put into his work is evident from the brief sections he wrote for Karel Reisz's book *The Technique of Film Editing*. He discusses how he introduced variation and interest into the editing of one of several motorcycle racing sequences in *Once a Jolly Swagman* (Jack Lee, 1948) (Reisz and Millar, 1968, pp. 80–1). Harris also discusses the famous opening of *Great Expectations* (1946) (pp. 238–40), but the extent to which he derived creative satisfaction from working on the prestigious, carefully planned projects directed by former editor David Lean is open to debate. One commentator quotes Harris as feeling somewhat stifled by the time of this fourth collaboration with Lean: 'I'm getting a bit tired of cutting off the number boards' (quoted in Brownlow, 1997, p. 220).

Harris edited in a classical style insofar as he disliked virtuosity for its own sake. He claimed to be 'completely unaffected by fashionable views or mere technical brilliance'. The biggest influences on him were the 'utter ruthlessness' of the editing in the early comedies directed by Frank Capra, and editor Duncan Mansfield's work on *The Front Page* (Lewis Milestone, 1931). As his comments about *Great Expectations* suggest, Harris believed editors should be intelligent, creative agents: 'the technician with nothing to say is ... the man most to avoid.' He experienced high-pressure, low-budget studio production at Twickenham and a nascent form of independent production with Lean at Cineguild when this company was granted considerable autonomy under Rank's Independent Producers initiative. As a pragmatic, seasoned professional, Harris saw the merits of both approaches. He believed producers should retain final say over the editing of standard commercial films but that 'creative' directors should be given more freedom (quoted in Reisz, 1951, p. 16).

Filmography

Take a Girl Like You (Jonathan Miller, 1970)
Three Sisters (Laurence Olivier, John Sichel, 1970)
A Man I Like (Claude Lelouch, 1969)
A Midsummer Night's Dream (Peter Hall, 1968)
Work Is a Four Letter Word (Peter Hall, 1967)
Mister Ten Per Cent (Peter Graham Scott, 1966)
He Who Rides a Tiger (Charles Crichton, 1966)
The Chalk Garden (Ronald Neame, 1964)
Sammy Going South (Alexander Mackendrick, 1963)
Billy Budd (Peter Ustinov, 1962)
Once More, with Feeling (Stanley Donen, 1960)
The Sundowners (Fred Zinnemann, 1960)
The Scapegoat (Robert Hamer, 1959)
Indiscreet (Stanley Donen, 1958)
Barnacle Bill (Charles Frend, 1957)
The Prince and the Showgirl (Laurence Olivier, 1957)
The Ladykillers (Alexander Mackendrick, 1955)
Out of the Clouds (Basil Dearden, 1955)
The Rainbow Jacket (Basil Dearden, 1954)
The Master of Ballantrae (William Keighley, 1953)
The Crimson Pirate (Robert Siodmak, 1952)
Where No Vultures Fly (Harry Watt, 1951)
Captain Horatio Hornblower (Raoul Walsh, 1951)
The Golden Salamander (Ronald Neame, 1950)
Oliver Twist (David Lean, 1948)
Once a Jolly Swagman (Jack Lee, 1948)
Blanche Fury (Marc Allegret, 1947)
Great Expectations (David Lean, 1946)
Brief Encounter (David Lean, 1946)
Blithe Spirit (David Lean, 1945)
This Happy Breed (David Lean, 1944)
Old Mother Riley's Ghosts (John Baxter, 1941)
Crimes at the Dark House (George King, 1940)
The Face at the Window (George King, 1939)
The Angelus (Thomas Bentley, 1937)
Beauty and the Barge (Henry Edwards, 1937)
Juggernaut (Henry Edwards, 1936)
Eliza Comes to Stay (Henry Edwards, 1936)
Spy of Napoleon (Maurice Elvey, 1936)

D'Ye Ken John Peel? (Henry Edwards, 1935)
The Morals of Marcus (Miles Mander, 1935)
Squibs (Henry Edwards, 1935)
The Kentucky Minstrels (John Baxter, 1934)
Lily of Killarney (Maurice Elvey, 1934)
The Wandering Jew (Maurice Elvey, 1933)
I Lived with You (Maurice Elvey, 1933)
The Shadow (George A. Cooper, 1933)
Frail Women (Maurice Elvey, 1932)
Condemned to Death (Walter Forde, 1932)
When London Sleeps (Leslie S. Hiscott, 1932)
The Missing Rembrandt (Leslie S. Hiscott, 1932)
Black Coffee (Leslie S. Hiscott, 1931)
The Sleeping Cardinal (Leslie S. Hiscott, 1931)
Lord Richard in the Pantry (Walter Forde, 1930)

Other editing credits:
Fools Rush In (John Paddy Carstairs, 1949) (supervising editor)
Take My Life (Ronald Neame, 1947) (editorial associate)
The Demi-Paradise (Anthony Asquith, 1943) (supervising editor)
Theatre Royal (John Baxter, 1943) (supervising editor)
When We Are Married (John Baxter, 1943) (supervising editor)
Old Mother Riley Detective (John Baxter, 1943) (supervising editor)
We'll Smile Again (John Baxter, 1942) (supervising editor)
Let the People Sing (John Baxter, 1942) (supervising editor)
The Common Touch (John Baxter, 1941) (supervising editor)
Pastor Hall, (Roy Boulting, 1940) (associate editor)
In the Soup (Henry Edwards, 1936) (supervising editor)
Man in the Mirror (Maurice Elvey, 1936) (supervising editor)
Dusty Ermine (Bernard Vorhaus, 1936) (supervising editor)
Broken Blossoms (Hans Brahm, 1936) (supervising editor)
The Triumph of Sherlock Holmes (Leslie S. Hiscott, 1935) (supervising editor)
The Last Journey (Bernard Vorhaus, 1935) (supervising editor)
Scrooge (Henry Edwards, 1935) (supervising editor)

RALPH KEMPLEN
Following a family tradition established by his bioscope showman father, Ralph
Kemplen entered the industry in 1928 as assistant editor to Arthur Tavares at
Gainsborough. He worked on *Balaclava* (Maurice Elvey, 1928) and later, under
Ian Dalrymple's supervision, cut parts of *The Ghost Train* (Walter Forde, 1931)

and *Sunshine Susie*. In the latter part of the 1930s Kemplen worked with Jack Harris at Twickenham Studios and began to freelance. During the Second World War he edited some training films for the Ministry of Information. In the 1950s he worked on a fairly regular basis for the Woolf brothers' Romulus and Remus production companies. Beginning with *The African Queen*, Kemplen forged a creative partnership with John Huston, which they revived in the 1960s. He continued working on major productions throughout the 1970s. Kemplen directed one film, *The Spaniard's Curse* (1958).

Credits for *Room at the Top* and *A Man for All Seasons* (Fred Zinnemann, 1966) consolidated Kemplen's reputation as a great dialogue editor. On the latter film Zinnemann invited Kemplen to contribute comments not only on the script but also on rehearsals. Other projects Kemplen had a considerable impact on included *The Good Die Young*. He recalled: 'I did a reconstruction whereby the three or four stories which were originally separate were made to run concurrently' (quoted in Musgrave, 1979, p. 16). His various achievements include the dynamically yet classically edited opening sequence of *Moulin Rouge*, and two sequences in *The Day of the Jackal* (Fred Zinnemann, 1973) he was particularly proud of: 'the sequence where the Jackal sets the sights on his gun, because of the economy of its cutting; the final section leading up to his death' (quoted in Sharples Jr, 1977, p. 13).

Filmography
The Dark Crystal (Jim Henson, Frank Oz, 1982)
The Great Muppet Caper (Jim Henson, 1981)
Escape to Athena (George Pan Cosmatos, 1978)
Golden Rendezvous (Ashley Lazarus, 1977)
The Odessa File (Ronald Neame, 1974)
No Sex Please, We're British (Cliff Owen, 1973)
The Day of the Jackal (Fred Zinnemann, 1973)
To Kill a Clown (George Bloomfield, 1972)
Goodbye, Mr Chips (Herbert Ross, 1969)
Oliver! (Carol Reed, 1968)
A Man for All Seasons (Fred Zinnemann, 1966)
The Bible (John Huston, 1966)
The Night of the Iguana (John Huston, 1964)
The Ceremony (Laurence Harvey, 1963)
Freud (John Huston, 1962)
The Roman Spring of Mrs Stone (José Quintero, 1961)
The Savage Innocents (Nicholas Ray, 1960)
Room at the Top (Jack Clayton, 1959)

Bobbikins (Robert Day, 1959)
Three Men in a Boat (Ken Annakin, 1957)
The Story of Esther Costello (David Miller, 1957)
Alexander the Great (Robert Rossen, 1956)
Carrington, V.C. (Anthony Asquith, 1955)
The Good Die Young (Lewis Gilbert, 1954)
Moulin Rouge (John Huston, 1953)
Beat the Devil (John Huston, 1953)
Women of Twilight (Gordon Parry, 1952)
Treasure Hunt (John Paddy Carstairs, 1952)
The African Queen (John Huston, 1952)
Pandora and the Flying Dutchman (Albert Lewin, 1951)
They Were Not Divided (Terence Young, 1950)
Trottie True (Brian Desmond Hurst, 1949)
The Romantic Age (Edmond T. Gréville, 1949)
Mr Perrin and Mr Traill (Lawrence Huntington, 1948)
Uncle Silas (Charles Frank, 1947)
Carnival (Stanley Haynes, 1946)
We'll Smile Again (John Baxter, 1942)
The Saint's Vacation (Leslie Fenton, 1941)
The Saint Meets the Tiger (Paul L. Stein, 1941)
Young Man's Fancy (Robert Stevenson, 1939)
Bedtime Story (Donovan Pedelty, 1938)
Behind Your Back (Donovan Pedelty, 1937)
Dusty Ermine (Bernard Vorhaus, 1936)
Broken Blossoms (Hans Brahm, 1936)
Scrooge (Henry Edwards, 1935)
The Private Secretary (Henry Edwards, 1935)
Death on the Set (Leslie S. Hiscott, 1935)
The Triumph of Sherlock Holmes (Leslie S. Hiscott, 1935)
Annie, Leave the Room! (Leslie S. Hiscott, 1935)
My Heart Is Calling (Carmine Gallone, 1934)
The Ghoul (T. Hayes Hunter, 1933)
There Goes the Bride (Albert de Courville, 1932)
The Midshipmaid (Albert de Courville, 1932)
The Frightened Lady (T. Hayes Hunter, 1932)

TONY LAWSON

A temporary job at a small documentary production company introduced Lawson to film-making. The congenial atmosphere in the cutting rooms convinced him to opt for a career in editing. From the mid-1960s onwards Lawson free-lanced as an assistant sound editor and assistant editor on features, working with Ann Chegwidden and Norman Savage. Lawson's break came on the contro-versial *Straw Dogs*. He got on well with director Sam Peckinpah, who was impressed by some promotional material he cut. After Savage and another edi-tor left the production, Lawson eventually gained a co-editing credit. During the 1970s he worked twice more with Peckinpah and spent two years with Stanley Kubrick on *Barry Lyndon*. Since then his most longstanding collaborations have been with directors Nicolas Roeg and, more recently, Neil Jordan. Lawson has often worked on films that have enabled him to experiment within the par-ameters of mainstream narrative cinema. He emphasises that alongside considerations of continuity, 'one of the things editors should be looking for too is conflicts and contrasts ... cut from a wide shot to a close shot, loud to soft, bright to dark, all those kind of things'.

Lawson sees film as a collaborative medium where it is nevertheless poss-ible to identify different directors' films. He tentatively speculates that 'a director can get to what he wants more easily, more fully, if the people that he surrounds himself with either understand him or they understand each other, essentially'. An example is the sequence in *Cross of Iron* where Sergeant Steiner (James Coburn) is caught in an explosion. A series of dissolves between shots of the blast and Steiner, some in slow motion, extend its impact. These are inter-cut with and superseded by a rapidly cut selection of shots of other characters, shots repeated from earlier in the narrative, imagined encounters by a lake, and shots of Steiner recovering in hospital. The latter include several extreme close-ups of a light being shone into his eye. Peckin-pah responded very positively to Lawson's work on this sequence because it was a successful experiment in a style of editing the director had become identified with. Lawson recalls: 'I got a piece of music [not retained in the fin-ished film], the Japanese Kodo drummers, which was just an extraordinary piece of music, and allied to the visuals turned this sequence into a quasi-reli-gious, mystical experience; near death. I know I hit Sam with that, because he called everyone in to see it.'

Filmography
The Good Thief (Neil Jordan, 2002)
Blow Dry (Paddy Breathnach, 2001)
Not I (Neil Jordan, 2000)
The End of the Affair (Neil Jordan, 1999)
In Dreams (Neil Jordan, 1999)
The Butcher Boy (Neil Jordan, 1997)

Michael Collins (Neil Jordan, 1996)
Othello (Oliver Parker, 1995)
Two Deaths (Nicolas Roeg, 1995)
Victory (Mark Peploe, 1995)
Tom & Viv (Brian Gilbert, 1994)
Friends (Elaine Proctor, 1993)
Wuthering Heights (Peter Kosminsky, 1992)
CrissCross (Chris Menges, 1992)
Cold Heaven (Nicolas Roeg, 1991)
Motion & Emotion (Paul Joyce, 1990)
The Witches (Nicolas Roeg, 1990)
Manifesto (Dusan Makavejev, 1988)
Track 29 (Nicolas Roeg, 1988)
Aria (Nicolas Roeg, 1987) (segment 'Un ballo in maschera')
Castaway (Nicolas Roeg, 1987)
Riders of the Storm (Maurice Phillips, 1986)
Insignificance (Nicolas Roeg, 1985)
Marie (Roger Donaldson, 1985)
The Bounty (Roger Donaldson, 1984)
Eureka (Nicolas Roeg, 1983)
Dragonslayer (Matthew Robbins, 1981)
Bad Timing (Nicolas Roeg, 1980)
Cross of Iron (Sam Peckinpah, 1977)
Barry Lyndon (Stanley Kubrick, 1975)
Straw Dogs (Sam Peckinpah, 1971)

Other editing credits:
Convoy (Sam Peckinpah, 1978) (uncredited)

RUSSELL LLOYD
Entering the film industry shortly after the coming of sound, Lloyd's first job was numbering rushes at London Films while *The Private Life of Don Juan* (Alexander Korda, 1934) was in production. Lloyd was one of several young British assistants working for the American editors Korda employed in the 1930s. The quality and extent of his contribution to *The Squeaker* (William K. Howard, 1937) was such that his senior colleagues Jack Dennis and William Hornbeck gave Lloyd an editing credit on the finished film, even though he had started on it as an assistant. The outbreak of war interrupted Lloyd's features editing career, although he worked on naval documentaries during this period, including *Close Quarters* (Jack Lee, 1943). After the war he spent several years

as a senior editor at Korda's reconstituted London Films, where he also co-
directed *The Last Days of Dolwyn* with Emlyn Williams.

From the 1950s onwards Lloyd edited a number of films for American directors working on Hollywood-financed productions in Britain, and established a
good working relationship with Fox's Darryl Zanuck. Beginning with *Moby
Dick*, Lloyd's collaboration with John Huston became one of the longest-
running editor–director relationships of the post-war period. It put him in a
select category, along with contemporaries such as Bert Bates and Ralph Kemplen, of British editors who worked primarily on Hollywood-financed
productions with sometimes very sizeable budgets. For example, Lloyd began
editing *Cleopatra* (Joseph L. Mankiewicz, 1963) before it was relocated from
Pinewood to Hollywood. His preference was always for a smooth, graceful style
of editing as opposed to more abbreviated cutting, and he disliked editing that
might even momentarily confuse an audience. One indication of Lloyd's classical approach is the elegant use of dissolves to signal the passing of time
throughout *The Man Who Would Be King*.

Filmography
The Dive (Tristan de Vere Cole, 1989)
Foxtrot (Jon Tryggvason, 1988)
Etter Rubicon (Leidulv Rissan, 1987)
Turnaround (Ola Solum, 1986)
Absolute Beginners (Julien Temple, 1986)
Where Is Parsifal? (Henry Helman, 1983)
The Link (Alberto de Martino, 1982)
The Fiendish Plot of Dr Fu Manchu (Piers Haggard, 1980)
Tristan and Isolt (Tom Donovan, 1980)
The Lady Vanishes (Anthony Page, 1979)
The Man Who Would Be King (John Huston, 1975)
In Celebration (Lindsay Anderson, 1975)
The Amorous Milkman (Darren Nesbit, 1972)
The Mackintosh Man (John Huston, 1973)
Love and Pain and the Whole Damn Thing (Alan J. Pakula, 1972)
Swedish Fly Girls (Jack O'Connell, 1970)
The Last Run (Richard Fleischer, 1971)
The Kremlin Letter (John Huston, 1970)
A Walk with Love and Death (John Huston, 1969)
Sinful Davey (John Huston, 1969)
Reflections in a Golden Eye (John Huston, 1967)

Casino Royale [John Huston's section only] (John Huston, Ken Hughes, Robert Parrish, Val Guest, Joseph McGrath, 1967)
After the Fox (Vittorio de Sica, 1966)
Return from the Ashes (J. Lee Thompson, 1965)
Ninety Degrees in the Shade (Jiri Weiss, 1965)
Of Human Bondage (Ken Hughes, 1964)
The Wild Affair (John Krish, 1963)
Bitter Harvest (Peter Graham Scott, 1963)
The Lion (Jack Cardiff, 1962)
The Unforgiven (John Huston, 1960)
Whirlpool (Lewis Allen, 1959)
The Roots of Heaven (John Huston, 1958)
The Naked Earth (Vincent Sherman, 1958)
Count Five and Die (Victor Vicas, 1958)
Heaven Knows, Mr Allison (John Huston, 1957)
Moby Dick (John Huston, 1956)
The Sea Shall Not Have Them (Lewis Gilbert, 1954)
Jhansi Ki Rani (Sohrab Modi, 1953)
Star of India (Arthur Lubin, 1953)
Decameron Nights (Hugo Fregonese, 1953)
Rough Shoot (Robert Parrish, 1953)
Saturday Island (Stuart Heisler, 1952)
I'll Get You for This (Joseph M. Newman, 1951)
Anna Karenina (Julien Duvivier, 1948)
A Man about the House (Leslie Arliss, 1947)
School for Secrets (Peter Ustinov, 1946)
So This Is London (James B. Clark, 1940)
Over the Moon (Thornton Freeland, 1937)
The Squeaker (William K. Howard, 1937)

Other editing credits:
Caligula (Tinto Brass, 1979) (uncredited)

REGINALD MILLS
As both assistant and fully fledged editor Mills worked with some of the most highly regarded figures within British film history. He assisted David Lean on films including *As You Like It* (Paul Czinner, 1936) and *Dreaming Lips* (Paul Czinner, 1937). After this Mills worked for Publicity Films at Merton Park Studios, directing and editing sponsored and advertising films. During the war he

served with the Army Kinematograph Unit. Mills then enjoyed a long stint as editor of all the classic post-war films directed by Michael Powell and Emeric Pressburger. Mills' love of music, ballet and opera made him well suited to experiment with them on the idea of the 'composed' film. Like many directors of that period, Powell was rarely seen in the cutting rooms while Mills was preparing his first cut. According to Mills' long-term assistant Noreen Ackland, Powell 'respected him a lot'. This is corroborated by the praise given to Mills' editing in Powell's volumes of autobiography (1987, pp. 583–4 and 652; 1995, p. 346).

Mills returned to directing and editing commercials in the latter part of the 1950s prior to renewing a fruitful collaboration with Joseph Losey on films including *The Servant* and *King and Country* (1964). Friction with Harold Pinter after editing *The Servant* contributed to a parting of the ways before the next Losey–Pinter collaboration. Mills' most sustained collaboration towards the end of his career was with Franco Zeffirelli. He finally realised a long-held ambition to direct a feature with the ballet film *Tales of Beatrix Potter* (1971). As an editor Mills insisted upon the paramount importance of the perfect timing of cuts. Although in certain respects a traditionalist who disliked some of the innovations of the 1960s, his editing, in the words of his obituarist, 'often had a great force and energy, almost a violence, that added a new element to the films concerned' (LH, 1990, p. 32). Mills was also a pioneer of the trend towards eliminating opticals from editing.

Filmography
The Boarding School (Chicho Ibáñez-Serrador, 1969)
Ring of Bright Water (Jack Couffer, 1969)
Romeo and Juliet (Franco Zeffirelli, 1968)
Dance of Death (David Giles, 1968)
Ulysses (Joseph Strick, 1967)
King and Country (Joseph Losey, 1964)
The Damned (Joseph Losey, 1963)
The Servant (Joseph Losey, 1963)
Circus of Horrors (Sidney Hayers, 1960)
The Criminal (Joseph Losey, 1960)
Blind Date (Joseph Losey, 1959)
Windom's Way (Ronald Neame, 1958)
Passionate Summer (Rudolph Cartier, 1958)
The Battle of the River Plate (Michael Powell and Emeric Pressburger, 1956)
Oh ... Rosalinda! (Michael Powell and Emeric Pressburger, 1956)
The Spanish Gardener (Philip Leacock, 1956)
The Sleeping Tiger (Joseph Losey, using Victor Hanbury's name, 1954)

Where's Charley? (David Butler, 1952)
Tales of Hoffmann (Michael Powell and Emeric Pressburger, 1951)
The Elusive Pimpernel (Michael Powell and Emeric Pressburger, 1951)
Gone to Earth (Michael Powell and Emeric Pressburger, 1950)
The Red Shoes (Michael Powell and Emeric Pressburger, 1948)
Black Narcissus (Michael Powell and Emeric Pressburger, 1947)
A Matter of Life and Death (Michael Powell and Emeric Pressburger, 1946)
What Would You Do Chums? (John Baxter, 1939)

Other editing credits:
The Champ (Franco Zeffirelli, 1979) (editorial consultant)
The Small Back Room (Michael Powell and Emeric Pressburger, 1949) (supervising editor)

JONATHAN MORRIS

Director Ken Loach's prolific output as a feature film-maker since the early 1990s owes a lot to the regular group of collaborators who have worked with him during this period. One of these is editor Jonathan Morris. Morris began his career as a child actor, appearing on stage and in films including *I Could Go On Singing* (Ronald Neame, 1963). After school he worked as a second assistant editor on television series such as *The Saint* and *The Champions*. Later Morris worked as a dubbing assistant at Tigon Films. With some exceptions, notably *Witchfinder General* (Michael Reeves, 1968), his experience there taught him that 'the great difference between editing as opposed to almost any other technique is that sometimes the best work is done on the worst films'. In the 1970s Morris opted for the relative security of a staff job at ATV (subsequently Central Television) where he met directors such as Ken Loach and John Pilger. When Central closed down their operations at Elstree, Morris and Steve Singleton established Parting Shots (later The Editing Partnership), which has provided editing facilities for Channel 4 and various other television and feature productions.

Morris and Loach's work together dates back to 1980s documentaries such as the controversial *Questions of Leadership* (1983). The politically expository nature of the documentary and feature films Loach directs means that for Morris 'the dialogue scenes that we do are really hard, really difficult ... a lot of footage'. Morris feels his relationship with Loach has developed over time: 'I have more influence with Ken now than I did fifteen years ago.' Loach will take note of his responses as the first viewer of the material: 'He may be watching me more than he's watching the rushes, to see how I react to something.' This relationship fed into editing the famous debate sequence in *Land and Freedom*

(1995), where Morris' 'energies were spent trying to cut it down'. He tried to view the sequence not from the perspective of 'the intellectual studying the Spanish Civil War, or politics in the twentieth century'. Instead, he imagined himself as an average cinemagoer 'sitting in the audience thinking, "I want to get on with the story", at the same time being aware that's what the film's actually about. So it's a delicate balance.'

Filmography
Sweet Sixteen (Ken Loach, 2002)
The Navigators (Ken Loach, 2001)
Bread and Roses (Ken Loach, 2000)
My Name Is Joe (Ken Loach, 1998)
Carla's Song (Ken Loach, 1996)
Land and Freedom (Ken Loach, 1995)
Ladybird Ladybird (Ken Loach, 1994)
Raining Stones (Ken Loach, 1993)
Riff-Raff (Ken Loach, 1991)
Hidden Agenda (Ken Loach, 1990)

TOM PRIESTLEY

As the son of author and broadcaster J. B. Priestley, Tom Priestley gravitated towards cinema partly because 'I wanted to try and find something that he hadn't done.' When studying at Cambridge University he attended film screenings every afternoon and particularly enjoyed Leslie Halliwell's programming at the Rex. Later Priestley secured a job as an assistant film librarian at Ealing Studios after a friend advised him Ealing was the best place to train. The first production Priestley worked on, as second assistant sound editor, was *Dunkirk*. Freelancing as an assistant to editor Peter Taylor, Priestley worked on *This Sporting Life*, which he describes as 'a wonderfully cinematic film, very strong and very unusual, and not really like the other Northern realist films; it had another element to it'. *This Sporting Life*'s production company, Independent Artists, 'had a policy of promoting new talent, which on the one side was quite altruistic and on the other side meant they could pay less'. This policy gave Priestley his first two editing credits, but after the company's demise he returned briefly to sound editing, working on several films including *Repulsion* (Roman Polanski, 1965).

Priestley's first real break was on *Morgan: A Suitable Case for Treatment*. This consolidated his reputation as one of the 1960s 'new, young editors' and led to work, in Britain and America, with new directors of that era including Jack Clayton, John Boorman and Lindsay Anderson. By the late 1970s Priestley was in a position where he could choose projects that fulfilled at least two out of three criteria: a good script; stimulating collaborators; an attractive location. He edited big productions such as *Voyage of the Damned* (Stuart Rosenberg, 1976) and supported new British features directors Derek Jarman, Michael Radford, Conny Templeman and Harry Hook. He has also taught at the National Film and Television School and directed two documentaries.

Priestley emphasises the importance of 'learning the material'. He spends a lot of time learning the rhythms of dialogue, camera movements, and movements of objects and people in the frame. The next stage involves deciding the extent to which different parts of the film should be cut with or against these various rhythms. After this the actual editing can proceed quite quickly. Another precept is 'to forget the previous film; don't bring any luggage with you'. Rather than applying a preconceived formula, editing decisions should always emanate from the material at hand. An example is the canteen sequence in *Nineteen Eighty-Four* (Michael Radford, 1984). This is played predominantly in medium close-up of Winston Smith (John Hurt) in front of an image of Big Brother.

> On the first cut ... more or less who was speaking was who you saw ... I then realised that the whole point was that the scene was totally centred on Winston ... because it was about him playing a role within the scene, because he's pretending to obey the rules.

Filmography
The Kitchen Toto (Harry Hook, 1987)
White Mischief (Michael Radford, 1987)
Nanou (Conny Templeman, 1986)
Nemo (Arnaud Sélignac, 1984)
Nineteen Eighty-Four (Michael Radford, 1984)
Another Time, Another Place (Michael Radford, 1983)
Times Square (Allan Moyle, 1980)
Tess (Roman Polanski, 1979)
Exorcist II: The Heretic (John Boorman, 1977)
Voyage of the Damned (Stuart Rosenberg, 1976)
That Lucky Touch (Christopher Miles, 1975)
The Great Gatsby (Jack Clayton, 1974)
The Return of the Pink Panther (Blake Edwards, 1974)
Alpha Beta (Anthony Page, 1973)
Deliverance (John Boorman, 1972)
Leo the Last (John Boorman, 1970)
Isadora (Karel Reisz, 1968)

Our Mother's House (Jack Clayton, 1967)
Marat/Sade (Peter Brook, 1966)
Morgan: A Suitable Case for Treatment (Karel Reisz, 1966)
Father Came Too! (Peter Graham Scott, 1963)
Unearthly Stranger (John Krish, 1963)

Other editing credits:
Lord of the Flies (Harry Hook, 1990) (supervising editor)
Rock Show (1979) (post-production)
Jubilee (Derek Jarman, 1977) (supervising editor)
O Lucky Man! (Lindsay Anderson, 1973) (supervising editor)

TERRY RAWLINGS

Shortly after completing two years' National Service Rawlings was offered a job
in the Rank film library. Intrigued by the film industry, he moved on to become
a dubbing assistant. The first project he worked on was *Town on Trial* (John
Guillermin, 1957). Several years as an assistant followed, often working with
Jack Harris, until Rawlings gained his first full credit as sound editor on *The Pot
Carriers* (Peter Graham Scott, 1962). He followed this with the prestigious *The
L-Shaped Room* (Bryan Forbes, 1962). Rawlings worked briefly as sound and
music editor on the first series of Granada Television's *World in Action*, which
taught him how to meet tight deadlines yet maintain high standards. During the
1960s and 70s he worked as sound, dubbing and music editor on films directed
by emerging new talents including Jack Clayton, Karel Reisz, Ken Russell and
Michael Winner. The passion for music he shared with editor Michael Bradsell
fed into films such as *The Music Lovers* (Ken Russell, 1970).

Rawlings' perception that sound editors were 'the poor relations of the cutting room' eventually led him to cross over into picture editing. He edited an
impressive run of films in the late 1970s and early 80s: *Alien*, *Chariots of Fire*
and *Blade Runner*. With his love of music and policy of 'always looking in
people's eyes when I'm cutting', Rawlings relished editing sequences combining
musical numbers and dialogue in *Yentl*. One example is when Yentl (Barbra
Streisand) eats at Hadass' (Amy Irving's) house and sees for the first time how
much Hadass loves Avigdor (Mandy Patinkin): 'It needed everybody's looks and
observing what's going on, but going to Yentl in the right places and getting all
the lines of dialogue in amongst the words of the song.'

From *Alien* onwards a recurring aspect of Rawlings' work has been experimentation with expressive dissolves. They feature prominently in *White of the
Eye* (Donald Cammell, 1987), a film he describes as a 'fantastic editing exercise'. The narrative is about a serial killer who murders women as a form of

bizarre ritual or artistic practice. The film is a virtual compendium of editing devices: unusually placed dissolves; flash-frames; freeze-frames; inter-cutting; flashbacks given a 'steely, grainy grey look' through treble duping. Rawlings recalls that he and Cammell 'would try so many different things', and says of their experiments:

> I'm not one for over tricksy editing. I don't think it's necessary all the time. But you're working with a story like that which is very hard to swallow, so you can take it a stage further so the audience are not offended so easily by what it's about, but are stimulated by it ... the editing takes you away for a second, but then it makes you concentrate more.

Filmography
The Core (Jon Amiel, 2003)
The Musketeer (Peter Hyams, 2001)
Entrapment (Jon Amiel, 1999)
U.S. Marshals (Stuart Baird, 1998)
The Saint (Philip Noyce, 1997)
GoldenEye (Martin Campbell, 1995)
Trapped in Paradise (George Gallo, 1994)
No Escape (Martin Campbell, 1994)
Sleepwalker (Jon Jacobs, 1993)
Alien³ (David Fincher, 1992)
Not without My Daughter (Brian Gilbert, 1991)
Bullseye! (Michael Winner, 1991)
Slipstream (Steven Lisberger, 1989)
The Lonely Passion of Judith Hearne (Jack Clayton, 1987)
White of the Eye (Donald Cammell, 1987)
F/X (Robert Mandel, 1986)
Legend (Ridley Scott, 1985)
Yentl (Barbra Streisand, 1983)
Chariots of Fire (Hugh Hudson, 1981)
The Awakening (Mike Newell, 1980)
Alien (Ridley Scott, 1979)
Watership Down (Martin Rosen, 1978)
The Sentinel (Michael Winner, 1977)
The Stone Killer (Michael Winner, 1973)

Other editing credits:
Blade Runner (Ridley Scott, 1982) (supervising editor)

ALFRED ROOME

One of twelve apprentices taken on straight from school in 1927 by Herbert Wilcox and J. D. Williams, Roome began as an assistant in the property department and cutting rooms. Moving from Wilcox's British and Dominions studio to British International Pictures, he worked as second camera assistant to Jack Cox on films directed by Alfred Hitchcock including *The Ring* (1928) and *Blackmail* (1929). At British International Pictures Roome was also one of director E. A. Dupont's assistant editors. He noted that the German director edited his films himself. Returning to Wilcox at the British and Dominions studio, Roome's first full editing credit was for the Tom Walls Aldwych farce *Thark* (1932). He continued this association, working closely with the writer Ben Travers, when Walls' production unit moved to Gaumont-British and Gainsborough.

Roome's growing reputation as a comedy specialist led to work on some of the cycle of Will Hay, Crazy Gang and Arthur Askey films produced at Gainsborough during the mid- to late 1930s. As Roome became a more senior figure during the 1940s he was often asked to come onto the studio floor to support new directors. He co-directed two films and progressed to associate producer status. Subsequently employed by Rank at Pinewood in the 1950s and 60s, Roome felt the films produced there were frequently quite poor but as 'technicians, we were quite happy because it kept us in work'. Roome often worked with directors Ken Annakin and Ralph Thomas during this period. He respected producer Betty Box's efficiency and commercial acumen, but sometimes challenged director Muriel Box, for whom he edited *To Dorothy a Son* (1954), because he felt the real power rested with her husband Sydney. Roome brought all his comedy experience to bear when in the late 1960s and early 70s he edited fourteen *Carry On* films. He knew, for example, that experienced performers like Sid James and Kenneth Williams could spoil someone else's line but gain an extra laugh 'by either making a remark or making some facial expression, which, if put in the right place, made the line entirely different'. The overall approach with regard to pacing these films was, 'just carry straight on ... if there's three gags or three laughs and [the audience] miss two of them, but get one, that's good enough'.

Filmography

Carry On Behind (Gerald Thomas, 1975)
Carry On Dick (Gerald Thomas, 1974)
Carry On Girls (Gerald Thomas, 1973)
Bless This House (Gerald Thomas, 1972)
Carry On Abroad (Gerald Thomas, 1972)
Carry On Matron (Gerald Thomas, 1972)

Carry On at Your Convenience (Gerald Thomas, 1971)
Carry On Henry (Gerald Thomas, 1971)
Carry On Loving (Gerald Thomas, 1970)
Carry On Up the Jungle (Gerald Thomas, 1970)
Carry On Again, Doctor (Gerald Thomas, 1969)
Carry On Camping (Gerald Thomas, 1969)
Carry On Doctor (Gerald Thomas, 1968)
Carry On Up the Khyber (Gerald Thomas, 1968)
Follow That Camel (Gerald Thomas, 1967)
Doctor in Clover (Ralph Thomas, 1966)
Deadlier Than the Male (Ralph Thomas, 1966)
The High Bright Sun (Ralph Thomas, 1965)
The Informers (Ken Annakin, 1965)
Hot Enough for June (Ralph Thomas, 1964)
Doctor in Distress (Ralph Thomas, 1963)
A Pair of Briefs (Ralph Thomas, 1962)
The Wild and the Willing (Ralph Thomas, 1962)
No Love for Johnnie (Ralph Thomas, 1961)
No My Darling Daughter (Ralph Thomas, 1961)
Doctor in Love (Ralph Thomas, 1960)
Conspiracy of Hearts (Ralph Thomas, 1960)
The Thirty-Nine Steps (Ralph Thomas, 1959)
Upstairs and Downstairs (Ralph Thomas, 1959)
Nor the Moon by Night (Ken Annakin, 1958)
A Tale of Two Cities (Ralph Thomas, 1958)
Across the Bridge (Ken Annakin, 1957)
The Big Money (John Paddy Carstairs, 1956)
The Black Tent (Brian Desmond Hurst, 1956)
The Woman for Joe (George More O'Ferrall, 1955)
You Know What Sailors Are (Ken Annakin, 1954)
Up to His Neck (John Paddy Carstairs, 1954)
To Dorothy a Son (Muriel Box, 1954)
Always a Bride (Ralph Smart, 1953)
Top of the Form (John Paddy Carstairs, 1953)
Encore (Harold French, Pat Jackson, Anthony Pelissier, 1952)
Penny Princess (Val Guest, 1952)
The Planter's Wife (Ken Annakin, 1952)
Hotel Sahara (Ken Annakin, 1951)
Highly Dangerous (Roy Baker, 1950)
Trio (Harold French, Ken Annakin, 1950)

Holiday Camp (Ken Annakin, 1948)
The Man Within (Bernard Knowles, 1947)
The Magic Bow (Bernard Knowles, 1947)
I'll Be Your Sweetheart (Val Guest, 1945)
Waterloo Road (Sidney Gilliat, 1944)
Give Us the Moon (Val Guest, 1944)
Miss London Ltd (Val Guest, 1943)
Kipps (Carol Reed, 1941)
Once a Crook (Herbert Mason, 1941)
The Frozen Limits (Marcel Varnel, 1939)
Where's the Fire (Marcel Varnel, 1939)
Shipyard Sally (Monty Banks, 1939)
Ask a Policeman (Marcel Varnel, 1939)
Bank Holiday (Carol Reed, 1938)
Alf's Button Afloat (Marcel Varnel, 1938)
Old Bones of the River (Marcel Varnel, 1938)
Good Morning, Boys (Marcel Varnel, 1937)
Oh, Mr Porter! (Marcel Varnel, 1937)
Pot Luck (Tom Walls, 1936)
Stormy Weather (Tom Walls, 1936)
The Man Who Changed His Mind (Robert Stevenson, 1936)
Boys Will Be Boys (William Beaudine, 1935)
Foreign Affaires (Tom Walls, 1935)
A Cup of Kindness (Tom Walls, 1934)
Dirty Work (Tom Walls, 1934)
London on a Night Like This (Tom Walls, 1933)
The Blarney Stone (Tom Walls, 1933)
Leap Year (Tom Walls, 1932)
Thark (Tom Walls, 1932)

Other editing credits:
Broken Journey (Ken Annakin, 1948) (supervising editor)
Bees in Paradise (Val Guest, 1944) (cutting)
Millions Like Us (Frank Launder, Sidney Gilliat, 1943) (cutting)
King Arthur Was a Gentleman (Marcel Varnel, 1942) (cutting)
The Young Mr Pitt (Carol Reed, 1942) (cutting)
For Freedom (Maurice Elvey, Castleton Knight, 1940) (cutting)
Ask a Policeman (Marcel Varnel, 1939) (cutting)
Band Waggon (Marcel Varnel, 1939) (cutter)

The Lady Vanishes (Alfred Hitchcock, 1938) (cutting)
Said O'Reilly to McNab (William Beaudine, 1937) (cutting)
Doctor Syn (Roy William Neill, 1937) (cutter)

PETER TANNER

The first film Tanner assisted on was *Lorna Doone* (1934), directed by Basil Dean during his time as head of Ealing Studios. Tanner returned to Ealing in the late 1940s and 50s to edit some of the most outstanding films produced under Michael Balcon's leadership. Prior to that he served his apprenticeship as assistant to Reginald Beck at Fox's Wembley Studios. Thanks to a training programme negotiated between Fox and the ACT, he went to Hollywood for several months and worked with editor Robert Simpson on *Always Goodbye* (Sidney Lanfield, 1938). Although Tanner was young enough to be called up for active service during the War, producer Sydney Box secured him exemptions to work on various documentary projects. He edited *We Serve* (Carol Reed, 1942), a film designed to recruit women to the Army, and *Failure of a Strategy* (David Lean, 1944), a newsreel compilation intended for exhibition in countries recently liberated by the Allies. With fellow editor Stewart McAllister, Tanner helped put together the first British documentary record of the newly liberated concentration camps for the German War Atrocities project.

Tanner joined Ealing for *Scott of the Antarctic*, where he was closely involved in 'matching [Vaughan Williams'] music to the rhythm of the cutting of the film' (quoted in Belfrage, n.d., p. 206). The project he enjoyed most was *Kind Hearts and Coronets*. During production Alec Guinness often visited the cutting rooms to remind himself, by listening to sound loops, of the different voices of the nine characters he was playing. Tanner spent ten years at Ealing, assisted initially by Seth Holt and later by John Jympson. Most of Tanner's subsequent career was spent freelancing on various features, interspersed with occasional television work. One regret was never working with Hamer again: 'I was going to do *Lady Windermere's Fan* with him just before he died, which would have been fascinating, because he would have been perfect for Wilde.' *Husbands* (John Cassavetes, 1970) was a challenge because of its long, improvised shots where the conception of a scene might change from take to take. Tanner's favourite film of the later part of his career was the little-known *Stevie* (Robert Enders, 1978). He occasionally published and lectured on his experiences as an editor, and emphasised that 'you should never be too old to learn, as well as never too old to experiment ... If it doesn't come off, nothing is lost, it just didn't come off. But there is always the chance that it will' (quoted in Belfrage, n.d., p. 206).

Filmography
Something to Believe In (John Hough, 1998)
A Month by the Lake (John Irvin, 1995)
Widow's Peak (John Irvin, 1994)
Taffin (Francis Megahy, 1988)
Without a Clue (Thom Eberhardt, 1988)
Hamburger Hill (John Irvin, 1987)
Turtle Diary (John Irvin, 1985)
The Monster Club (Roy Ward Baker, 1980)
A Game for Vultures (James Fargo, 1979)
Stevie (Robert Enders, 1978)
The Thief of Baghdad (Clive Donner, 1978)
Wombling Free (Lionel Jeffries, 1977)
Nasty Habits (Michael Lindsay-Hogg, 1977)
Hedda (Trevor Nunn, 1975)
The Beast Must Die (Paul Annett, 1974)
The Maids (Christopher Miles, 1974)
And Now the Screaming Starts! (Roy Ward Baker, 1973)
The Belstone Fox (James Hill, 1973)
Asylum (Roy Ward Baker, 1972)
What Became of Jack and Jill (Bill Bain, 1972)
I, Monster (Stephen Weeks, 1971)
The House That Dripped Blood (Peter Duffell, 1970)
Husbands (John Cassavetes, 1970)
The Best House in London (Philip Saville, 1969)
Diamonds for Breakfast (Christopher Morahan, 1968)
The Crooked Road (Don Chaffey, 1965)
A Jolly Bad Fellow (Don Chaffey, 1964)
Tamahine (Philip Leacock, 1964)
The Last Days of Sodom and Gomorrah (Robert Aldrich, 1962)
Greyfriars Bobby (Don Chaffey, 1961)
Hand in Hand (Philip Leacock, 1960)
Light Up the Sky (Lewis Gilbert, 1960)
A Terrible Beauty (Tay Garnett, 1960)
The Angry Hills (Robert Aldrich, 1959)
A Question of Adultery (Don Chaffey, 1959)
Davy (Michael Relph, 1957)
The Man in the Sky (Charles Crichton, 1957)
Who Done It? (Basil Dearden, 1956)
The Night My Number Came Up (Leslie Norman, 1955)

Touch and Go (Michael Truman, 1955)
Lease of Life (Charles Frend, 1954)
The Maggie (Alexander Mackendrick, 1954)
The Cruel Sea (Charles Frend, 1953)
The Gentle Gunman (Basil Dearden, 1952)
I Believe in You (Basil Dearden, 1952)
Secret People (Thorold Dickinson, 1952)
Pool of London (Basil Dearden, 1951)
Cage of Gold (Basil Dearden, 1950)
The Blue Lamp (Basil Dearden, 1950)
Kind Hearts and Coronets (Robert Hamer, 1949)
Scott of the Antarctic (Charles Frend, 1948)
Sabotage at Sea (Leslie S. Hiscott, 1942)
Murder in the Family (Albert Parker, 1938)

Other editing credits:
Sky Bandits (Zoran Perisic, 1986) (supervising editor)

LESLEY WALKER

Keen to work in the arts, Walker fell into editing by chance. Her first job was in a film laboratory, where she worked as a runner, negative cutter and receptionist. In this capacity she got to know many film editors. Walker's next job was as cutting room secretary and assistant editor at a company producing commercials and Children's Film Foundation films. Over the next ten years she assisted John Bloom and Tom Priestley. Walker has edited commercials, worked occasionally for television, and taught at the National Film and Television School, but her primary focus since the late 1970s has been editing features. She has worked with directors as diverse as Mike Leigh, Derek Jarman, Richard Attenborough and Terry Gilliam. Walker has also worked as a film doctor, but will only do so if both producer and director request this, because she believes creative ownership ultimately resides with the latter.

Walker considers one of her main responsibilities to be shaping the dramatic arc of a film, ensuring that its overall narrative development is properly measured and integrated. Close attention to the minutiae of actors' performances is also high on her list of priorities. When it is appropriate to the material Walker also

> quite likes mistiming and not necessarily matching shots up ... I will mess around with, shall we say, convention ... I cross the line, actually, in *The Fisher King* [Terry Gilliam, 1991] ... Although the audience doesn't quite know what you've done it actually makes you sit up and think something's happened, but it hasn't.

One example is when Jack Lucas (Jeff Bridges) chases fantasist Parry (Robin Williams) across a park. At one point rapidly edited shots of Parry running alternately from screen left to right and screen right to left are inter-cut with equally rapid shots of him dashing past Jack. The shots of Parry are 'mistimed', effectively crossing the line, since it would be impossible for him to repeatedly turn around so often and so quickly. Rather than endow Parry's movements with logical continuity Walker's editing shifts him partly into another dimension where normal rules of coherent space and time do not apply.

Filmography
The Sleeping Dictionary (Guy Jenkin, 2002)
Nicholas Nickleby (Douglas McGrath, 2002)
All or Nothing (Mike Leigh, 2002)
The Body (Jonas McCord, 2000)
Grey Owl (Richard Attenborough, 1999)
Fear and Loathing in Las Vegas (Terry Gilliam, 1998)
In Love and War (Richard Attenborough, 1997)
Emma (Douglas McGrath, 1996)
Mary Reilly (Stephen Frears, 1996)
Jack and Sarah (Tim Sullivan, 1995)
Born Yesterday (Luis Mandoki, 1993)
Shadowlands (Richard Attenborough, 1993)
Waterland (Stephen Gyllenhaal, 1992)
The Fisher King (Terry Gilliam, 1991)
Shirley Valentine (Lewis Gilbert, 1989)
Cry Freedom (Richard Attenborough, 1987)
Mona Lisa (Neil Jordan, 1986)
Letter to Brezhnev (Chris Bernard, 1985)
Meantime (Mike Leigh, 1981)
Richard's Things (Anthony Harvey, 1981)
Eagle's Wing (Anthony Harvey, 1979)
The Tempest (Derek Jarman, 1979)
A Portrait of the Artist as a Young Man (Joseph Strick, 1979)

Other editing credits:
Kin (Elaine Proctor, 2000) (uncredited)
The Woodlanders (Phil Agland, 1998) (uncredited)

NOTES

All unattributed quotations are drawn from the interviews conducted for this book, apart from quotations from Teddy Darvas, Alfred Roome, and Noreen Ackland's comments about female assistants and heavy work, which are drawn from their interviews for the BECTU History Project.

1. Unattributed (2000), is a rare profile of a black British editor, Oral Norrie Ottey, whose credits include *Bhaji on the Beach* (Gurinder Chadha, 1993) and *Plunkett & Macleane* (Jake Scott, 1999).

2. Wood (1973), profiles Hafenrichter. Thompson and Bordwell (1983), covers Hornbeck's career, although it says little about his time working in Britain.

Bibliography

ACTT, *Action: Fifty Years in the Life of a Union* (London: Pear Publications, 1983)

Anderson, Lindsay, *Making a Film: The Story of Secret People* (London: Allen and Unwin, 1952)

Arroyo, José (ed.), *Action/Spectacle Cinema* (London: BFI, 2000)

Attenborough, Richard, *In Search of Gandhi* (London: The Bodley Head, 1982)

Barr, Charles, *Ealing Studios*, second edition (London: Studio Vista, 1993)

Barr, Charles, *English Hitchcock* (Moffat: Cameron and Hollis, 1999)

Bates, Bert, letter to *Guild of British Film Editors Newsletter*, no. 30, March 1970

Beck, Reginald, letter to Russell Lloyd published in *Guild of British Film Editors Journal*, no. 49, June 1977

Belfrage, Colin, *All Is Grist* (London: Parallax Press, n.d.)

Bergfelder, Tim, 'The Production Designer and the Gesamtkunstwerk: German Technicians in the British Film Industry of the 1930s', in Andrew Higson (ed.), *Dissolving Views: Key Writings on British Cinema* (London: Cassell, 1996)

Bergfelder, Tim, 'Surface and Distraction: Style and Genre at Gainsborough in the Late 1920s and 1930s', in Pam Cook (ed.), *Gainsborough Pictures* (London: Cassell, 1997)

Birt, Dan, 'The Principles of Film Recording', *Close-Up*, September 1931

Bordwell, David, *Making Meaning* (Cambridge, MA: Harvard University Press, 1989)

Bordwell, David, 'Intensified Continuity: Visual Style in Contemporary American Film', *Film Quarterly*, vol. 55, no. 3, Spring 2002

Bordwell, David, Staiger, Janet and Thompson, Kristin, *The Classical Hollywood Cinema* (London: Routledge, 1985)

Brennan, Michael, 'HD Shooting – Cut the Hype!', *High Definition*, issue 2, June 2003

British Pathe, Newsletter, Summer 2002

Brown, Geoff, 'Money for Speed: The British Films of Bernard Vorhaus', in Jeffrey Richards (ed.), *The Unknown 1930s: An Alternative History of the British Cinema 1929–1939* (London: I. B. Tauris, 1998)

Brownlow, Kevin, *The Parade's Gone By* (London: Secker and Warburg, 1968)

Brownlow, Kevin, *David Lean* (London: Faber, 1997)

Brunel, Adrian, 'Dangers of Quickies to British Technicians', BFI Adrian Brunel Special Collection, n.d.[a]

Brunel, Adrian, 'Outline of Scheme for Enlargement of Brunel and Montagu Ltd', BFI Ivor Montagu Special Collection, n.d.[b]

Brunel, Adrian, *Film Craft* (London: George Newnes, 1933)

Brunel, Adrian, *Film Production* (London: George Newnes, 1936)

Brunel, Adrian, *Nice Work: The Story of Thirty Years in British Film Production* (London: Forbes Robertson, 1949)

Burton, Alan, O'Sullivan, Tim and Wells, Paul (eds), *The Family Way: The Boulting Brothers and British Film Culture* (Trowbridge: Flicks Books, 2000)

Charity, Tom, 'The Turner Prize', *Time Out*, 22 December 1999

Chibnall, Steve, *J. Lee Thompson* (Manchester: Manchester University Press, 2000)

Ciment, Michel, *Conversations with Losey* (London: Methuen, 1985)

Cole, Sidney, *Film Editing* (London: BFI, 1944)

Cole, Sidney, 'The Film Editor', in Oswell Blakeston (ed.), *Working for the Films* (London: Focal Press, 1947)

Combs, Richard, '*Petulia* and Friends', *Film Comment*, vol. 35, no. 1, January–February 1999

Crittenden, Roger, *Thames and Hudson Manual of Film Editing* (London: Thames and Hudson, 1981)

Crittenden, Roger, 'Cinematic Detection: A Case Study', *Journal of Media Practice*, vol. 1, no. 1, 2000

Dalrymple, Ian, 'Commercial Cutting', in Adrian Brunel, *Film Craft* (London: George Newnes, 1933)

Dalrymple, Ian, 'The Crown Film Unit, 1940–43', in Nicholas Pronay and D. W. Spring (eds), *Propaganda, Politics and Film, 1918–45* (London: Macmillan, 1982)

Dixon, Wheeler Winston, *The Charm of Evil: The Life and Films of Terence Fisher* (Metuchen, NJ: Scarecrow Press, 1991)

Dmytryk, Edward, *On Film Editing: An Introduction to the Art of Film Construction* (Boston and London: Focal Press, 1984)

Dyer, Richard, *The Matter of Images: Essays on Representation* (London: Routledge, 1993)

Eberts, Jake and Ilott, Terry, *My Indecision Is Final* (London: Faber, 1990)

Eisenstein, Sergei, Pudovkin, Vsevolod and Alexandrov, Grigori, 'Statement on Sound', in Richard Taylor and Ian Christie (eds), *The Film Factory: Russian and Soviet Cinema in Documents 1896–1939* (London: Routledge, 1988)

Ellis, John, 'Made in Ealing', in Tony Bennett (ed.), *Popular Fiction* (London: Routledge, 1990)

Elsaesser, Thomas, *Fassbinder's Germany* (Amsterdam: Amsterdam University Press, 1996)

Eyles, Allen, 'Cutting Remarks', *Stills*, no. 19, May 1985

Fairservice, Don, *Film Editing: History, Theory and Practice* (Manchester: Manchester University Press, 2001)

Fitzgerald, Theresa, interview with Alexander Mackendrick, *Screen International*, 29 September 1990

French, Philip, 'Memo to British Directors: Make More Films', *The Observer*, Review, 9 April 2000

French, Philip, 'Hollywood Shifts Chabrol into Top Gere', *The Observer*, Review, 9 June 2002

Frend, Charles, 'Cutting Room Practice', *British Kinematography*, vol. 8, no. 3, 1945

Gifford, Denis, 'Fitz: The Old Man of the Screen', in Charles Barr (ed.), *All Our Yesterdays: Ninety Years of British Cinema* (London: BFI, 1986)

Gladwell, David, 'Editing Anderson's *If...*', *Screen*, vol. 10, no. 1, January–February 1969

Glen, John, *For My Eyes Only* (London: Batsford, 2001)

Goldman, William, *Adventures in the Screentrade* (London: Macdonald, 1984)

Goodhew, Philip, 'It Was Grim, I Was Happy', *Sight and Sound*, vol. 7, no. 7, July 1997

Gribble, Bernard, 'Report from the City of Angels', *Guild of British Film Editors Journal*, no. 46, December 1975

Hacker, Jonathan and Price, David, *Take Ten: Contemporary British Directors* (Oxford: Clarendon Press, 1991)

Hankinson, Michael, 'The Routine of Editing', in Adrian Brunel, *Film Craft* (London: George Newnes, 1933)

Harper, Sue, *Women in British Cinema: Mad, Bad and Dangerous to Know* (London: Continuum, 2000)

Hartman, Andy, transcript of discussion with founders of Avid, 11 April 2000, <www.calvin.edu/admin/irc/cmp/video/avidhist.html> (visited June 2002)

Hepworth, Cecil, *Came the Dawn: Memories of a Film Pioneer* (London: Phoenix House, 1951)

Higson, Andrew, *Waving the Flag: Constructing a National Cinema in Britain* (Oxford: Clarendon Press, 1995)

Hill, John, *Sex, Class and Realism: British Cinema 1956–63* (London: BFI, 1986)

Hill, John, *British Cinema in the 1980s: Issues and Themes* (Oxford: Clarendon Press, 1999)

Honess, Peter and Urioste, Frank, 'Two Long-Time Friends Talk about Their Work', <www.editorsguild.com/newsletter/SepOct01/honess_urioste_two.html> (visited January 2002)

Houston, Penelope, 'The Innocents', *Sight and Sound*, vol. 30, no. 3, Summer 1961

Hudson, Roger, 'Putting the Magic in It', *Sight and Sound*, vol. 35, no. 2, Spring 1966

Hunningher, Joost, 'Putting Student Collaboration before Authorship', *Journal of Media Practice*, vol. 1, no. 3, 2000

Hutchings, Peter, 'Beyond the New Wave: Realism in British Cinema, 1959–63', in Robert Murphy (ed.), *The British Cinema Book*, second edition (London: BFI, 2001)

Igel, Rachel, 'I'll Let the Film Pile Up for You', <www.editorsguild.com/newsletter/Directory/tomasini.html> (visited June 2002)

Koszarski, Richard (ed.), *Hollywood Directors 1941–1976* (New York: OUP, 1977)

Lawson, Tony, letter to *Sight and Sound*, vol. 8, issue 5, May 1998

Lean, David, 'The Film Director', in Oswell Blakeston (ed.), *Working for the Films* (London: Focal Press, 1947)

LH, Reginald Mills obituary, *Film and Television Technician*, no. 540, August–September 1990

LoBrutto, Vincent, *Selected Takes: Film Editors on Editing* (New York: Praeger, 1991)

LoBrutto, Vincent, *Sound-on-Film: Interviews with Creators of Film Sound* (New York: Praeger, 1994)

Lovell, Alan, 'The British Cinema: The Known Cinema?', in Robert Murphy (ed.), *The British Cinema Book,* second edition (London: BFI, 2001)

Low, Rachael, *The History of the British Film, 1918–1929* (London: Routledge, 1997a)

Low, Rachael, *Film Making in 1930s Britain* (London: Routledge, 1997b)

MacCabe, Colin, *Performance* (London: BFI Film Classics, 1998)

McFarlane, Brian, *An Autobiography of British Cinema* (London: Methuen, 1997)

McGilligan, Patrick, *George Cukor: A Double Life* (London: Faber, 1991)

McGrath, Declan, *Editing and Post-Production* (Hove, E. Sussex: RotoVision, Screencraft series, 2001)

Manvell, Roger, *Film* (Harmondsworth: Penguin Books, 1944)

Medhurst, Andy, 'In Search of a Rogue', *Sight and Sound*, vol. 1, issue 1, May 1991

Minns, Adam, 'Blow for UK as Production Collapses', *Screen International*, issue 1378, 25 October 2002

Mitchell, Julian, 'Immersed in HD', in *HD World* (supplement), *TV Technology and Production*, vol. 20, issue 7, October 2002

Monk, Claire, 'The British Heritage Film Debate Revisited', in Claire Monk and Amy Sargeant (eds), *British Historical Cinema* (London: Routledge, 2002)

Montagu, Ivor, 'Working with Hitchcock', *Sight and Sound*, vol. 49, no. 3, Summer 1980

Morris, Mark, 'Chaos Theory Hits L.A.', *The Observer*, Review, 7 May 2000

Murch, Walter, *In the Blink of an Eye: A Perspective on Film Editing* (Los Angeles: Silman-James Press, 1995)

Murphy, Robert, 'Under the Shadow of Hollywood', in Charles Barr (ed.), *All Our Yesterdays: Ninety Years of British Cinema* (London: BFI, 1986)

Murphy, Robert, *Sixties British Cinema* (London: BFI, 1992)

Murphy, Robert (ed.), *The British Cinema Book,* second edition (London: BFI, 2001)

Musgrave, Peter, 'A Portrait of Ralph Kemplen', *Guild of British Film Editors Journal*, no. 52, June 1979

National Film Theatre programme booklets (London: BFI, November 1983, October/November 1999)

Oldham, Gabriella, *First Cut: Conversations with Film Editors* (Berkeley: University of California Press, 1992)

Ondaatje, Michael, *The Conversations: Walter Murch and the Art of Editing Film* (New York and London: Knopf/Bloomsbury, 2002a)

Ondaatje, Michael, interviewed on 'Front Row', BBC Radio Four, 31 October 2002b

Perkins, Roy, 'The Director as Author within the Process of Cinema Production', unpublished MA dissertation, Goldsmiths College, University of London, 1993

Petrie, Duncan, *The British Cinematographer* (London: BFI, 1996a)

Petrie, Duncan (ed.), *Inside Stories: Diaries of British Film-Makers at Work* (London: BFI, 1996b)

Powell, Michael, *A Life in Movies: An Autobiography* (London: Methuen 1987)

Powell, Michael, *Million Dollar Movie* (New York: Random House, 1995)

Pudovkin, Vsevolod, *Film Technique and Film Acting* (London: Vision, 1958)

Rayns, Tony, '*Petulia*', in John Pym (ed.), *Time Out Film Guide*, fifth edition (London: Penguin, 1997)

Reed, Kimberly, 'Time Code', <www.dv.com/magazine/2000/0800/reed0800.html> (visited June 2002)

Reisz, Karel, 'The Editor: Jack Harris', *Sight and Sound* supplement: Films in 1951

Reisz, Karel, *The Technique of Film Editing* (London: Focal Press, 1953); revised edition with additional text by Gavin Millar, 1968

Richards, Jeffrey, *Thorold Dickinson: The Man and His Films* (London: Croom Helm, 1984)

Rivers, John, 'John Glen', in Yoram Allon, Del Cullen and Hannah Patterson (eds), *Contemporary British and Irish Directors* (London: Wallflower Press, 2001)

Salt, Barry, *Film Style and Technology: History and Analysis* (London: Starword, 1992)

Sarris, Andrew, 'Notes on the Auteur Theory in 1962', in Gerald Mast, Marshall Cohen and Leo Braudy (eds), *Film Theory and Criticism* (New York: OUP, 1992)

Sarris, Andrew, 'The Care and Feeding of Auteurs', *Film Comment*, vol. 29, no. 1, January–February 1993

Saxon, David, 'Does Anyone Know What the Editor Does?', *The Hollywood Reporter*, 9 July 1984

Schatz, Thomas, *The Genius of the System: Hollywood Filmmaking in the Studio Era* (New York: Pantheon, 1988)

Screen Digest, 'Report on the Implications of Digital Technology for the Film Industry' (London: Department for Culture, Media and Sport, Creative Industries Division, September 2000)

Seidenberg, Robert, 'Behind Every Blockbuster', *American Film*, vol. 15, no. 9, June 1990

Sharples Jr, Win, 'Prime Cut', *Film Comment*, vol. 13, no. 2, March–April 1977

Sherman, Eric, *Directing the Film: Film Directors on Their Art* (New York: AFI/Acrobat Books, 1988)

Sinyard, Neil, *Jack Clayton* (Manchester: Manchester University Press, 2000)

Spittles, Brian, *John Ford* (Harlow: Longman, 2002)

Stafford, Roy, *Non-Linear Editing and Visual Literacy* (London: BFI, 1995)

Stewart, Hugh, 'The Function of Editing in Film Making', *British Kinematography*, vol. 13, no. 6, 1948

Stollery, Martin, *Alternative Empires: European Modernist Cinemas and Cultures of Imperialism* (Exeter: Exeter University Press, 2000)

Stollery, Martin, *Trainspotting* (London: York Press, 2001)

Sweeney, Mary, 'What I've Learned as a Moviemaker', *MovieMaker*, vol. 1, issue 8, July 2002

Tanner, Peter, 'Kind Hearts and Coronets', *Amateur Movie-Maker*, June 1960

Tanner, Peter, 'Editing: Theory and Practice', *The Photographic Journal*, vol. 102, no. 11, November 1962

Taylor, John Russell, *Hitch: The Life and Work of Alfred Hitchcock* (London: Faber, 1978)

Thompson, Kristin and Bordwell, David, 'From Sennett to Stevens – An Interview with William Hornbeck', *The Velvet Light Trap*, no. 20, Summer 1983

Truffaut, François, 'Une certaine tendence du cinéma français', *Cahiers du cinéma*, no. 31, January 1954

Unattributed, 'A Cut above the Rest', *Black Film Maker*, vol. 3, no. 8, 2000

Unattributed, interview with Peter Honess, *Hollywood Reporter*, <www.hollywoodreporter.com/Jan02> (visited January 2002a)

Unattributed, 'Footsteps on the Beach: Cast and Crew', <www.thaistudents.com/thebeach/masahiro.html> (visited March 2002b)

Unattributed, 'Quantel Thinking', <www.quantel.com/domisphere/infopool.nfs/html> (visited June 2002c)

Unattributed, report in *High Definition*, issue 2, June 2003

Vaughan, Dai, *Portrait of an Invisible Man: The Working Life of Stewart McAllister, Film Editor* (London: BFI, 1983)

Walker, Alexander, *Hollywood, England* (London: Harrap, 1974)

Walter, Ernest, *The Technique of the Film Cutting Room* (London and New York: Focal Press, 1973)

Wanstall, Norman, letter to *Guild of British Film Editors Journal*, no. 50, March 1978

Wapshott, Nicholas, *The Man Between: A Biography of Carol Reed* (London: Chatto and Windus, 1990)

Williams, Raymond, *Culture and Society 1780–1950* (Harmondsworth: Penguin, 1958)

Williamson, Judith, *Deadline at Dawn: Film Criticism 1980–1990* (London: Marion
    Boyars, 1993)

Wilson, Freddie, 'A Museum of Recollection', *Guild of British Film Editors Journal*,
    no. 53, 1979

Wollen, Peter, *Signs and Meanings in the Cinema* (London: Secker and Warburg, 1969);
    fourth revised edition, 1998

Wood, Ean, 'Oswald Hafenrichter', *Guild of British Film Editors Journal*, no. 42,
    November 1973

Wood, Linda, 'Julius Hagen and Twickenham Film Studios', in Jeffrey Richards (ed.),
    The Unknown 1930s: An Alternative History of the British Cinema 1929–1939
    (London: I. B. Tauris, 1998)

Wood, Linda, 'Low-Budget British Films in the 1930s', in Robert Murphy (ed.),
    The British Cinema Book, second edition (London: BFI, 2001)

Wyeth, Peter and Grantham, Bill, 'Cutters Way', *Stills*, no. 11, April–May 1984

Young, L. L., 'Angela's Ashes: The Novel, the Film, the Moviola', *ACE Magazine*,
    Autumn 1999

Yule, Andrew, *Enigma: David Puttnam, The Story So Far* (Edinburgh: Mainstream,
    1988)

JOURNALS

ACE Magazine
Film and Television Technician
Guild of British Film Editors Journal
Journal of Media Practice
Screen International
Sight and Sound
Stills
TV Technology and Production

SPECIAL COLLECTIONS

BECTU History Project interviews with: Noreen Ackland; Reginald Beck; Richard
    Best; Anne Coates; Sidney Cole; Charles Crichton; Teddy Darvas; Geoffrey Foot;
    Leslie Norman; Alfred Roome; Hugh Stewart; Peter Tanner.

Adrian Brunel Special Collection held at the British Film Institute Library.

Ivor Montagu Special Collection held at the British Film Institute Library.

INTERVIEWS CONDUCTED FOR THIS BOOK

(Except where indicated, all interviews were conducted by Roy Perkins)

In the USA:
Dede Allen, Los Angeles, 4 May 2000.
Anne Coates, San Francisco, 12 May 2000.
Antony Gibbs, Los Angeles, 5 May 2000.
Bernard Gribble, Los Angeles, 6 May 2000.
Mike Le-Mare, Los Angeles, 8 May 2000.

In the UK:
Noreen Ackland, London, 3 November 2000.
Tariq Anwar (by fax), 29 June, 27 July 2000.
Mick Audsley, London, 17 March 2000.
Stuart Baird, London, 22 June 2000.
Richard Best, London, 3 November 2000.
John Bloom, London, 13 July 2000.
Jim Clark, London, 10 March 2000.
Frank Clarke, Devon, 19 February 2000.
David Gladwell, London, 17 February 2000.
Tony Lawson, London, 26 October 2000.
Russell Lloyd (with Martin Stollery), Sussex, 10 February 2000.
Jonathan Morris, London, 28 June 2000.
Tom Priestley, London, 28 July 2000.
Terry Rawlings (with Martin Stollery), Herts., 6 April 2000.
Peter Tanner (with Martin Stollery), Bucks., 16 March 2000.
Lesley Walker (with Vivien Pottersman and Martin Stollery), London, 9 March 2000.
Mel Worsfold (film engineer), London, 10 July 2002.

Select Glossary

A and B rolls: Assembly of original material in two separate rolls to allow optical effects to be made by double printing.

Acmade: British manufacturer of editing equipment.

ADR: Automatic Dialogue Replacement. Clean dialogue re-recorded to picture playback, replacing the dialogue tracks shot during filming. ADR can be used to change the inflection of an actor's lines, and to insert dialogue re-written during post-production where lip movements are not visible.

Assembly: The first stage of editing when the filmed scenes, often cut over length, are put together in script order.

Avid: Manufacturer of the most widely used professional computerised editing system, often synonymous with **non-linear editing**.

CIR splicer: Italian-designed device for joining two pieces of film, where the adjacent frames are butted together, and joined with removable transparent tape.

Clapperboard: A chalkboard for identifying shots, usually photographed at the head of each take. The board's hinged clapper produces a reference point for **rushes** synchronisation before editing.

Cutting copy: The print, consisting of the structured film rushes, which progresses through the various editing stages to **fine cut**. Sometimes referred to as the work print.

Dailies: See **Rushes**

Digital Betacam: High-level professional broadcast TV acquisition format (see **Digital Video**).

Digital Video (DV): A video signal comprised of binary digits, as opposed to a continuously variable analogue image, required for storage and manipulation on **non-linear** computer workstations.

Dissolve: An optical effect combining a gradual fade out with a gradual fade in, where one image appears to merge with the next.

Dubbing: The final mixing of separate soundtracks onto one master track.

Dubbing (or sound) editor: Editor responsible for preparing separate soundtracks prior to dubbing.

Dupe, duping: Producing a duplicate copy from the negative or positive print.

Emulsion: The light-sensitive coating on film stock which forms the photographic image.

Fade: Appearance of an image from, or disappearance of an image into, black.

Final Cut Pro: Non-linear editing software (developed by Apple), aimed initially at the consumer market but increasingly used in professional applications.

Fine cut: The end stage of picture cutting where all structural adjustments and editing refinements have been made, with the approval of director and producer.

Flatbeds: Table-style editing machines, such as the **Prevost**, **Steenbeck** and **KEM**, designed to run large rolls of film and sound forwards or backwards at variable speeds, with a screen large enough for more than one person to sit at.

Frame: The individual photographic image on a strip of film. 35mm feature films are shot at a rate of twenty-four frames per second at standard running time.

Freeze-frame: An optical effect where a single frame image is repeated, producing the illusion of stopped action.

Grading: The laboratory process of balancing the varying tonal values between scenes within the final film print.

Grip: Camera support crew.

High Definition (HD): A professional digital video system that produces pictures of approximately 1,000 lines of resolution, compared to the 400 to 500 lines of consumer DV (see **Digital Video**).

iMac: Popular consumer computer manufactured by Apple.

Iris: An optical circular **wipe** that expands or contracts, characteristic of silent films.

Joiner: See **Splicer**

Jump-cut: An edit which breaks continuity by removing frames from within the same shot, or which cuts two similar shots together, producing a jump effect.

KEM: See **Flatbeds**

Lightworks: A non-linear editing system widely used in feature film editing.

Looping: See **ADR**

Matte: A camera or laboratory process that allows a separately shot image to be combined into the original negative using a masking process.

Media 100: A mid-range non-linear editing system, commonly used for broadcast and industrial video production.

Moviola: An upright, rather than table-style motorised editing machine requiring standing operation and only able to run shorter lengths of film. The Moviola's small screen is best suited to individual working.

Negative cutting: The matching of the camera-original negative to the finally approved cutting copy.

Non-linear editing (NLE): The electronic editing of a film assisted by computer, which usually dispenses with cutting the film print. Some editors prefer to conform the computerised edit back to film, which can then be projected to check pacing and effect.

Optical effects: Shots processed in the film laboratory, such as **dissolves**, **fades**, **freeze-frames**, **wipes** and **irises**. In computerised rather than film editing these effects can be tested immediately.

Pic-sync: A **synchroniser** with a small screen.

Pinnacle: Manufacturer of post-production software and hardware.

Post-synching: Recording and matching sound to picture after the film has been shot.

Prevost: See **Flatbeds**

Principal photography: The standard six- to eight-week period when the main cast and crew are contracted to film the script.

Release print: The fully graded print of the completed film with synchronous soundtrack, approved for cinema projection.

Rewind: A geared device mounted on the cutting bench for rewinding the film.

Rough cut: The second stage in the editing process (referred to variously by editors as 'first cut' or 'editor's cut') between **assembly** and **fine cut**, when evaluation of the film's structure begins to take place.

Rubber numbering machine: A machine which stamps a matching code along picture and sound rushes, providing logging data and synchronised reference points for editing.

Rushes (Dailies, in US): The first prints made from camera-original negative (usually processed overnight following the day's shooting); when synchronised with sound they provide the raw material from which the film is edited.

Shooting ratio: The relationship between the amount of footage shot and the length of the completed film.

Splicer (or **Joiner**): Device used for joining two pieces of film, originally by cementing overlapping adjacent frames (see **CIR splicer**).

Steenbeck: See **Flatbeds**

Synchroniser: An editing device for keeping two or more print, negative or soundtracks locked in alignment with each other, using a common drive shaft with sprocketed wheels for film transport.

Synching up: The exact alignment of picture and soundtracks in the **synchroniser**, using the **clapperboard** as a reference.

Takes: Repeated recordings of the same shot, numbered progressively until acceptable to director and key production crew.

Trims: Frames of film removed by the editor at any stage of cutting.

Trim bin: A bin that supports a frame for hanging and filing trims, which are then easily accessible to editor and assistant.

Wipe: An optical transition where one shot is succeeded by another, usually by means of a horizontal, vertical or diagonal line traversing the frame.

Work print: See **Cutting copy**

Index

Page numbers in *italics* indicate illustrations and captions; page numbers in **bold** indicate main entries in the section of filmographies. n following a page number indicates that the reference is to the notes on the page cited. Film titles cited only in the lists at the end of filmographies are not included in the index.